SNOUTS
IN THE
TROUGH

SNOUTS
IN THE
TROUGH

A TRUE STORY OF
THE UNDERWORLD AND
THE BROTHERHOOD BEHIND THE BADGE

ANDREW FRASER

hardie grant books

MELBOURNE · LONDON

Published in 2010 by Hardie Grant Books

Hardie Grant Books (Australia)
85 High Street
Prahran, Victoria 3181
www.hardiegrant.com.au

Hardie Grant Books (UK)
Dudley House, North Suite
34–35 Southampton Street
London WC2E 7HF
www.hardiegrant.co.uk

Cataloguing-in-Publication data is available from the National Library of Australia.
Snouts in the Trough
ISBN 978 1 74066917 7

Cover design by Design by Committee
Front cover image courtesy of Getty Images
Author photograph by Lindey Allen
Typesetting by Kirby Jones
Typeset in Sabon 11/16pt
Printed and bound in Australia by Griffin Press

10 9 8 7 6 5 4 3 2 1

'This is, in the end, the story of how corruption can arise and how it can be avoided; it is a story whose relevance never vanishes, a warning from the past.'

—*Inquisition* by Toby Green

acknowledgements

Thanks to Malcolm and Gillie Rosenes for having the intestinal fortitude to come forward for the first time and tell it like it was in the Victoria Police.

Special thanks to all the people (and they know who they are) who have provided me with interviews, background material and some very juicy snippets of information.

And finally to Sandy Grant and all those at Hardie Grant Books who had the ticker to take this book on, which on any assessment, is a very controversial project.

contents

PART TWO   BARBARIANS AT THE GATE

INTRODUCTION

On 23 September 1999 at 3.35 am my life as a lawyer came to a screeching halt when I was arrested on a number of drug charges. The most serious of these was being knowingly concerned with the importation of a commercial quantity of cocaine—the result of a serious addiction I had managed to acquire.

The Drug Squad officer leading the raid on my house was Detective Sergeant Rosenes and boy, was he ever happy with himself. I can still see his smug smile as he quizzed me, before searching my house and later my office in central Melbourne. The rozzers found no cocaine, but there was plenty of other evidence of my raging habit and I was charged, processed and finally granted bail. Each appearance at court brought with it a continuing supercilious attitude from all of the drug squad, in particular Detective Sergeant Rosenes, Detective Steven Paton and Detective Senior Sergeant Wayne Geoffrey Strawhorn, as they gathered like vultures around my carcase. Right at the forefront was Rosenes, to the extent that one day I had to tell my barrister to get him out of my face or I would not be responsible for my actions—I'd belt him right there in the court foyer and hang the consequences.

I was subsequently convicted and went to jail for five long, hard years, along the way losing everything I had worked for nearly thirty years to achieve. But the worm was about to turn. Prior to my case being heard Sergeant Rosenes and Detective Steven Paton were themselves charged with corrupt activities as sworn police officers—including drug trafficking. I was overjoyed to see these blokes brought undone and subsequently go to jail themselves. The icing on the cake would surely be for the kingpin Detective Senior Sergeant Wayne Geoffrey Strawhorn to come a cropper. He had been the instigator of my arrest and a man I knew to be corrupt. I did not have to wait long for my wish to come true and for Strawhorn to be charged, convicted and sentenced. Oh happy day—this bloke whom I had known to be crooked for years had finally been brought to book.

On the subject of which, when I left jail the publishers Hardie Grant talked me into writing my first memoir, *Court in the Middle*, and the next year a sequel, *Lunatic Soup*. My life had been reinvented as a writer, believe it or not, compliments of Hardie Grant, and for that I am grateful.

In view of all this you are probably wondering how I came to be writing the story of my sworn enemy, Detective Sergeant Malcolm Rosenes, and the Brotherhood of Victoria Police. Well, life is full of contradictions and a beauty was about to come my way. My literary agent Victor Susman met a friend at a function who told him Malcolm Rosenes had a book in mind and that he was interested in me writing it for him. Victor contacted Malcolm, keeping him well away from me. They met a couple of times and one way or another I came to the decision that I was prepared to give Malcolm the benefit of the doubt and at the very least meet Rosenes to see what he had to say.

When I did Victor held his breath as he knew full well my

attitude to the drug squad in general and Rosenes, Paton and Strawhorn in particular. To say things were frosty between us is an understatement as Malcolm recounted what he considered to be his tale of woe as a cop in jail. His concept was for a jail diary and I was not remotely interested in writing it for him. As the meeting proceeded I told Malcolm that his diary had no public appeal, that the public interest in a corrupt cop having a hard time of it in the nick would be nil. Bad luck, you were caught out and got a jail sentence. In my view he had copped his right whack and I had not one skerrick of sympathy for him.

Then I leaned over the table and eyeballed Malcolm. I told him then that there was a story he had which I would be very interested in writing. 'What is that?' he asked me. 'Easy', I said, 'all I want you to do is for once in your life tell the truth, the whole truth and nothing but the truth as far as the rotten and corrupt Drug Squad is concerned. I want the whole sordid story, warts and all.' To Malcolm's eternal credit he did not even blink. He looked me straight in the eye and replied 'OK'. In the end I got much more than the Drug Squad episodes. This book shows how Malcolm's descent into corruption follows his rise through the ranks.

I suppose everybody is entitled to a second chance and I was prepared to give him just that on the strict understanding that the minute I thought he was bullshitting me the gig was up. Malcolm felt that by telling all, he could finally lay to rest the ghosts of a life gone wrong. In the light of his unhesitating answer in the affirmative I decided to write this sorry tale which includes aspects of my prosecution that make my blood boil.

I have been impressed by Malcolm's forthrightness even when it places him in a very bad light. The story discloses matters which even as a hard-bitten criminal lawyer stagger me and on occasions I have felt sick at the breathtaking revelations made to me. I had harboured suspicions for years but their confirmation bowled me over.

The downfall of Malcolm Rosenes came when he took a promotion to the drug squad. That's when he finally became caught in the web of corruption woven by all and sundry and degenerated into a world of intrigue and lawlessness. Here he ran the ill-fated and inaccurately named 'Chemical Diversion Desk', with Strawhorn as his superior officer.

Ultimately he was charged with trafficking a commercial quantity of ecstasy while a serving police officer, along with drug and other charges. When the music stops there is always someone left without a chair and this time it turned out to be Malcolm.

Strawhorn desperately ran around behind the scenes and tried to rearrange those deck chairs on the Titanic but there is only one way that ship was heading and that was down. He continually tried to stay out of the water but ultimately it was to no avail and I am pleased to report that despite his efforts to deflect blame to anyone other than himself, Strawhorn succumbed to the inevitable and has only recently been released from jail. He is currently serving a number of years' parole.

More of that later, but be under no misapprehension about the fact that there are plenty to blame for all that went wrong in the Drug Squad.

On the night of his arrest, while lying on the ground in a Caulfield park with Inspector Peter De Santo's foot on his head and a gun in his ear, Malcolm Rosenes assented to Ethical Standards' request to 'tip in' and tell all about corruption in the Drug Squad.

Malcolm was debriefed and the transcripts of that debrief, together with many hours of interviews, form the basis of this book. There are thousands of pages of debrief, all of which the powers that be, including the Victorian Government, have been in possession of since 2000. It discloses corruption on a grand scale. As I write precious little has been done.

PART 1

ON A WING AND A PRAYER

Skilled police are acutely conscious of how laws can be circumvented or broken without penalty. The better they are at their job, the more they learn. It is no accident that the police officers most admired for their skill by colleagues include some who become corrupt.

—The Fitzgerald Inquiry

Chapter One

A NICE LITTLE PICKLE

'If you can't annoy somebody, there's
little point in writing.'

—Kingsley Amis

In July 1987 the ABC's 'Four Corners' screened a programme entitled 'The Moonlight State' which blew the lid off police corruption in the State of Queensland like nothing previously. Add to that the fearless reporting of journalist Phil Dickie from the *Courier Mail* in Brisbane on endemic corruption inside the Queensland Police Service and the cat was out of the bag for the corrupt coppers of that state. Luckily for posterity and the future integrity of the Queensland Police Service, Parliament and Queensland itself the then premier Joh Bjelke Petersen was out of the state. In his absence his Deputy Bill Gunn appointed Tony Fitzgerald QC to set up a six-week inquiry into allegations against specific coppers, the idea being to look like the Government was doing something on one hand while keeping a very tight lid on the seething undercurrent of corruption existing at the time in Queensland. Like each State Government in this

7

country, Queensland was terrified of its Police Union and the disproportionate political power those unions exercise, and was endeavouring to placate it with a fairy floss Inquiry.

If the Government of the day thought they had appointed a tame silk to quietly sweep the accumulated filth under the carpet then it had made a mistake. Fitzgerald is a man of enormous integrity, who fearlessly grabbed the Royal Commission and ran with it, harassing and pressuring the Government until his terms of reference were widened twice and Queensland had a real inquiry on its hands. The outcomes would reverberate throughout Australian society for years to come. What a pity successive Victorian governments have lacked an equal dose of intestinal fortitude and addressed like issues with like commitment. Instead a predictable pattern has emerged where corruption is ignored, or not dealt with in an accountable or transparent manner, if at all.

In Queensland progress was made: Fitzgerald pursued corrupt coppers and politicians with vigour and guts and ended many a shining career with his breathtaking revelations. A Chief Commissioner of Police ended up in the nick and the Premier himself stood trial but was acquitted in what can only be described as highly suspicious circumstances.

The two most significant lessons from the Fitzgerald Inquiry were that if you have a sufficiently robust Royal Commission then real benefits to the community can be achieved and that no one is above the law. Fitzgerald's achievements have resonated across the entire country and Victoria is not immune, as we shall see.

Let's jump forward to July of 2009, when the *Australian* reported that twenty-five senior police officers had been charged in Queensland with illegal and improper dealings with serving prisoners in order to obtain evidence and/or intelligence. When this was reported Fitzgerald noted that his Royal Commission had been held twenty years earlier and that the lessons then learned appeared to have been forgotten. In his view the only way to continue to confront the ever present threat of corruption was to maintain extreme vigilance and if necessary hold a Royal Commission every twenty years or so in order to flush out corruption.

Also in 2009, Fitzgerald launched a stinging attack on the Victorian Government on the subject of corruption but to date the silence from the Government has been deafening. The last thing they need is an exposé of corrupt practices within its police force. The only thing wrong with the ostrich approach to life is while you are busy closing your eyes to the obvious you won't see who is sneaking up from behind and is about to insert the rough end of the pineapple into your delicate areas. As I write I note with interest that the Premier has, yet again, announced that one of the key issues the next election is to be fought on is law and order. Bring it on.

The current Labor Government in Victoria has presided over a period of unparalleled corruption in the Victoria Police resulting in two of the force's most elite squads being disbanded due to endemic corruption. By the way the previous Kennett Liberal government cannot sneak away unnoticed either. A number of the disclosures in this book relate to incidents that were well known during the reign of Kennett yet he too did nothing. In fact for the last twenty years not a sausage has been done to root out and deal with corruption in the police force in this state.

Corruption takes many forms; it's not just nicking a few dollars during a raid on a drug dealer. Inappropriate use of position, interfering with the administration of justice, perjury, violence, drug dealing and, of course, theft are all forms of corruption. While this book tells only one story, it discloses a culture of corrupt activities in many forms carried out by the most senior officers down to the most junior, all of whom have sworn to 'Uphold the Right' and many of whom are still in 'the job'.

But we need to set the scene for this culture in which politics ignores the issues under its nose so let's start with the one thing all pollies in Victoria are terrified of, the Police Association. This organisation is really nothing but a trade union and if you don't believe me then check their website; not one word about community safety, public service or stamping out crime unless it is couched in terms relating to the ever-more strident call by the Association for more coppers. The Association takes a combative approach each time the topic of corruption is raised. Weeding out corruption will not be helped as long as one of the main functions of the Association is to fund coppers who have been pinched for doing the wrong thing.

Luckily for the Association Victorian Premier Steve Bracks came to the rescue and in a secret deal prior to the 2006 election, he pledged in a letter entitled 'Record of Commitments' that the Government would cave in to police strong arm demands to reimburse Police Association legal costs for police who were investigated by the Office of Police Integrity (OPI), a body set up after immense public pressure to investigate crooked cops. The deal was done to encourage the police to support the government's re-election. When the deal came to light it was too late, the election had been called and won by Bracks. Imagine for one moment if the same deal had been done with for instance the Builders Labourers or Wharfies. There would have been a hue and cry of deafening proportions and rightly so, this deal was dishonest and in my view illegal. Typically the stonewall tactic is adopted until the stink dies down and it is business as usual.

The 'Brotherhood' that is the Victoria Police is discussed more than once in this book. When it comes to serving justice (as they have sworn to do) or staying staunch with the Brotherhood, there is no contest. The very people they have sworn to protect run a sad second in an uneven two horse race. Don't take my word for it. Judge Michael Strong, head of the OPI, states this very fact in an OPI Annual Report tabled in Parliament. Judge Strong reported:

> It is a common feature of OPI public hearings that police witnesses receive considerable support from other police. Most of those offering support have no particular day to day contact with the witnesses, nor have they any insight into their relevant conduct except through what has been revealed at the public hearings. The unquestioning loyalty that causes some police to close ranks to ward off external scrutiny is discussed in detail in the forthcoming OPI report 'The Armed Offenders Squad—a case study'. In that case, the Police Association organised a rally to support squad members who later pleaded guilty to charges of assault and misleading the director by lying in hearing.
>
> The ability to engender support and attract loyalty for conduct that undermines the integrity of Victoria Police reflects the worst aspects of an outmoded police culture and adherence to 'old style' policing methods. It appears as a recurring theme in almost all of the cells identified by OPI. Whilst members may engage in separate, discreet activities, they are often protected by an outmoded police culture that turns a 'blind eye' to inappropriate activity, or demands loyalty to a code of silence.
>
> Loyalty to a code of silence, in the context of OPI's coercive powers, creates a further demand on those who adhere to it. Too many police witnesses required to answer questions under oath in OPI hearings seem willing to sacrifice their credibility rather than break the 'code'. Like my predecessor, I am gravely concerned at the apparent disregard some police have for the oath

or affirmation to tell the truth when they give evidence. Perjury is a serious crime. The fact that the perjurer is a police sworn to uphold the law is an aggravating circumstance.

This is a damning indictment indeed and his Honour has hit the nail on the head.

ALL GOOD THINGS MUST COME TO AN END, EVEN WHEN THE odds seem to be in your favour. The Drug Squad was disbanded on 14 December 2001 and the Armed Robbery Squad disbanded on 8 September 2006. Each hit the dust in spectacular circumstances with a number of Drug Squad coppers going to jail for drug trafficking and Armed Robbery coppers charged with serious assault.

The dogs had been barking at the goings on of these two squads for many years to no avail. The Armed Robbery Squad's violence was legendary, as was their innate ability to only ever recover a proportion of the proceeds of any bank robbery, even if the crooks were nabbed at the door of the bank they had just robbed! My original law firm acted for one of the first companies to install security cameras in the ANZ bank and it was related to me on more than one occasion that after an armed robbery, if the company was quick, they would be in time to recover half the money—such was the reputation of the Armed Robbery Squad (or the 'robbers' as they were nick-named).

I personally appeared in many armed robbery cases where only small percentages of proceeds of robberies were recovered but the best was a famous case where the armed robbers were being hotly pursued by the coppers from the very doors of the bank they had just stuck up. The crooks were arrested and guess what? Even though they had been pursued from the doors of the bank not one cent was recovered. The police evidence was that while in pursuit in outer western Melbourne, where it's as flat as a strap and there's nothing but open paddocks, they observed a plastic shopping bag being thrown from the car. When the cops went back a few minutes later no bag could be found. Not so, according to the accused crooks who all gave identical instructions: the coppers recovered the bag and had a 'whack up' of the proceeds of the robbery at the scene.

The Drug Squad's reputation was for taking guns, drugs and money when searching houses. My client Lewis Moran used to complain bitterly about the Drug Squad members who regularly raided Moran's house. Lewis told me he didn't mind being 'fined' occasionally but on an almost weekly basis it was a bit over the odds. Similar stories were related to me by many clients with monotonous regularity over many years and I certainly don't believe that they were all lying.

What happened after the revelations were made about the Armed Robbery and the Drug Squad? On both occasions a great deal of noise was made that the 'bad eggs' had been rooted out and the other police in those squads had been redeployed within the force. At the time the Drug Squad was disbanded there were approximately 60 serving officers and to suggest that banging up a few corrupt coppers solves the problem is laughable. What happened to the senior ranks running this debacle? Where have those with large clouds over their heads gone? After the initial flurry of excitement the Government quietly swept the whole mess under the carpet and there it stays until someone has the spine to rip it off and show the mess for what it is.

Don't think the trouble is confined to the Drug and Armed Robbery Squads either. In 2004 the internal business and IT governance procedures were rearranged within the Victoria Police with a view to making the whole question of awarding lucrative IT contracts and general spending of huge amounts of taxpayers' money on computer equipment more accountable, transparent and professional. Nothing further is heard of this until November 2009 when all hell breaks loose because 39 million dollars of the Victorian taxpayers' hard-earned has gone down the drain due to maladministration, incompetence and probably dishonesty within the very same IT department that was restructured in 2004 in order to avoid precisely this catastrophe.

The contracts complained of were mostly with multinational behemoth IBM and where do you suppose many of those who awarded the juicy contracts now work? IBM! Thank you very much.

The Victorian Ombudsman tables a report annually to State Parliament and the current report discloses that a number of police have been charged with serious criminal offences. Why are those accused not named? Why the big secret? I am happy to report that former Deputy Commissioner Noel Ashby was charged with perverting the course of justice and perjury and escaped prosecution on a technical hitch: a stuff-up by the OPI. But that's nothing compared to the case of Detective Senior Sergeant Paul Dale, who was charged with murder.

In December 2009 the Office of Police Integrity tabled its annual report in Parliament in which ongoing corruption was discussed and charges against senior police for a variety of offences were recommended. The disturbing aspect of those recommendations is that these are *senior* officers. And in the same week as this report was released, another senior detective in the highly secretive Security Intelligence Group was suspended for leaking sensitive matters of national security to the *Australian* newspaper about Somali terrorist activities.

But let's go back a few years, and look at how one ordinary young man got caught up in this sorry business.

Chapter Two

NEVER LET YOUR RIGHT HAND KNOW WHAT YOUR LEFT HAND IS DOING

'Life is not meant to be easy, my child;
but take courage—it can be delightful.'

—George Bernard Shaw

When Malcolm Rosenes started work with the Victoria Police, he was looking forward to what he thought would be an honourable career, something his family could be proud of. In the thirty or so years that followed, he gradually let go of everything he valued: his respect for his fellow officers, his honesty and ultimately, his humanity. It wasn't until he found himself serving time for his part in trafficking a commercial quantity of ecstasy and drug offences that he had time to reflect on what had happened to him. Much of what I am about to tell you sickens me. I am still shocked at what he saw and at the way he said and did nothing to prevent the rampant corruption and greed that went all the way to the top. He is aware that in relating all of this, he is not casting himself in a very good light—there is very little in these pages that will give comfort to his wife and children. I know he will be eternally sorry for the grief and shame he brought upon them.

I offer his story to you knowing that some will dismiss the entire contents of this book as fiction, the ramblings of a bent copper. I can only offer you this assurance—everything here has been known to the Victoria Police watchdog, the Ethical Standards Department (EDI), since 2001.

Following the demise of the Drug Squad and under enormous pressure from the public the Government begrudgingly set up the Office of Police Integrity (OPI) but they are yet to land a knockout punch in any direction, try as they may. I believe that as a society we deserve a better system, where those facing charges can expect to have untampered with and unbiased evidence put before the courts. Juries deserve to hear the whole story, the true story before delivering their verdicts. Young men and women entering the police force deserve a career they can be proud of, where proper checks and balances are in place and rogue coppers are ruthlessly weeded out before they can wreak havoc.

It is my hope that this book will shock those in power out of their complaisance and that we will have the Royal Commission into Police Corruption in the state of Victoria that we, as an enlightened first world society have a right to expect.

I am writing this book to set the record straight about the corruption that went on over twenty-eight years (1975–2003) while Malcolm was a serving detective sergeant in Victoria Police. This corruption started at the earliest time in his police career. First, I would like to tell you a bit about him: his name is Malcolm Rosenes and this book is one man's story of his journey through the Victoria Police.

Malcolm's father, Slawek Rosenes, was born into the Jewish

faith in Lodz, Poland, in 1902. His father's father was a Rabbi. The family held quite some social standing within the tight-knit Jewish community in Poland. Slawek was educated in Poland and became a fashion designer and tailor by trade, something that was later to save his life. When Slawek grew up he moved to Germany which, on reflection, wasn't a good place to be if you were Jewish in the 1930s but he had his own business in which he tailored and manufactured coats, jackets and suits for men and he was good at his job and much sought after. Prior to World War II, when the persecution of the Jews in Germany began, Slawek was forced to wear the yellow star on his jacket and was subjected to the prejudice and hatred that gradually manifested in Germany. Upon outbreak of war, all the Jews in his town, as elsewhere, were herded into a ghetto and Slawek spent the entire war in concentration camps. He was married and had two infant children. His wife and two children died in the camps, an experience those of us lucky enough to live in this country can only imagine. The great unanswered question for him was how could his darling boy and girl die in such an awful way, while he lived to a ripe old age, and by coming to Australia was given another life altogether. It all seemed so unfair to him.

However because of his tailoring expertise he was of value to the Germans in manufacturing uniforms for the German military and that kept him alive for the entire war. Finally he was transported in cattle trucks in the middle of winter to the infamous Auschwitz death camp where Hitler was playing out his 'final solution', the extermination of the entire Jewish people. As the war was clearly going against Germany, no more uniforms were required so Slawek was assigned to munitions production. It was at this stage that, no longer being indispensable, he was selected for extermination. Luckily for him it was by now August 1945 and the Americans liberated Auschwitz a few days before he was due to be sent to the gas chambers.

No matter what trials and tribulations Malcolm may have endured in his life he knows that nothing could possibly come close to the horror of those dark days in the death camps. Their impact on his father was profound. He steadfastly refused to talk about his experiences for many years until Malcolm's own sons finally persuaded their granddad to open up to them: it was a cathartic experience for all of them.

At the end of the war, Slawek had had enough of the tailoring business. It bought back too many memories of German uniforms and the hell associated with them. Instead he opened a mixed business, a corner store, and quickly became rather successful, ending up with three shops.

He also remarried. Sarah was a German Jew Slawek met in Auschwitz—she was Malcolm's mum. Malcolm's brother Hank was born in Germany in 1947. But with fears of a Nazi resurgence because of a re-emergence of Jewish persecution Slawek walked away from Germany as a displaced person. Malcolm's mum, dad and brother Hank immigrated to Australia and arrived in 1949. Malcolm was born on 30 July 1953 in Carlton.

When he was four, his mum died at the young age of thirty-nine of peritonitis following a burst appendix. In those days, as they were not wealthy and were recent immigrants, there was little affordable medical care available. His mother battled on, she didn't let on that she was feeling unwell, merely taking an aspirin and going to bed. By the time it became obvious that she was very ill, it was too late. After his mum's death, his father, Slawek, couldn't cope with the two little boys because he was working two jobs to try and make a fresh start in his newly adopted country. He worked permanent nightshift on the Holden production line at General Motors in Fishermans Bend and during the day he put his tailoring skills to good use by manufacturing jeans in the garage at home and then selling them on the weekends in his stall at the Victoria Market.

Malcolm's father worked very hard to be a good provider, but he never really recovered from the war and was very introverted, completely unable to express any emotion or love towards the two boys. Without his wife, he was unable to cope, so he sought help from the Jewish Welfare Society.

Jewish Welfare undertook to look after Hank and Malcolm and placed them both in an orphanage called The Francis Barkman Home in Balwyn which accommodated about 60 Jewish orphans. A matron and staff at the home cared for them. Life was spartan and as they did not receive money from their father they were unable to buy themselves even little treats to help dispel the monotony of the orphanage.

Malcolm lost nearly all contact with his father at this stage. Jewish Welfare was a very generous group of people and, as a result of that, he was sent to the new Jewish private school called Mount Scopus College but he was like a fish out of water. He was a son of a refugee who had no money and essentially no family and the rest of Mount Scopus came from the affluent Jewish establishment of Melbourne. They had money, family and connections. He didn't fit in at all well. Even though he desperately wanted these new kids to be his friends it didn't happen. He even failed fourth grade.

Most kids had a parent or foster parents and they would all be taken from the orphanage for the weekend. Even though Malcolm had a dad, he never communicated with him or with the home. In the death camps you kept your mouth shut and said nothing to anyone. That way you might just stay alive. This life robbed Malcolm's father of any ability to communicate with his sons.

Each Friday night Malcolm would get himself dressed with all the other kids into his best clothes and he would sit and wait, and wait, and his dad never turned up. He would hear nothing. The feeling of utter desertion was devastating to a little boy of six or seven. He would cry himself to sleep in his best clothes. It's something that has never left him.

He didn't fit in at school. He didn't fit in at the orphanage. He felt rejected and unloved by his dad. It was only many, many years later when his father was in his nineties that he started to open up, not to Malcolm but to Malcolm's young sons who regularly, persistently questioned him about his life and, particularly, life in the ghetto and in Auschwitz.

For Malcolm his clearest recollection as a child was a desperate desire and need to be accepted, to fit in. Because no one came to take him out on weekends he was left on his own in the orphanage all weekend and this was a real nuisance to the matron as he was the only small child there. There was nothing to do but to think and worry about his situation and as a result, he continually wet his bed until the age of about eleven. As punishment, on Monday he was forced to wash his own soiled sheets in front of the rest of the home. He can still recall the humiliation.

Malcolm's father remarried when he was about nine years of age. His new wife, Maria, a Russian Jew, already had a son who was then approximately fourteen years old. Slawek had left General Motors by then and bought a delicatessen in Bay Street, Port Melbourne. Finally Malcolm had cause to be excited because he thought he would be leaving the orphanage and going to live at home in a family environment again. Malcolm's brother, who was seven years older than him, left the orphanage and went to live in Bay Street. But his new stepmother already had a son and the house behind the deli was small. Malcolm was left in the orphanage, his desertion and desolation total. He rarely went to Bay Street but when he did he was the outsider and was regularly ignored by his stepmother. He was also mistreated by his new stepbrother. He felt utterly alone and abandoned. His overwhelming desire was just to belong and that became the motivating force in his life.

Whilst the matron at the orphanage was good enough to him, he was always hungry—there was never enough to eat. All the other kids had some sort of financial support which enabled them to buy little bits and pieces to augment the diet that was provided, but his father never gave him any pocket money. And it was only on a couple of occasions when he came back from the odd weekend with his father, that he would load his son up with stuff from the shop. He would give him Kit Kats and Chocolate Royals which were a treat indeed. But immediately he got back to the orphanage he would share them with his best mate and they would eat the lot in one sitting on Sunday night, the two of them hiding under the stairs gutsing themselves until everything was gone and they felt sick. If anyone found the treats, they would have to be shared with everybody.

Because he was always hungry, he would sneak scraps from the playground rubbish bins at Mount Scopus. He ate other kids' sandwiches that they had thrown away. The upshot of this was a severe dose of hepatitis that landed him in Fairfield Infectious Diseases Hospital for three months. He was found to be extremely undernourished and unwell. During the entire three months he was in Fairfield Hospital he did not receive one visitor either from the school, the orphanage or from his family, no get well cards, no books, nothing. Two aspects of his childhood were to haunt him: the overwhelming feeling of rejection and the desperate desire to belong. He didn't know what to do or how, just that he wanted to belong and be accepted.

When he returned to the orphanage he found out that because he had contracted hepatitis, every kid in the place had had to have a shot in the bum to inoculate them against hepatitis and he became even more unpopular.

When Malcolm was thirteen, the Francis Barkman Home was sold and Jewish Welfare instead established three smaller houses in the Caulfield area. The idea of these houses was that the children would live in a normal home environment with foster parents. In the home he went to he continued to be deprived of food and there was no improvement in terms of attention, love or encouragement. In fact one evening one of the foster parents who was an art teacher bought another artist home to have Malcolm and another boy pose nude for the two of them to draw. Malcolm and his mate went to bed and the next thing they knew these blokes were in bed with them. He must have blocked everything out because he can't remember what actually happened. It seems that it didn't matter where he turned, there were people that always wanted to hurt him.

When he was about fourteen years of age, the focus of the home changed from being for orphans to also taking in kids that had been in trouble. There was a girl who was a heroin user and a prostitute living in the house and also Malcolm first met George Gerard Kaufman there. Kaufman had been in trouble with the police and many years later was to become the infamous Armadale Rapist. It was quite a large house and there were about thirteen kids living there. Even at that stage it was obvious to Malcolm, not withstanding his inexperience, that Kaufman was not a nice person. He recalls going to the Ajax Swimming Pool in Alma Road, St Kilda with Kaufman and the others and while they were in the swimming pool he would go over the road into the park and do a bit of 'poofter bashing' or roll the drunks and steal their wallets. They knew what was going on but were too scared of Kaufman, who was older, to say anything about it to anybody. Because Kaufman was uncontrollable he ended up in Turana Youth Training Centre, a junior jail if you like, a sign of things to come. The kids from the home all visited him while he was at Turana.

Years later Malcolm would see Kaufman in St Kilda, when he had graduated to doing burglaries and was a serious heroin user. It was in the course of doing these burglaries that over the years he became the Armadale Rapist.

There was certainly no encouragement for Malcolm to study. He struggled all the way through school and felt like Mount Scopus couldn't wait to see the back of him. He left around the third year of high school and went to Prahran Technical School. He enjoyed the Tech and wanted to become a plumber. His old man wouldn't have a bar of him being a plumber even though he had had little input into his son's life. He was more interested in him studying and getting a profession. When his father put his foot down, Malcolm craved his approval enough to abandon the idea of plumbing as a career.

Because his stepmother had made it very clear that she did not want him at the deli in Port Melbourne he remained at the homes until he was sixteen when he was able to leave of his own accord. Even though Jewish Welfare obviously meant well the bulk of his childhood had been emotionally cold and loveless and he couldn't wait to escape and forge his own way in the world.

When Malcolm was seventeen he finally got to move in with his dad because his stepbrother had gone to live with his natural father. In many ways Malcolm hated his father for not taking him into his home earlier and Malcolm never developed a relationship with his stepmother, other than one of hostility, which made him anxious that he would be rejected by his Dad and cast out into the world alone again.

In 1999, at age 87, Malcolm's stepmother had a stroke and died. Notwithstanding what had gone before, he took his dad in and he lived with Malcolm and his family until, at the age of 95, he was too frail to be cared for and he was accepted into the Montefiores Home for the Aged. There he stayed until he died in 2004. Unlike his father's attitude to his small son whom he left in the orphanage, Malcolm and his wife and kids visited the old man every week in the home until he died, during Malcolm's time in prison. When he died a lot of Malcolm's demons died with him.

Sadly the prison authorities refused permission for Malcolm to attend his dad's funeral. From bitter personal experience I am able to vouch for this callous behaviour. My own father fell ill while I was at Fulham Prison near Sale, one of the privately run prisons in Victoria. I was escorted to Melbourne to say my goodbyes and was told point blank by the operations manager, Andy Walker, that I would be refused any request to attend the funeral should Dad die while I was still in prison. Luckily he did not pass away until after my release.

MALCOLM'S UPBRINGING LED HIM TO SEARCH FOR A CAREER where he could belong, and to him the police force looked like just the sort of place where you could be a part of things. You could also do good for the community, something he had experienced little of. All he knew was people did bad things to those they were supposed to care for and protect. Man's inhumanity to man knew no bounds.

In the Jewish community at that time, joining the police force as an occupation was at the bottom of the barrel. This was because of what so many Jews had suffered in the concentration camps. While the camps were Nazi-run, the actual day-to-day running of the camps was done by the camp police. Even though they were all Jews, they were the ones responsible for picking out who lived and who died. Therefore the standing of police no matter where they were was the lowest of the low in the minds of the Jewish community. Malcolm's father was not at all happy that he chose that career.

He was lucky to be accepted into the force because at about eighteen years of age, Malcolm found himself in trouble. At the time he was working at a service station in Caulfield but still living behind the shop in Bay Street, Port Melbourne. He bought himself a single shot .22 rifle and used to go rabbit shooting on the weekend. This was back in the days before you needed a firearm to be registered and anyone could walk into a gun shop and buy a .22 or a 12 gauge shot gun without any documentation required. This .22 always lived on the back seat of his Volkswagen. One day he was driving down a one-way street in Prahran and came upon a truck parked across the laneway with a number of cars banked up. After sitting there for quite some time with the drivers becoming rather agitated, he got out and walked up to the truck driver and asked him how long he would be. He told Malcolm to piss off, that he was busy unloading his truck. Malcolm went back to the car and waited until the truck driver had finished unloading his truck and moved out of the way. As he was driving past he reached into the back seat, grabbed the .22, pointed it at the truckie and threatened him. As it happened the gun wasn't actually working at this stage. It didn't matter, because almost as soon as he arrived home, there were coppers everywhere. They ran through the house, arrested and handcuffed him and took him off to the Prahran cop shop. The bloke he was working for paid $50 to bail him out and he was charged with assault with a weapon and threatening words and had to front the Magistrates Court at Prahran.

Malcolm's older brother briefed a young barrister who had plenty of dash in him and appeared destined for greater things. He had a real go and Malcolm left the Prahran Magistrates Court that day with a good behaviour bond. That barrister is now His Honour Mr Justice Phillip Cummings of the Supreme Court of Victoria.

When Malcolm applied to join the Police Force in 1975, he was questioned about this incident by the Deputy Commissioners who conducted the interviews in those days and he told them that he had been young and immature. They asked him, 'What will you do if you join the Force and we give you a gun? It is an extremely onerous responsibility.' Malcolm replied, 'This happened when I was eighteen. I am now twenty-two, seeking to join the Force. Things have changed—I have matured.' Not withstanding that prior conviction, the Police Force accepted him. He at last had a family.

Off he trotted to the Police Academy in Mount Waverley and the first thing he was told was that it was a live-in twenty-week course. He would be living in a four-man bunk room or a two-man small bedroom. The thought of this brought back unbearable memories of life in the orphanage and then in the home. He discovered that there was a special dispensation for married men, who didn't have to live at the Academy. He saw a chance. He went to see the Academy, telling them, 'I am Jewish, I can't eat the food that you provide here, because it is not Kosher and I have my father's house to go to.' He was given special dispensation to live at home, and there he stayed until graduation.

While they were in the Academy it was like being at uni. Everybody was head down and arse up studying, desperately trying to get all their studies done by graduation day. There wasn't much emphasis on the Brotherhood at this stage. That came immediately after you had graduated. Once you had the blue uniform on and you had your police identification badge, known as a 'Freddie', you could do no wrong in those days and that become apparent on day one. After graduation, he was so excited, here he was at the grand old age of twenty-two and a fully fledged copper, tearing home in his car from the graduation ceremony. He was just around the corner from the Police Academy in Waverley Road when he was pulled over for speeding. He immediately showed his Freddie to the motor-cycle copper who took one look at it and said, 'Oh, sorry mate, on your way, just slow down a bit.'

In those days, once you had the uniform on, you were part of the Victoria Police family. You looked after your own and it was obvious from day one that all you had to do was show a fellow officer your identification and all your sins would be forgiven. This would ultimately lead to Malcolm's downfall.

This sort of dispensation also extended to your family. If, for instance, one of your kids got into a blue and had been arrested, all you needed to do was ring up the officer concerned, explain who you were, explain who your son was, and all would be forgiven—away your boy walked, no questions asked. The motto should be: 'All for one and one for all … no matter what!'

Welcome to the Brotherhood!

MORE IMPORTANT BY FAR FOR MALCOLM THAN BECOMING A copper was meeting his wife Gillian in 1979. She was not Jewish but he fell in love with her and they married in 1984 and their three boys came along in 1986, 1988 and 1989. Throughout all that he has inflicted upon Gillian and the boys he is grateful and humbled to say that they stuck by him through thick and thin, and that the one constant he has been lucky enough to maintain is their love and support. In jail when all seemed dark and there was no tomorrow he was secure in the knowledge that they would be there at the end of jail and that single thought maintained him through those difficult days.

Chapter Three

THE GETTING OF WISDOM

'A sadder and a wiser man/
He rose the morrow morn.'
—'Rime of the Ancient Mariner', Samuel Taylor Coleridge

By 1971 Victoria Police needed a drastic overhaul of its organisational structure and the Government appointed a Pom, Sir Eric St Johnston, to make changes. Sir Eric's report contained many recommendations but one of the most significant was an overhaul of the promotional system. No longer were promotions to come by seniority alone, rather on merit. This met with substantial resistance from the Police Association and in reality took many years to be properly implemented.

Significantly, in 1975 the Bureau of Internal Investigations (BII) came into being, the forerunner of the much-maligned Ethical Standards Section (known in the force as 'the toe cutters'), supposedly to allay the public's growing concern about police corruption. The establishment of BII made precious little difference, mainly because the Brotherhood was so entrenched and coppers did not like ratting on coppers.

Into this state of affairs Malcolm graduated from the Police Academy in late 1975, a fully fledged member of Victoria's finest. His first posting was to the old and now defunct Russell Street Police Station. Like all young coppers he was busting to sink his teeth into some real cop work, just like on 'Homicide' or the other TV cop shows. Unfortunately the reality of policing lacked the glamour of the kind you saw on the telly. In those days, every new recruit started their tour of duty in Russell Street and from there gained experience in policing and then started applying for vacancies advertised from time to time in the police gazette for postings at metropolitan police stations or up the bush.

Central Melbourne in the mid seventies was not the throbbing metropolis it is now with its vibrant night life. As an inexperienced uniformed police constable it could be just plain boring. You would arrive at work for a 7 am shift and assemble in a large muster room (commonly known as the 'Bullring') which held about 60 or 70 young policemen. The day's activities comprised waiting in the muster room for someone in the front office at Russell Street Police Station to press a buzzer when members of the public arrived with their complaints or accident reports or inquiries. A bell rang in the muster room and the next available policeman trotted off down the corridor to meet whatever problem presented itself to him and that became the day's task. If you were lucky enough to get out of the Bullring and be paired up with another policeman, you would walk the beat in the city streets of Melbourne. You would be looking out for petty crime and if you were really lucky maybe you would score a shoplifter at Myer or, even better, a pub brawl. That would be the most exciting part of your day in policing. All this was supposed to take place under the watchful eye of a supervising sergeant.

Day shift ran from 7 am to 3 pm, afternoon shift from three to eleven and nightshift from eleven to seven. Even if you were working nightshift there wasn't a great deal to do because there weren't the 24-hour night clubs, or the current explosion of bars that run day and night and the out-of-control drug consumption that there is now. From about 2 am the city was dead which was about the time the night clubbers had wended their way home. You would walk the beat back then and a street assault would be considered a big pinch.

What if you were on afternoon shift or nightshift? If you were lucky enough to get into a divisional van, and there were only two covering the entire City of Melbourne, you drove the van with an experienced sergeant as observer, who was not necessarily pleased to see you. In those days if you wished to be promoted you first completed the exams for that rank and once the promotion came through as a sergeant you had to go back to Russell Street, into uniform for six months, before you could apply for a posting as a sergeant—and didn't the new sergeants detest this procedure. They hated being away from their normal police station and being under the scrutiny of a lot of officers who all worked out of Russell Street, particularly the commanders and the commissioners. Everything to do with senior management was at Russell Street and you were forever bumping into senior officers.

If you were lucky enough to get out in the divvy van you would be pulling over motorists for traffic offences, still pretty mundane work. You looked forward to the nightshift and while on nightshift you wouldn't see many cars in the city but you would see the various delivery and service vehicles. It was likely you would see the Woodruff's Dairy trucks making their deliveries throughout the city. In the very first weeks of Malcolm's time at Russell Street a police radio call came to the divvy van over the official police radio frequency with a message to stop the Woodruff's truck and pick up the milk. The first time it happened Malcolm wondered what the hell this was all about. Was someone having a joke? No, the deal was for the van to collect free milk from Woodruff's and take it back to Russell

Street for use in the muster room. And that was not all. The messages came in thick and fast: collect milk for the City Watch House, collect milk for the CIB and the Armed Robbery Squad and on it went to the degree that it seemed Woodruff's were supplying every squad in Russell Street, all for nothing. It must have been a substantial cost for old man Woodruff to wear.

This was so familiar to everyone at Russell Street that whenever the Woodruff's truck was double parked, rather than pinch the driver for a traffic offence the coppers would merely pull up behind it and snip him for a couple of bottles of milk to take home.

As with every rort it came to a sad end. Coppers rorting the Woodruff's trucks got to the stage where every second copper in Melbourne was pulling over Woodruff's trucks and asking for free milk. Old Man Woodruff said, 'Enough is enough.' It turned out he was actually losing money on his deliveries to the city so he sent out the order that there was no more free milk for the coppers. This was relayed back to the powers that be at Russell Street. But the order came back, 'Well if that's Woodruff's attitude, bugger him, every Woodruff's truck that is committing any traffic offence, no matter how minor, is to be pinched.'

As I said, in those days, the city was quiet after 2am, so often the trucks nipped the wrong way down one-way streets, double parked or turned against red traffic lights because there was absolutely no traffic in town. Well, Malcolm and his colleagues were told to even up with Woodruff's and did they ever. Every time a truck did anything wrong and I mean anything, even forgetting to indicate in a deserted street, they would pull the truck over and pinch the driver. This went on for some time until Old Man Woodruff finally flew the white flag, surrendered and the free milk was back on for everyone at Russell Street, including the brand new product on the market, Big M flavoured milk—which everybody loved.

This was a great introduction to corruption for a young copper, first the free milk, and then the improper use of collective police power to wage a campaign against Woodruff until he caved in. It didn't occur to Malcolm that these goings on were corruption. The officers and sergeants all copped their free milk for home as well as the station and as everyone was into it, it was accepted as normal practice. He never questioned or challenged any of these practices and my bet is his life would have taken a much different path had he had the guts to challenge such practices or at the least not become involved.

Another minor abuse of their position was cops wearing the 'discount suit', the police uniform. Very early on Malcolm was talking to a sergeant in the van one night and mentioned that he was thinking about buying a new TV. He replied, 'Make sure you wear your discount suit when you go to the shop as coppers always receive a good discount if they're in uniform.' He soon discovered the other constables were already in on this rort.

The worst job you could possibly get as a young copper on the beat was to have to stand on the steps at Parliament House. It was the most boring job in the Victoria Police force at that time. There you were, hanging around Parliament House like a shag on a rock, not a thing happening, not a person stirring, and worse than that, every once in a while an officer would drive by, stop, hop out with his clipboard, take your name and rank and make sure that you were standing up, that you weren't asleep or had nicked off somewhere else. Just around the corner in Exhibition Street was the old Forensic Science Laboratory (FSL) and there was always a junior police officer on duty there too. At the end of four hours, half way through the shift, you were allowed to swap over. After four hours of being bored rigid, not to mention being frozen to the bone in winter outside Parliament House you would trot around and be on guard duty at the Forensic Science. This was fantastic because it was a really interesting place full of neat stuff for a nosy young cop to fiddle with.

In those days, nobody cared about maintenance of exhibits, nobody cared about continuity of exhibits and nobody cared about contamination of exhibits. Wandering around the FSL as a young bloke was a real buzz. Your eyes were out on stalks. You could walk into any room at Forensics—where there might be for instance a reconstruction of a murder scene. You could trot around and pick stuff up, looking at it, handle it and generally play with everything. You were able to read all sorts of highly confidential reports and test results, pick up photos and look at them, even pick up the guns and look at them. Virtually every exhibit in every room at Forensic Science would have been touched or handled in an unauthorised manner by an unauthorised person at that time—it helped the nightshift go a bit quicker. It would have been interesting to know what a defence lawyer's reaction would have been if he had known what had happened to vital exhibits in important cases.

After years in uniform, promotion started to enter Malcolm's head. The first step was to try and be seconded to the crime cars. It was not a promotion in rank but it was certainly a promotion within the job and was considered a foot on the first rung of the ladder. Each local station in those days had their own crime car unit. Off you went in plain clothes, even carrying a shooter! This really was just like being on the TV. Crime cars dealt with the more serious crime in the area, but not crime that required the CIB, which was another step up the ladder. It was the CIB's job to investigate burglaries or serious assaults and then if that serious assault turned out to involve Homicide, then the Homicide Squad was called in: if it was a serious burglary that turned out to involve a safe-breaking, it would be referred onto the Breakers Squad and so on. Nevertheless, this was the real deal, and after the boredom of Russell Street, very exciting.

Promotions took a long time to attain, not like today when a university degree is rewarded with promotion irrespective of how well you go as an operational copper. But being academically sound does not necessarily make you a good copper and in the old days you earned your stripes first, quite literally, by walking the beat and working your way up, no short cuts. It was expected you would be in uniform for some considerable period of time, usually about eight years, before you were even eligible to apply to become a detective. If you were accepted for detective training school, and passed your qualification, you became a senior detective and were assigned to one of the local Criminal Investigation Branches (CIB). Invariably you would be placed in one of the large police stations like Dandenong, Frankston, Preston, Broadmeadows, where there was always plenty of action, a lot to learn and a good earn to be had.

If after a few years there you turned out to be any good, you really hit the jackpot by being transferred to one of the heavy hitters, in every sense of the word, like the Armed Robbery Squad. That was where you could start to make serious money and the giggle continued all the way up until that squad was disbanded in 2006 for belting a bloke in the interview room. If that was the criteria for disbanding a squad it is a modern miracle there are any squads left, with the exceptions of the Homicide and Fraud squads.

Most policemen, once they got into the squads, were happy to remain a senior detective; this is where the real action and the dough are. Often a bloke would remain a senior detective for ten or fifteen years before he would even entertain thoughts of applying to become a sergeant.

Once you became a sergeant the rule was that you could not accept your promotion and remain in your present station or squad. So if you were a senior detective in the Armed Robbery

Squad you couldn't stay there and take your promotion as a sergeant. It was a must that you returned as a uniform sergeant to Russell Street, usually for about a year. Then when a vacancy arose back in your squad, you could re-apply to go back as a detective sergeant. The theory was that you trained to be a sergeant in a controlled atmosphere in Russell Street.

Nice idea but in reality the sergeants at Russell Street did no more than mark time and teach starry-eyed junior constables bad habits which quickly became ingrained. It didn't take long for the penny to drop that the sergeants were slack, with scant attention to detail, and that this attitude was then accepted by the young constables and on it went.

Malcolm soon saw that the sergeants loathed being back at Russell Street and back in uniform. All they wanted was for their penance to pass quickly so they could jump back into the action. Rule number one with all the sergeants was to do as little as possible until such time as they went back to either the local CIB or to the squads. Often on nightshift if you were in the divvy van with one sergeant in particular, you'd drive into the Fitzroy Gardens, drive down one of the pedestrian walkways, right into the middle of the gardens, into a secluded spot and it was time for a sleep. You would literally sleep nightshift away and accomplish nothing.

Not all the sergeants were only marking time at Russell Street, some were much smarter than others and used their time to select what they saw as potential in young constables. The sergeant would make a point of cultivating a particular kid, invite him/her to visit his station and if all parties thought it was a good fit then when the constable completed the Russell Street stint he could apply for a vacancy at that station.

Malcolm struck up a relationship with a sergeant who came from Fitzroy, a real old fashioned inner suburban working class station and he wanted him to check the place out with a view to applying to be Fitzroy bound. He hadn't witnessed any real violence until then; sure a drunk from time to time threw the odd cut lunch (punch) at him, but nothing serious.

One night on his way out for dinner with his girlfriend he decided to drop in and check out the Fitzroy station. He was stunned; the whole joint was like something out of a Charles Dickens novel, ancient and badly run down. You could smell the despair and decay. He was directed to the cells for a look and was appalled to see a number of coppers giving a bloke a good old-fashioned flogging. What was his offence to warrant this? Giving cheek to the sergeant? This bloke was in a bad way. If this was life at Fitzroy then he wasn't going to have a bar of it. He didn't apply for Fitzroy.

Violence was an accepted part of police life and it didn't matter what Force Command gave out to the media—gratuitous violence was there to stay. It continues today, you only have to look to the antics that gave rise to the disbanding of the Armed Robbery squad a few years ago—when they were filmed bashing a suspect senseless in an interview room—for reinforcement of this proposition. To suggest that with the disbanding of the 'Robbers' violence miraculously dissipated from the force is frankly an insult to the intelligence of the public.

Some of the sergeants were entrepreneurial, and they would use the time to go round and replenish domestic freezers and pantries until such time as they were on nightshift again. During that time Malcolm learnt invaluable lessons such as how to go to the Four'N Twenty Pie factory to score pies, pasties and sausage rolls. Even though it was outside the Russell Street area, a sergeant was able to make the decision to move outside the area whereas the young constables couldn't. They were taken to places like the Tip Top Bakers where the blokes would get bread and bread rolls and cakes, not for the police stations but for themselves. As a young copper, going to these places wasn't your rort so you could not call the shots but the sergeants always made sure the driver copped his fair whack of the contraband. This was Malcolm's first experience of the 'sling', a tradition that remains alive and well in the Victoria Police Force.

When you were driving around in the divvy van, you always had to be with a sergeant. They knew where all the illegal two up games were held in the Melbourne precinct and would often drive past them. You would see the cockatoo (look out) at the front and he would not even bother racing inside to warn the operators of the game that the coppers were in the vicinity. The van would pull up out the front and without exception the sergeant would tell you to wait in the van while he went into the game in full uniform. A short time later he would emerge and jump back in the car. Nothing was ever said. Looking back it's clear that he was picking up his cash sling for not interrupting the game.

This was the introduction of a young copper to the workings of the Victoria Police Force. By the way, the miserable bastards never cut the young constables in on any cash slings—most coppers are greedy.

Malcolm soon tumbled to the fact that if you kept your eyes open there was a rort around every corner. As a young bright-eyed copper, it was hard to support your family on his wage so he also drove cabs part-time, even though you weren't supposed to. You never bothered seeking clearance from above—you just did it. You would make sure you went to places like the Italian Waiters Club, which in those days was a famous sly grog establishment in Melbourne, in uniform while on duty to be certain they knew exactly who you were. Then later on, while on nightshift or while driving a cab, you would wander back into the club and sit down and have a feed and have some grog and at the end all you had to do was flash your Freddie. Malcolm remembers his sergeant even telling him 'Make sure you take your hat off when we are in there', 'Why?' 'So he recognises you when you go back later for your free feed.' What a beauty! Thank you very much, no charge, see you later.

Bear in mind these coppers were supposed to be pinching these clubs to stamp out sly grogging in the City of Melbourne. Instead, in return for a free feed, these blokes got a clear run at it. You couldn't get a legal drink to save yourself in the middle of the night in Melbourne in those days.

In those days the coppers were something akin to a large social networking organisation. Melbourne was, as it is still, with the addition of junkies to the equation, full of old drunks, vagrants and homeless people and a lot of these old blokes were real old school crooks. Some went right back to the thirties. Malcolm remembers locking up somebody who had been an associate of Squizzy Taylor's (a famous gangster from the 1920s). These poor old blokes had been drinking methylated spirits and were not well, lying unconscious in the gutter. The coppers would stop and fill up the divvy van with these poor old blokes and then either take them to the Salvation Army Gill Memorial Home or if they were too pissed, back to the city watch house and put them into the cell known as the 'drunks tank' where they were left till they sobered up, usually for four hours. They'd give them a feed and then put them back out on the street. The Salvos did a lot better than the police in that they would try to keep them there, do their best to keep them off the grog, wash them up, feed them and try and keep them on the straight and narrow. The Salvos are the one organisation that keeps picking people up, it doesn't matter how many times they fall down. I reckon the Salvos do a terrific job, they are a good mob, they stand for and practice what all human beings should be irrespective of religion—good people who try and help their fellow man and on any assessment that is admirable.

By far the best thing about working at Russell Street on nightshift, even though it was a shocking shift, was the infamous Nightshift Barbecue. It wasn't just Russell Street that did the Nightshift Barbecue; every major police station that had a nightshift did the same thing. The Russell Street Nightshift Barbecue was always held in Royal Park at the end of weekly nightshift and everything that was consumed at the barbecue was 'donated' by various publicans, sly groggers, legitimate businesses, two up operators—the lot.

The barbecue itself started at about 2 am on the nightshift, which had commenced at 11 pm, so there was never any policing done on the last night of nightshift. The entire shift was spent either setting up the barbecue or going round collecting goods to be consumed at the barbecue. They didn't miss anyone, stamping them for contributions to the barbecue. Everybody was visited by the nightshift party and donations kindly accepted. The function was immense. Not just Russell Street nightshift coppers were there but day shift and afternoon shift would turn up, and from surrounding police stations: Carlton, Fitzroy, City West and Richmond. Coppers from anywhere and everywhere would front; it was bigger than ten bears! Don't forget they were all supposed to be on duty, yet they all hit the sauce, because huge amounts of grog had been donated by publicans, licensed bottle shops and even the sly grog merchants. About once a month the owner of a famous Greek restaurant in Melbourne would turn up with the souvlaki which he had made himself as a special treat for the boys and a thank you for looking after him. The barbecue was a weekly occurrence, not just for special occasions, and the amount of work not done on those nights was breath taking.

Things got progressively more out of hand the larger the party became; blokes discharging firearms in a public park and all driving home pissed off their heads were but a couple of the popular party tricks. Eventually the barbecue was banned, but not to be deterred its organisers went underground. It was still held but at varying locations. Never let it be said that coppers lack ingenuity.

From a professional perspective the most interesting and informative part of Malcolm's first posting was as security at the Beech Inquiry. The Beech Inquiry was not a Royal Commission but an inquiry by the soon-to-be His Honour Mr Justice Barry Beech QC of the Supreme Court of Victoria into alleged corruption in Victoria Police.

As a young constable on duty, Malcolm saw the sergeants who were his mentors at Russell Street being hauled up before the Beech Inquiry under allegations of loading blokes up with false evidence, verballing them, that is, making false statements that were attributed to them, copping bribes and robbing people. Malcolm found it hard to correlate this with the antics of the sergeants in the divvy van or in the crime cars in his formative days at Russell Street. Looking back however he realised these blokes were the ones that either went to sleep on divisional van duty on nightshift or spent the shift driving all over Melbourne rorting for their own ends. It's now clear to him that what they were doing in those days was actually teaching the young coppers the ropes, showing them how to rort. They were nothing but bad influences ingraining bad habits that last a lifetime. In his experience young coppers didn't turn their minds to the question of possible corruption. This was the way it was done and you had senior officers telling you precisely that.

ONE OF THE GREAT JOBS FOR A YOUNG COPPER AT RUSSELL Street was to drive the duty officer around. By the way in those days 'great job' equalled 'slack job'. Even in Malcolm's infancy in the job one of the first things he noticed was everyone's aversion to paperwork. It was better to advise some punter at the enquiry desk there was nothing you could do for him rather than find yourself saddled with a mountain of paperwork you could never get on top of. Slackness was a way of life.

A duty officer was of the rank of inspector or above and they were supposed to be independent. They would, for instance, come into the interview room after a crook had been interviewed, interview register under his wing, and send the interviewing coppers out of the room before enquiring whether the crook had any complaints about their treatment by police and if they didn't, the duty officer would sign off the interview register and the crook was processed. In those days, all the crooks were old school and even if they had been belted unconscious they would say that they were satisfied with their treatment by the police. The duty inspector's job was pretty easy.

However, there was more to being an inspector than met the eye. As Malcolm drove one particular duty inspector around, now retired, he would be asked to go to various houses around the suburbs and wait while he went inside. These were ordinary suburban houses with no criminal connections whatsoever. He would be in the house for half an hour or so then come out again. It was clear that he was shagging various women all over Melbourne and he was doing it while on duty, the young coppers acting as his personal limousine drivers.

I'VE HAD MY OWN EXPERIENCE WITH A DUTY OFFICER, WHO IS still in the job, and his so called 'independence'. Jason and Mark Moran had given themselves up to the Major Crime Squad one Friday evening and I had made an arrangement with Detective Sergeant Brian 'the skull' Murphy that I would attend at St Kilda Road with my two clients. It was agreed both would be placed in one interview room and I could be present while they were interviewed. I arrived at St Kilda Road with my clients. No Brian Murphy: the skull had, out of the blue, gone home early. Instead, when we arrived, they grabbed each Moran, put them in separate rooms and told me to fuck off. I said, 'that's not the arrangement I had with Brian Murphy' and was told, 'Murphy's not here, you're not listening, fuck off.' I refused to go and the detective, who was a very large unit, grabbed me by the back of the collar and the back of my pants and literally threw me out of the Major Crime Squad office. I was furious and had to endure various Major Crime coppers laughing at my expense.

I went downstairs and called for the duty officer to make a complaint. I waited and waited and kept asking and waiting until finally a couple of hours later the duty inspector appeared. He took one look at me and said, 'What are you doing here?' (The duty inspector and I didn't exactly hit it off.) I said 'I'm here to make a complaint.' He said, 'What's the complaint?' I said 'I was thrown out of the Major Crime Squad and told to fuck off.' He looked at me then and said, 'Yeah, what a good idea, fuck off' and turned and walked away. No complaint was ever taken. That's an independent inspector for you.

It transpired that the reason I was kept waiting was so that they could charge both my clients, get them to the old City Watch House and have their bail refused without any legal representation. By the time the penny dropped I thought: two can play at that game. I attended the watch house, ascertained which Justice of the Peace had been used and drove off to Carlton to pick him up so I could make a bail application. Once upon a time if bail was refused and your clients were unrepresented you could find representation and make another application, which is precisely what I did. All the Majors had shot through and bail was granted. The coppers were not happy when they realised I had short-sheeted them.

Life was pretty rough and tumble in those days.

Chapter Four

HARD MEN—THE PAINTERS AND DOCKERS

'I must go down to the seas again, to
the lonely sea and the sky.'

—John Masefield

While stationed at Russell Street Malcolm was occasionally sent for temporary postings at nearby stations if they were down on staff. One such posting was a short stay at the old Flinders Lane Police Station. In this almost derelict building was a run down police station, only open to the public during business hours. The station also had an afternoon shift where they closed up and two of them headed off on foot patrol around Flinders Lane and Degraves Street, and the Flinders Street Station area. One evening, close to knock off time, about 10.30 pm, Malcolm pulled over a car in Elizabeth Street near Flinders Lane that didn't have its headlights on. It was being driven by a young woman and she had a girlfriend with her. It was her last night of freedom, as she was soon to be married. He took the details of her licence and decided not to issue the ticket. Then he arranged to meet the girls at the Flinders Lane Police Station at the end of their shift to have a drink with them.

Close to 11 o'clock the two constables headed back to the station to finish their paperwork and the girls turned up. They invited them into the station, which was closed at that time. Nothing untoward was happening when lo and behold, within a few minutes of the girls arriving, the duty officer, Inspector Jackson, walked into the police station and there they were, a couple of young coppers with two unauthorised females in a police station. They tried to explain as best they could that they were intending to take them out after work and that they had pulled the girls up without headlights and let them go with a warning. The shit hit the fan. Inspector Jackson entered in the Occurrence Book that there were two unauthorised females in the police station. Malcolm was to report to Russell Street the following morning at the start of the day shift.

The next day he reported as ordered and met with Senior Sergeant Alan Jeans, (coach at St Kilda football club), who announced that his behaviour was so unprofessional that it warranted a substantial punishment. Malcolm was sent to Victoria Dock Police Station to do penance there for at least six months. He was not happy, because the girls being at the station was entirely innocent. Jackson had misread the situation totally but it was useless arguing—a constable versus an Inspector, no contest—so he copped it sweet. To make matters worse, he was also told that he had to write the young lady a ticket for driving without headlights and post it to her in the mail. Boy, didn't that go down well when she got the ticket just before her wedding. She rang him and let him have it down the phone.

In those days the wharves and waterfront were run by the Federated Ships Painters and Dockers Union and I mean *run*. The union was hardcore and often bloody-minded; they nearly sent the stevedoring companies to the wall with their work practices and militancy. There was a period when you could not even get a job on the docks unless you had form and preferably had been to jail. It follows that the docks were full of hard men who couldn't care less about some snotty nosed copper trying to poke it into their business. He pulled his head in or they would pull it off.

These were the halcyon days on the wharves; if you needed a new TV all you had to do was have a beer in a certain pub and not only was the telly the right price but delivery was thrown in for good measure. I regularly heard of entire containers going missing and I clearly recall being in a pub in Port Melbourne one night and noticing every bloke in the bar had brand new runners on—all the same brand. We can assume they didn't come from a special at Kmart!

Violence (many a bloke allegedly went for a swim off the end of Station Pier in Port Melbourne wearing nothing but his concrete boots) was another hallmark of the P&Ds as they were nicknamed, together with allegations of stand over tactics and even money laundering. All of which conspired to bring about the P&Ds demise in the form of the Costigan Royal Commission constituted in 1980 to enquire into the activities of the union, and running for four long years. The Royal Commission was long and thorough and while the findings failed to land a knock out punch against the Union its real force was dissipated if for no other reason than Costigan made such a pest of himself and applied such pressure that business started being done elsewhere, effectively ending the stranglehold the Union had over the wharves and stevedoring companies.

When Malcolm was sent to Victoria Dock the P&Ds were at their zenith. The dock area was another world which operated by its own set of rules, all backed by Union enforcers and the executive of the P&Ds.

Malcolm quickly gleaned from other coppers that Victoria Dock was the place they sent the bad apples, the recalcitrants, the old drunks, the trouble-makers and the coppers they couldn't sack and wanted out of the public eye until they retired. What a great career move—here he was being sent to purgatory, not exactly a ringing endorsement of how he was travelling as a copper. Still, it would expose him to real criminals, lots of old school crooks who knew the ropes, and if he kept his wits about him he would learn a lot—which is precisely how things turned out.

Things didn't get off to a flying start. The senior sergeant was already suspicious of him because he had been sent down to Victoria Dock as punishment. Even though nothing had happened with the women at Flinders Lane, rumours were rife that dirty deeds went on before the inspector arrived. On one hand Malcolm was a bit of a hero for supposedly rooting on the job but on the other the officers thought he was not to be trusted without strict supervision. It was in this climate that he commenced his duties at Victoria Dock.

He approached his stint on the waterfront with some trepidation but once there he found that he enjoyed the work. Instead of every sergeant and officer being on his case it was a pleasant surprise to find the constables were left pretty much to their own devices. They worked in plain clothes and drove around the docks and surrounding areas in unmarked police cars and of course, they carried a shooter. It felt like being on the film set of *On the Waterfront* as some sort of Marlon Brando-type. He learnt who all the good crooks of Melbourne were by observing the Painters and Dockers around the place. He learned how the wharfies worked and how they didn't work; he saw the thieving that went on, not only by the wharfies but also by the coppers who worked on the Dock. The theft carried out by each was on a grand scale; it was open season on anything not nailed down and some things that were.

The Painters and Dockers couldn't have cared less about the police presence on the docks; in fact they treated the force with utter disdain. It cut both ways. The coppers knew where the crooks were during business hours, and that made pinching them easy. For instance if a stick up took place and a P&D was a suspect it was a relatively easy task to ascertain whether he was at work at the relevant time. Police presence on the docks also made intelligence gathering simple. They took photos of the wharfies, their cars, and who they hung around with—all vital information that was passed on to other squads on a needs basis.

What about this for an odd job? Weekly they drove the Armaguard van in full police uniform, doing the payroll delivery. What was that all about? I bet that somewhere, somehow a senior copper was copping a sling.

What always amazed Malcolm about Victoria Dock was that the sworn members of the Victoria Police were paid their wages by the Melbourne Harbour Trust, the police station was provided by the Melbourne Harbour Trust and the police vehicles were serviced and owned by the Melbourne Harbour Trust. If that were to happen today, you would have to think that was a conflict of interest, wouldn't you? Whose orders were you supposed to follow?

They felt like some sort of private army operating in another dimension. The job wasn't taxing. It was essentially driving from wharf to wharf, theoretically keeping an eye on the wharfies, in the vain hope you could stop the pilfering, which was of plague-like proportions. How could the coppers possibly stamp out pilfering when they were some of the main offenders? Remember, the majority of the coppers at Victoria Dock were only going one way in the force: out. Before that happened they were determined to make every post a winner and didn't they work hard at it. Talk about leaving the monkey in charge of the bananas! For the bad eggs of the force, most of them didn't give a bugger what was going on with the P&Ds because they were too bust pinching stuff flat out themselves.

Containers came and went at the docks, but nothing like those huge things you see today. Back then the majority of the cargo coming into Victoria Dock was in tea chests and big hessian bales—easy to breach. For example, and this is tiny in comparison to what else went on, there would be a tea chest full of tea that had been rammed (on purpose) by the wharfies using the forklift. Obviously it was damaged goods. Would the coppers on patrol make a damage report or quarantine the damaged goods until they could be assessed for insurance? No, they would always be telephoned by one of the officers in charge at the station to collect enough tea not only for the station but for all those who wanted to take some home. There you'd be, standing on the wharf taking orders over the two-way radio like some bloody clerk in a grocery store. Tea, coffee, sugar and meat, along with all sorts of weird and wonderful consumables that had been 'damaged'—they'd just help themselves.

The difficult part for the P&Ds was getting their ill gotten gains past the security gates because the coppers who manned them randomly searched the blokes or their cars. On the other hand it was easy for the coppers to get their loot home; they were able to walk off the wharf, straight through the gates manned by coppers who had just minutes before picked up their share of whatever the rort of the day had been: one of the early examples Malcolm witnessed of the Brotherhood in action.

There were other times when small articles like underwear or even an item as inexpensive as handkerchiefs would be given to the police to take back to the police station to share among the others. Malcolm could not believe the pettiness of some of the coppers. If it was there to pinch they were into it like a chicken into hot gravy, whether they needed the item or not. On one occasion he saw a copper take perhaps over two hundred handkerchiefs. What in heaven's name are you going to do with two hundred hankies?

While the use of containers wasn't what it is now, there were proper containers on the wharves back then. Even so, security wasn't what it is, nor were the manifests as detailed and closely scrutinised as now. Regularly when electronic goods, such as TVs, stereos or air conditioners, came onto the wharf, somehow the container would be breached. Those items were not available on the wharf but after work, if you wanted to place an order with certain blokes down at the pub, then you could pick up the TV or the air conditioner or other electrical goods, or get free home delivery for larger items. *That's* customer service.

Just down the road from Victoria Dock was and still is the Seatainers Terminal. This was a huge complex even back then and it was owned and run privately by the Seatainers company. A bloke by the name of Jack Ford was the head of security there. Jack Ford had been named in the Kaye Royal Commission as being a corrupt police officer who had taken bribes to turn a blind eye to illegal abortions. As a result of that, in addition to being expelled from the force, he went to jail. On release, up he bobs, bold as brass, and lands a plum job as head of security for a huge multi-national where honesty is paramount. Jack Ford was neither and Malcolm couldn't work that one out in a million years: how a publicly named corrupt cop, newly released from jail, scored a job on the wharves as head of security for Seatainers. It beggared belief.

Everyone at the station knew Ford had been to jail. They were regularly called to Seatainers by Ford when a container had been breached or contraband had been found in a Painter and Docker's car as he was leaving the wharf. Off they had to go to Seatainers to charge that particular person with theft. Ford's life just rolled on as if he had never been inside.

THIS SORT OF BUSINESS ON THE WHARVES WENT ON FOR A LONG, long time. To give you an example, I'll tell you about a little episode that demonstrates how the endemic corruption persisted for many years after Malcolm moved on from the docks. Much later, while Malcolm was in the Drug Squad, they learnt that the old school Melbourne crooks, Lewis Moran and Graeme Kinniburgh (known as 'the Munster'), had imported a container of hashish into Melbourne docks. Coincidentally both Lewis and the Munster were old P&Ds who had first met working on the docks as young blokes. They became lifelong best mates. Somehow, Moran and Kinniburgh got word that the container was 'off', which meant that the coppers had got wind of the fact that they had brought in this container and the coppers were all over it like a rash. To go near it would certainly result in getting pinched. Once a container is 'off' it is very difficult to get it off the wharf. I can't say it doesn't happen, but it is difficult. There are other possibilities though. Among the thousands and thousands of containers on the wharf, the easiest thing in the world is for one of them to get 'lost', and this is what Moran and the Munster managed to do with their container. The Drug Squad had had it parked in a designated spot so it could be watched around the clock. They had been watching it day and night and after some months one night it disappeared into thin air right from under their noses, literally. The container, which the Drug Squad knew was full of hashish, disappeared, though it could not have left the wharf.

Over the years it didn't matter how hard the Drug Squad searched or watched, they couldn't locate this container. One of them had had a look in the container when it first arrived. That's how they knew the hash was in it and they also knew what it looked like and how it was packaged. Years later, this very same hashish started turning up on the streets and to this day, they don't know how Kinniburgh and Moran accessed the container, let alone got the stuff off the wharf.

It is now a matter of public record that Lewis Moran sold ten kilos of hashish directly to Malcolm while he was still in the Drug Squad. Each block of hash was wrapped in newspaper and when they got it back to the Drug Squad and unwrapped it, they realised that the newspapers were about fifteen years old. The hash was as hard as a rock and had dried out. Even now, the police don't know where that container is. It's probably still sitting at some secret location on the wharf, still half full, because both Kinniburgh and Moran were murdered during the so-called Gangland Wars.

It was painfully apparent to everyone concerned that somebody on the wharf had to be turning a blind eye, and therefore in on the rort, for this container to be continually accessed and hashish removed. But who, why, when or how, we will never know. Just one of the eternal mysteries of the Melbourne Docks.

THE GREATEST COVER-UP THAT MALCOLM EVER WITNESSED WAS during his time on the wharves in the late seventies. Victoria Police were changing over from the old .32 automatic pistols that they were using as service firearms to the Smith & Wesson .38 revolvers. The police operating at the dock were told that there was a container full of the new revolvers coming in from America. This was top secret because of the nature of the cargo. They were ordered to watch the container's every move, making sure that the Victoria Police received the delivery intact. Handguns are a top shelf underworld item, eagerly sought after by the very blokes unloading the container. Malcolm was one of the officers down on the wharf watching the container being unloaded. Somehow the Painters and Dockers had got wind of the contents of the container. By the time it was unloaded and taken off the wharf there were at least 100 pistols missing. How such a thing happened Malcolm could not work out but it was clear that the P&Ds had helped themselves to a large number of firearms. The police were then ordered from the very top not to talk to anybody and not to bother looking for the guns, because they would be long gone.

Someone, somewhere got their hands on a load of brand new shooters. Why keep it dark? Well, it's bloody embarrassing for coppers to admit they can't keep an eye on their own stuff.

Another tale from those times. Putty Nose Nicholls, who was the head of the P&Ds, had a son who also worked on the docks. One afternoon Malcolm and his fellow coppers on the docks saw a car tear through a police checkpoint at Webb dock, where they were searching cars for hot gear. To run the gauntlet is almost an admission of guilt so Malcolm and his partner jumped in a car and gave chase and what a chase it was: through the streets of Port Melbourne, through Footscray and finally to Williamstown, where the car came to an abrupt halt outside a house and the driver bolted inside. As they ran in the back door after him a lunatic appeared wielding a pitch fork, lunged at Malcolm's mate and injured him. They were in plain clothes and hadn't had time to identify themselves as police so anything could have been on the cards. The bloke with the fork was off his head, screaming and shouting, and Malcolm thought he would kill one of them for certain. Malcolm pulled his gun, aimed it at the bloke with the pitchfork and yelled that they were police and to put the fork down. The man hesitated but finally complied. Malcolm was so scared that if he had made one false move he would have shot him for certain.

The bloke with the pitchfork turned out to be Putty Nose Nicholls himself and it was his son they had been chasing. All ended well with the son giving himself up and no one getting killed. What a willing old customer Putty Nose had been, even when faced with two blokes with shooters aimed straight at him.

MANY YEARS LATER, WHEN MALCOLM WAS IN THE ST KILDA Crime Cars squad, he still wasn't able to get away from the Painters and Dockers and was called on regularly to help out other coppers investigating the P&Ds. Malcolm knew how they thought and also who was who at the zoo. One afternoon when he was on patrol he was called to the old Bayview Hotel in Cecil Street, South Melbourne. The Bayview was not as flash as it is now. These days it's a trendy gourmet pub: Lamaro's. Back then it was the blood house where all the P&Ds drank. Malcolm's car had been chasing a bloke called Victor Allard all the way from the docks and as they tore down Cecil Street they saw him dart down a side street. Malcolm jumped out of the car and charged in the front door of the pub in time to hear two shots ring out. It turned out Vic had run in the door off the side street, and as they say, fell on a couple of bullets, and there he was lying in a pool of blood. They closed the pub down, locked all the doors and started asking everybody for witness statements. Nobody had seen anything—what a surprise. They approached Allard, who was lying on the floor waiting for an ambulance to arrive. They asked him if he knew who had shot him, and was he prepared to make a statement. To which he told them to: 'Fuck off, coppers'. And that was the end of that. They never solved that shooting and no one was ever charged. Allard was shot to death in Fitzroy Street some years later after he had been promoted from Painter and Docker to drug dealer.

AS A YOUNG CRIMINAL LAWYER I WANTED TO BE WHERE THE action was and nowhere was better on that score than acting for the P&Ds. By the late seventies I had met and was acting for Lewis and his brother Tuppence Moran, so called because he was tuppence short of a pound. Lewis was a terrific source of work and this was well known in the legal profession, so much so that before I became partners with Brian Rolfe and Bob Galbally they tried to lure Lewis away from me, but Lewis was staunch and stuck.

Lewis introduced me to a few old P&Ds and it wasn't long before the work started flowing. My first big break was a call to meet a bloke by the name of Anthony Farrell, alias 'The Mushroom', at the P&D watering hole The Southern Cross in Port Melbourne. The Mushroom had hit a hurdle over the far from outrageous allegation that he was a heroin dealer. In those days this pub was renowned as being as rough as hessian underpants and it was with some trepidation that I approached the bar on a summer's afternoon. Here I was, in my lawyer's suit, while everyone in the bar was in P&D bib and brace overalls. As I walked in the door of the bar the joint fell silent. They all thought that being there in a bag of fruit, I must have been a copper. It was only when the Mushroom (as he was invariably referred to) approached me and introduced himself that things settled down again.

I was having trouble hearing over the general din and the TV going flat out, broadcasting the races. A bloke with Mushy yelled out to turn the TV down but he was ignored. Without further ado he hauled a pistol out of his overalls and blew the telly away. Without blinking an eye he put the gun away, saying 'I told youse to turn the fucking telly down.' This was the first actual pistol I had ever seen. In the years to come I saw many more, usually when clients had been on the wrong end of one.

The P&Ds were on the books. Like Malcolm I'd been introduced to a world with its own laws.

Chapter Five

HOT WHEELS: THE STOLEN MOTOR VEHICLE SQUAD

'Everything happens to everybody sooner
or later, if there is time enough.'

—George Bernard Shaw

In 1978 Malcolm left the madhouse that was Victoria Dock and sat his exams for promotion to the rank of Senior Constable. He passed and became a senior detective. His first posting was to the old Bureau of Criminal Intelligence (BCI) where he undertook basic observation work, which for a still-young copper felt just like being in ASIO, sneaking around like a spy.

Here he was under the command of Fred Silvester, an old-fashioned copper who did everything strictly by the book and woe betide anyone caught trying to take a shortcut during an investigation. This was the one unit Malcolm was involved with where there was never any shifty business. It comprised three sections: tactical, surveillance and 'technical', in which the unit carried out telephone tapping and breaking into people's houses to plant listening devices. He never knew when the target might return home unexpectedly—it was very exciting work.

Malcolm only stayed at BCI for a couple of years and was not far off completing his stint when he decided to go with a couple of mates to the TokH hotel in Toorak for a drink one night. It turned out to be the best move he ever made. He met a girl that night called Gillie and they hit it off straight away. They spent the night chatting, thoroughly enjoying each other's company. His mates gave him stick about it next morning but he didn't care, it was love at first sight. They're still together all these years later.

The issue of money was always present, living on a copper's wage. There was never enough, especially with a wedding pending. Malcolm's brother went into a business in a nightclub known as Madison's, a very flash joint for the times. There were always dickheads trying to sneak in, so Malcolm got a job on the door. Being a copper from the docks he had a fair handle on most of the crooks' heads from around town and it was his job to point them out so they could be refused admission.

This was back in the days when security licences were unnecessary and stacks of coppers had jobs bouncing. The word got out that off duty coppers were giving blokes gratuitous floggings and trouble was brewing at Force Command. So Malcolm moved off the door to mix cocktails. He worked Wednesday, Thursday, Friday and Saturday nights from 9 pm to 3 am and in that time he learned more about what was going on in Melbourne than he did in a fortnight as a copper. No wonder every man and his dog chased extra work.

The head of the Crime Department visited one evening and advised that crooks were getting in. He wanted them stopped, so Malcolm went back to vetting who came in. There was no problem from the Commander about the extra job; he just wanted the crooks kept out.

Coppers always turned up to drink and he looked after them with that terrific new invention that all coppers perfected in the years to come: the drink card. They all drank for nothing. After all you had to look after your mates in the Brotherhood.

Malcolm's first real posting as a detective was to the Stolen Motor Vehicle Squad. Now he was part of a fully fledged detective unit pinching real crooks. No more sneaking into some poor bastard's house while he was at the movies and bugging him. Now he was a detective, a far cry from Russell Street as a constable still wet behind the ears. He was in a CIB squad and wasn't he shit hot?

With most of the Force the best thing to look forward to was the Friday afternoon piss up. The Stolen Car Squad was no exception. In fact they took it to another level. The interview room was transformed into a bar with a table positioned across the doorway, the grog was stacked behind the table in the interview room, complete with ice troughs. A couple of detectives manned the bar. Cheap grog is a copper's delight and they had it by the bucketful. Beer and spirits were provided to all those from the Stolen Motor Vehicle Squad, the Arson Squad, Homicide Squad and any other squads that were invited to come along and partake on any given Friday.

The grog was well below retail and even below the prices charged at the Police Club bar. How did they do this? Malcolm's contacts on the docks.

The Stolen Car Squad had many vehicles that it used in its day-to-day activities: utilities, panel vans, station wagons and of course the four wheel drive. It was like a posse in the movies, with Malcolm leading the charge to the docks to meet captains of ships coming from interstate that he had got to know while in his previous posting. There they bought stacks of alcohol at wholesale less excise. They were able to pull this stunt thanks to the good old Aussie Constitution, section 92, which states that there shall be free trade between the states. The police paid no excise because the booze was coming directly from another state. What a ripping rort—no one could match their rock bottom prices.

Malcolm phoned the captain and made the necessary arrangements to pick up; it was as easy as that. They stacked the cars to the roof with enough grog to last the bar the month until the ship returned. They cleaned up out of this little earner. Of course, the cars that were used were police vehicles and no one obtained permission before using them for a non police activity. You have to wonder how it would have looked if they'd had a crash on the way back to Russell Street with all that grog sloshing around in a police vehicle.

While they were picking up the alcohol the captain always offered them other goods, like boxes of meat and chicken fillets, which they purchased at ridiculously low prices and later raffled at the Stolen Car Squad party. There was plenty of gambling activity too, for example playing punch boards, where you pushed out a number on a perforated board with the chance of winning five, ten, fifty or a hundred dollars. These were hugely popular and the social club did very, very well. They would also on-sell slabs of beer to the Armed Robbery Squad and other squads so they, in turn, could sell cheap beer to their members.

The Friday afternoon get togethers were legendary throughout Russell Street and every man and his dog would lob, including the superintendents of the Russell Street CIB and chief inspectors from the other squads. All the officers came in for a 'quiet one' because it was the cheapest and coldest beer in the building. All this took place in direct defiance of an edict from the Chief Commissioner that there was to be no alcohol consumed on the Russell Street premises—the entire Russell Street complex was supposed to be dry. Not a word was ever said by anyone about the Chief Commissioner's order; they were having too good a time.

Once everybody had finished drinking their cheap beer at the Stolen Car Squad, they moved down to Delaney's Hotel on the corner of Russell and Latrobe streets. There they would continue drinking until closing time and beyond, because though the publican closed the doors, he continued to serve the police. At the end of the night they would use the Squad's cars to organise lifts home. No such thing as a designated driver back then; even the driver was as pissed as a parrot!

There were often vehicles damaged on the drive home, followed by a cover up on the part of everyone involved. The worst occasion was that of a Detective designated to drive the senior sergeant and two others home all the way to the outer suburb of Mount Evelyn. He reached Mitcham station, let the senior sergeant off near his home and was continuing down the Maroondah Highway when, taking a corner too fast, he rolled the unmarked police car, not once or twice, but several times. Luckily he survived the accident and had the common sense to grab his briefcase and leave the scene of the crime. He knew if he stayed away for four hours he could refuse to be breath tested. The accident happened at about ten on a Friday night and the detective was found wandering around at 5 am the following morning, claiming to have amnesia. The Brotherhood sprang into action. Rather than pinch him with leaving the scene of an accident he was offered sympathy as a person who had been seriously injured, and taken to hospital. By pulling this stunt the detective evaded the breathalyser, any subsequent blood test or any sanction whatsoever. The police car was a write off and nothing further was done about it—the whole untidy incident had been swept well and truly under the carpet.

This incident in no way stalled the momentum of the Friday afternoon piss up and the Stolen Car Squad continued its legendary status as the place to be after work on a Friday. In fact it wasn't after work for many, as they usually kicked off the bar at about 2 pm so that anybody who was working the afternoon shift effectively did not work, and the rest were out of action from lunchtime onwards because they were setting up the bar.

IT WAS IN THE STOLEN CAR SQUAD THAT ONE OF THE GREATEST rorts of the lot reared its head. The American airline Continental had just opened a trans-pacific route to Australia, and in order to get bums on seats or some other reason that only those in the know would be able to explain, Continental offered senior officers in the police force free flights or ridiculously cheap flights if you were in one of the squads. And when I say cheap, I mean a return flight to Los Angeles from Melbourne via Sydney was something like $50 or a $100, depending on who you were. These tickets were too good to be true and these days it would be obvious that it was improper and easily construed as improper inducement to police. Not to be deterred, the coppers flocked to take up these free or cheap seats and many, many police had their first overseas trip compliments of Continental Airlines. This rort continued for three or four months until the cat got out of the bag and it was obvious that very senior police officers were availing themselves of free trips courtesy of this deal. There was hell to pay over this, and an ESD (Ethical Standards Department) investigation, which went absolutely nowhere. Unfortunately for all concerned the media got wind of the rort and started pursuing the coppers about improper inducements. The police did what they do most effectively and put up the shutters, trying to stonewall the media until they lost interest.

It was too late. The media had hold of it and weren't letting go. It ended up plastered all over the front pages and a number of senior officers were named. The official word in response was that some of the senior officers had been disciplined and some counselled. Malcolm couldn't believe that was all that happened to them. He hadn't taken a flight because he was newly married with a young family and couldn't afford it even at the prices on offer.

While in the Stolen Car Squad Malcolm was involved in a huge pinch in which he stumbled on a racket run by police. If the Force were brutally honest with Joe Public they'd admit that not many of the big pinches come from Sherlock Holmes-style detective work, but rather from stumbling across criminal activity by accident or through information received from the public.

For many, many years some Lebanese blokes, the Hassan Brothers, had operated a huge panel-beating and spare parts business in Shepparton. Highly successful, they were pillars of the community. Every Friday afternoon, the brothers would personally turn up at the Shepparton station laden with free grog and every policeman in Shepparton would get on the piss compliments of the Hassans for hours. From all accounts it was a ripping session, and what bloke is able to resist the lure of free grog? As matters transpired the motive behind the largesse of the brothers was not that they thought coppers were good blokes. They were operating a massive stolen car racket in Shepparton, right under the coppers' noses. The modus operandi was simple. Stolen cars were ferried from Melbourne en masse every Friday evening to the Hassan Brothers' various establishments throughout Shepparton and surrounding areas and there the cars would be re-birthed, or taken to pieces, stripped down and given new identities. This was achieved by attaching forged compliance plates to the car, filing numbers off chassis and engine blocks and re-stamping them with new numbers so that they could re-sell the cars. They also conducted a massive spare parts business and it turned out that anything not required for the re-birthing or spare parts business was taken out and buried on country properties by a local earthmoving contractor whenever he dug a new dam in the Shepparton area.

This lurk went on for years and the coppers at Shepparton all went to Hassan's to have their cars panel beaten, to pick up spare parts or to have their cars serviced. Then the Stolen Car Squad got wind of this nice little enterprise. They were ordered from the highest echelons of the police force under no circumstances to let anybody at Shepparton know that they had commenced an operation on Hassan's. This operation was fantastic police work and they were all very excited at the prospect of such a huge pinch.

Serious surveillance commenced. They observed what time the Hassans arrived at the police station and what time they usually left and that gave them a handle on their time table. For weeks they watched the convoy of stolen cars from Melbourne to Shepparton. They recognised a number of professional car thieves driving these cars and then all heading back to Melbourne in one car after leaving three or four cars at Hassan's. This was a big, well-organised operation that had obviously been going on for years.

One Friday afternoon, the Squad grabbed a young car thief, known to them as a heroin addict, arrested him, took him back to Melbourne and grilled him. There's nothing like the prospect of not having your next hit to act as an incentive to tip in. He duly went to water and tipped everybody in, telling the Squad precisely how the operation worked. They were off and running and executed numerous search warrants simultaneously in the Shepparton area, recovering truck loads, quite literally, of evidence. There were stolen number plates and car pieces, all pointing to the fact that there had been hundreds and hundreds of cars dealt with in this way.

At the end of this extremely successful series of raids the Hassan Brothers and a whole heap of other people who were involved with them were all charged, went to court and received heavy jail sentences.

Bearing in mind the local coppers' friendly relationship with the Hassans, what happened to the police? In the wash up no police were even interviewed. The Squad were rightly ecstatic at the results of the bust—and equally pleased no coppers got hit by friendly fire.

At the start of this book I complained about the police tactic of stonewalling and then, after the noise dies down, sweeping everything under the carpet. You may have noticed an emerging trend of that by this point in Malcolm's story of his life in the Force.

I PERSONALLY HAD DEALINGS WITH THE STOLEN CAR SQUAD. In the early eighties I bought a second hand Porsche from a reputable dealer. At about the same time there was a bit of a scare about a re-birthing racket involving Porsches. An inspector knew I had bought the car and as I was leaving the Melbourne Magistrates court one morning he and one of his sidekicks loomed up and said they were seizing my car on suspicion it was a re-birth. Needless to say I failed to see the humour of this and fired up. The upshot was the car stayed where it was, a Porsche expert was called who confirmed the car's bona fides and we all went on our merry way.

It was a couple of years later that I bumped into the inspector, who admitted the whole thing was carried out with the sole intention of winding me up. Boy, did it ever work!

ONE THING THE POWERS THAT BE IN THE FORCE LIKE TO DO IS to move you around from posting to posting, the theory being that corrupt practices cannot take hold if you're moved often enough.

For whatever reason, Malcolm was moved to Doncaster CIB in 1984 but as it turned out he was only at Doncaster for about six months before Task Force 'Wheels' at the Stolen Car Squad was formed and because of his experience he was seconded back to the Squad.

Far more important and exciting than his change of station was getting married to Gillie. They became engaged in 1983 and from the outset things had gone against them. First off he was engaged to a 'schiksa' (a derogatory term for a non-Jewish woman) and this did not sit well with his family or friends. Secondly he did not live in one of the Jewish areas of Melbourne, preferring to live in Templestowe, where they built their home. So from the outset, they had led a fairly isolated existence.

They married in a civil ceremony. They could not marry in a synagogue because Gillie was not Jewish. To her eternal credit Gillie, knowing how important Malcolm's religion was to him, embarked on the long road to converting to the Jewish faith. This journey usually takes about one year but for Gillie it took ten because Malcolm was a policeman and policing is not an acceptable occupation for a Jew, dragging out the process. When she completed the conversion process in 1994 they married again, only this time it was a real, traditional Jewish wedding in a synagogue.

TASK FORCE WHEELS WAS EASILY THE BIGGEST THING GOING AT the Stolen Cars. It was a joint Task Force with the Australian Federal Police into the importation of cars, mostly Mercedes Benz, from Singapore and Hong Kong where the cars are built with a right hand drive so they don't need converting for our roads. The police referred to these Mercedes as 'Hong Kong Holdens' because over there everyone appears to drive a Benz and they were as common as Holdens are here. The cars imported were shit heaps and should not have been registered. Someone was making a big quid and the Squad wanted to find out whom.

The scam worked like this: a car came into the country from Hong Kong or South Africa and somehow, even though they did not comply with Australian Design Rules, they ended up registered and sold to the unsuspecting public.

It soon emerged that any Benz with the rego prefix of BXA or BZA was suspect. It then transpired that the majority of these cars ended up being sold out of Riverside Motors in South Yarra.

There are two things all the consumer protection legislation in the universe cannot legislate against: greed and stupidity. By way of example, at that time, a given model of Benz retailed in Australia legitimately for say, $25,000. At Riverside the same model sold for $17,000. What the punter didn't know was that the car had been purchased overseas for two thousand and, after all shipping costs, a grand total of four thousand. Not a bad mark up in anyone's language.

Riverside advertised Benzes which at first blush appeared to be at very reasonable prices with no mention made of the fact the car was an import with dodgy provenance and did not comply with Australian Design Rules. They sold like hot cakes.

It wasn't long before the inherent problems started to surface: rust, mechanical problems, the lot. Think of a car problem and these things had it. The burning question was: how were these cars getting registered? The Squad dug deeper and ascertained that the cars were bypassing Victoria Police testing centres and the Road Traffic Authority. A sergeant at Yarra Glen, an outer Melbourne suburb, was doing the registering and copping a two hundred dollar sling in cash for every registration. There had been heaps of these regos and the sergeant concerned had made a pile. The Roadworthy certificates were bodgies into the bargain and it became clear he didn't even inspect the cars. Often they weren't even driven to Yarra Glen. Sometimes the dealers would collect the plates sight unseen from Yarra Glen where the registration had taken place and he copped his two hundred.

Not a bad lurk, but one that was bound to come unstuck, particularly once the Squad started delving into the bona fides of the Roadworthy certificates only to discover that they were written out in bulk, the cars never inspected at all. The number plate prefixes BZA and BXA had been assigned to Yarra Glen, a significant piece of evidence in convicting the crooked sergeant.

Once a pattern emerged they started seizing the suspect cars and boy didn't this ruffle a few feathers. People reacted very badly once they were told their cars were suspect, possibly forfeits. The seized cars went to forensics for further examination and it emerged that the cars were unroadworthy, and in some instances, plain dangerous to drive.

This was terrific work, done with a clear conscience and no shifty tricks, just five police working long hours to obtain a fantastic result. The entire house of cards came tumbling down around the participants' ears. For some time the word 'import' became a dirty word in the used car industry to such a degree that even legitimately imported cars had their resale value decimated.

Everyone in the rort was charged including the sergeant who went down big time and ended up in jail for a lengthy whack. While still basking in the glow of a job well done everyone in the Task Force received a Commissioner's commendation for their efforts, and the team were very satisfied.

Then, out of the blue a couple of coppers with very heavy reputations contacted each of the Task Force members and threatened them for putting their mate the corrupt sergeant behind bars. Physical violence was threatened, and the threats were taken very seriously. Collectively they were shitting themselves for some time.

In the Task Force traditional policing was the order of the day: collect information, identify possible suspects, investigate. If all the evidence stacked up, charge and obtain a conviction. No funny business, no rorts. Malcolm should have maintained this attitude to all his future policing but he got caught up in the culture with how things were done. He should have listened to Gillie when she pointed out the undesirables he was associating with because on each and every occasion she turned out to be spot on. He used to say to Gillie, 'Ask me no questions and I will tell you no lies.' He couldn't be told. He knew it all and as they say, pride comes before a fall.

Chapter Six

L!FE ON THE STREET

'Believe those who are seeking the
truth. Doubt those who find it.'

—Andre Gide

By 1986 Malcolm had been around the block a few times and he was eligible to sit his sergeant's exams, which he passed. Before his first posting as a sergeant he took six months' long service leave on half pay. His brother had recently purchased the Wattle Gully goldmine at Bendigo and it was his job to maintain security, making sure none of the gold was pinched by the miners. As a serving copper he could not officially be paid so Gillie went on the payroll instead.

The miners are suspicious of security in the first place and when they found out Malcolm was a copper they decided to take matters into their own hands. They set a booby trap in the dunny he used by placing a stick of gelignite under the toilet. He went to the toilet and as he walked away there was a huge explosion, the dunny blown to pieces. Miners don't muck around.

The job was supposed to last six months but the company

sold to a multinational after two months and he copped severance pay. He used this pay for an overseas holiday and then his next son was born, so he decided to cancel the balance of his leave and return to work.

His first posting as a uniform sergeant was to the St Kilda Police Station. Talk about welcome to the real world! As a criminal lawyer in the seventies and eighties doing the rounds of the suburban courts I found that the Prahran and St Kilda courts were always frantically busy. The cells were packed with junkies, dealers, prostitutes and pimps to say nothing of those arrested for assault or burglary—a veritable smorgasbord of offending. It was common to be locked in a holding cell with your client and a host of other crooks, as the genius who designed the cells invariably overlooked the fact that defendants usually retain lawyers who would probably like some instructions before court. It was a very intimidating situation, especially if a fight broke out, which happened regularly.

Malcolm had already seen his fair share of action but nothing could possibly prepare him for the pressure cooker the old St Kilda Police Station was. The volume of work hit from day one and there was no stop to the running or rorting until the day he left St Kilda.

In those days, the St Kilda Police Station was a rabbit warren of an old building with the CIB over the road on the other side of Chapel Street and just to confuse matters further the inspector's office down the road. This made for poor communication and administration but hey, who cares, coppers make it up as they go along any way. Because St Kilda was always the hub of prostitution and drug dealing in Melbourne along with most of the burglaries, assaults and other street crime that went with it, the coppers were as busy as one-legged arse kickers and as a result developed a real siege mentality. So much so, they called themselves the St Kilda Police Force.

Everybody knew where the drug dealing was taking place in those days, and that was St Kilda. But some bright spark in the Government had the brilliant idea that they should clean up the streets of St Kilda because it was becoming trendy and touristy. As a result, this fragmented the drug industry. Instead of drugs being essentially contained in and around St Kilda, after the crackdown in Fitzroy Street, the heroin industry suddenly dispersed and fragmented, springing up in Footscray, Dandenong and Springvale in particular. Where one head had been before all of a sudden a hydra appeared, and it became impossible for the coppers to even remotely get a handle on who was dealing drugs and where, because most of the drug dealers became highly mobile, moving from suburb to suburb to sell their product. Well done to the genius who thought of that. When drug dealing was essentially restricted to Fitzroy Street, it was easy. Everyone knew who was dealing with minimal surveillance and they also knew how to deal with them, but not now. That was the real start of the boom in the drug industry in this state.

Malcolm's first introduction to corruption at St Kilda was on a relatively minor scale. They used to purchase the old *Truth* newspaper and look up the ads for prostitutes. St Kilda was the hub of prostitution at the time and most of the girls lived and worked there. They would ring and make a booking and then turn up in their police uniforms, ostensibly to raid the premises. When Malcolm first saw the next little trick he could not believe it. The sergeant he had executed the warrant with went to the bedroom and had sex with the girl. They then searched the house, knowing she kept her money there, and took it. Needless to say the girl started to complain and carry on so the sergeant told her that if she kept blueing about it, he'd pinch her as well for good measure. Of course she shut up and he walked out, having had a root and with a pocket full of cash to boot. Not bad for a morning's work.

No junior ranks ever went on these raids. Often when the warrants were executed four or five sergeants would raid a couple of girls working out of a flat. The girls would be intimidated by the appearance of four or five sergeants. They would have no option but to turn on the free sex and lose their money as well. Up to five burly sergeants having sex with one girl: it was called a 'daisy chain'.

THE MOST DIFFICULT THING I FOUND IN ACTING FOR PROSTITUTES was that they hate paying, and if there is one thing lawyers loathe it's clients that don't cough up, so acting for a working girl was always interesting from the outset. On more than one occasion I heard a complaint exactly the same as the story related above, and I thought the girls must have been lying. Not that I believed everything the police said about their innocence either (not by a long chalk). But stealing in such a brazen manner was fraught with danger. I suppose the police worked on the premise that if push came to shove who would be believed: five coppers or a couple of girls of dubious reputation? Just goes to show, you learn something every day.

As a newly promoted sergeant, even though Malcolm had the three stripes, it was the more experienced senior constables who ran the show when they were out on patrol together. They had the years of experience at St Kilda and Malcolm was learning the ropes, even though he was theoretically in charge.

On one such patrol with one of these senior constables, they picked up a prostitute who had been working the street. She jumped in the back seat of the police car and Malcolm was directed to drive to a quiet location up a laneway where he thought the senior constable would have a quiet chat with the prostitute. He imagined she was an informer or giving information on a casual basis. It was still early in the afternoon and to his amazement, the senior constable jumped out of the passenger seat and got in the backseat with the female. The next thing he was copping a blow job in the back seat. Malcolm sat in the driver's seat dumbfounded. She didn't even want to be driven back to where she had been picked up. She just got out of the car and the constable hopped back in the passenger seat, looking very pleased with himself, like nothing had happened. He merely looked at Malcolm and smiled.

That wasn't the only example of such behaviour. When the nightshift wound up many coppers would literally stumble off to the houses or flats where they knew prostitutes plied their trade and they would go in, ten or more, and engage in sex with one of the girls, free of charge. This was commonly known as 'the train' where one policeman would shag the girl and the next one would line up to follow. Malcolm heard of these goings on on not just one occasion but many. Needless to say, the women complained, but their complaints were never accepted at the police station, so no action was taken. After all, boys will be boys. Any such complaint was treated as bullshit and senior officers would say as much to a working girl. They all stuck together, irrespective of rank, and yet again Malcolm saw the strength of presenting a united front to the world and the power of the Brotherhood.

Back in those days in St Kilda there was no security for exhibits and the coppers were regularly pinching people with substantial quantities of drugs or other illegally gained goods. Once the goods were logged and the person charged and processed, the exhibit would have a tag put on it and be placed in the storeroom. There was no drug safe, therefore, once again, no evidence of continuity. The bigger problem was however, that often when the matter was going before the courts, you would go into the storeroom to retrieve the bag of drugs that you had seized from a particular offender only to find that the drugs were missing. This did not happen once or twice—it happened on a regular basis. And it was not only the drugs that went missing, other items such as jewellery or weapons also evaporated into thin air.

Continuity of an exhibit is crucial to any prosecution. If the police cannot demonstrate that an exhibit is one and the same as the exhibit allegedly seized then the exhibit is of no evidentiary value with the inevitable result the prosecution usually fails. Therefore coppers must be able to prove the chain of hands that an exhibit has passed through to prove that it *is* the actual exhibit seized. In instances like this it would have been impossible to prove without the police witness manufacturing a chain of continuity and therefore perjuring himself.

The St Kilda Police Station was a complete bun fight but never more so than when St Kilda Court sat. The courthouse was adjacent to the police station. This was back in the days before defendants' prior convictions were computerised. It meant that for a sling the prosecuting sergeant could allege in court that there were no prior convictions known against an offender. This was, of course, complete and utter bullshit as everybody, the Magistrate included, often knew that a particular person had prior convictions, and sometimes plenty of them. However, if no prior convictions were alleged, then a person received a lesser sentence than one with prior convictions. To do this the prosecutor had to have been got at not to mention that a particular person had any priors. This was not only copping a sling, but perverting the course of justice and this happened many times at the St Kilda, Prahran and Elsternwick courts, which were the courts that the St Kilda Police visited.

On numerous occasions I have had precisely this happen to clients. Caught completely by surprise you could not agree your client had no priors because that would be misleading the court, a very serious matter indeed. Instead I would say to the court that 'there is nothing alleged against my client'. Semantics at its best!

At the Elsternwick Magistrates Court a second division of the court sat, which was chaired by the Justices of the Peace. The Js as they were called dealt with very minor matters to relieve some of the pressure on the Magistrate. Three Justices of the Peace sat and the Chairman was an old Jewish man by the name of Arnold Koppel. Mr Koppel was well known to the police in St Kilda and surrounding areas as he owned a bakery. The standing deal for every copper in the St Kilda station was to turn up to Mr Koppel's bakery and help yourself to whatever you wanted, absolutely free, no questions asked.

Old Arnie had a bit of a soft spot for this fine young Jewish sergeant and there was regularly a bottle of scotch from Mr Koppel for Malcolm. The downside was that once Mr Koppel found out Malcolm was Jewish, every member of the Jewish community, and it's a big Jewish community in St Kilda, would refer anyone in bother direct to him to look after. He was inundated. The problem with old Arnie was that he kept sticking his nose into other people's business because he considered himself to be an upstanding member of the Jewish community and a senior member at that. An example. On one occasion there was a fire where a business had burnt down and the family stood to collect a windfall from the insurance company. 'Buckets' Anderson, so called because of his big thirst, who was the inspector in charge of the Arson Squad, commenced investigating. The Squad found an incendiary device on the premises and immediately the fire was categorised as arson, therefore there would be no insurance pay out. Out of the woodwork, Mr Koppel appeared to try and smooth things over on behalf of the family. He went into Buckets' office and a short while later he left. What transpired is that he had given Buckets a watch on behalf of the family so that he would turn a blind eye to evidence of arson. Unbeknown to Mr Koppel, after he left, Buckets appeared at the door of his office and yelled out to all and sundry sitting in the main office area: 'Look what the old bastard tried to do. He's given me a $20 watch to try and bribe me not to investigate a million dollar fire. This is what I think of that.' And he chucked the watch in the bin.

Watches were a favourite sling for Arnie. There was a young Jewish bloke who was a bit of a tearaway, always in strife. As per usual Arnie stuck his bib in and called the sergeant concerned over to the boot of his car. He opened it and there was a boot-load of Seiko watches. The sergeant took one and the matter stopped there, no pinch. About six months later the same lout got into more bother and Arnie rang to see what he could do. 'Fuck him,' said the sergeant. 'I'm charging him this time and that's it.' All Arnie said in response was: 'Sergeant, do you have the time please?' He had the drop on the copper and he knew it. Problem solved.

Mr Koppel regularly sat as Chairman of the Justices at the Elsternwick Magistrates Court and it was always the best court for someone in trouble in Melbourne to appear in, particularly if he was Jewish. Prior convictions would regularly go missing. Young blokes would get pat on the head after pat on the head and Arnie would dish out a good behaviour bond.

Mr Koppel regularly turned up at the station unannounced with a box full of presents for the police. They might be watches, bottles of scotch or crates of bread or cakes; he kept fronting up, labouring under the misapprehension that by giving the policemen gifts, he could do what he liked. They always viewed Mr Koppel as an eccentric old man rather than a criminal, even though what he did was clearly criminal and a dreadful abuse of the position he held.

St Kilda had a large Jewish population and Malcolm, being Jewish, was regularly asked by the Bureau of Criminal Intelligence to check out members of the community under suspicion of committing criminal offences. He enjoyed this investigative aspect of the work and it was a precursor of things to come.

One bloke whose criminality was not in doubt was Jack Kranz, or Pfefferkranz. He was a receiver of stolen goods and an operator of girls of the night—a pimp. When Malcolm was at Victoria Dock Jack Kranz would regularly drive straight through the check point in his Rolls Royce with a car full of girls into a prohibited area and down to the ships. He would put the girls onto the ships to do their work while he waited and then drive them back out through the same security gates after having slung the sergeant on the desk on the way through. Don't forget that the docks are a quarantine threshold with not only police but Customs officers present to stop people coming ashore and supposedly strictly monitored. These activities made a farce of that.

This laxity at the docks was not just an innocent caper. Heroin and the offending that went along with its insidious presence was only just starting to become a problem on the streets of St Kilda, and the working girls were some of the first to get into it. With security on the wharves having more holes than Swiss cheese, this is how the smack came ashore, with Jack Kranz front and centre. What an easy gig for Jack. He had carte blanche to take his girls on and off the wharves to visit ships in port and he was never stopped or checked. It was easy to get the heroin off the docks in his carload of girls.

Kranz would also regularly turn up at the St Kilda station in his Rolls Royce and drop off slabs of beer, Cryovac packs of meat and bottles of scotch to say nothing of the ready access he had to jewellery and colour TVs and other electrical goods (obviously hot). He made no effort to disguise these transactions which were usually conducted in the reception area of the police station, all in cash and all at the right price. Picture for yourself the sight of uniformed police purchasing stolen goods in the foyer of the cop shop in full view of everyone. This brazen behaviour was a regular occurrence.

On a Friday afternoon, Kranz would often turn up and bring a truck-load of grog with him. It was always the officers who invited him upstairs to the police mess room where all ranks, from inspector down, would have a drink with him. One of the senior sergeants at St Kilda even went into business with Kranz in a trout farm.

Years later Kranz popped up again when Malcolm was in the Drug Squad. Undercover police were issued with different firearms to regular police: automatic Berretta pistols. Only two people in the Drug Squad had access to the safe where the Berettas were kept: Dave Reid and another inspector called 'Knuckles' Notman, a nickname acquired in his days in the Breaking Squad. One of the pistols went missing and Notman had been the last person to sign that pistol out—he was going to cop the flack for it. After the pistol had been missing for some time, it mysteriously re-appeared in a plain brown paper bag. It transpired that Reid had taken the gun, as nobody ever used it and theoretically it wouldn't be missed. The pistol was then given to Kranz for uses unknown. When the shit hit the fan, Reid had to retrieve the pistol. Luckily Notman, who was the fall guy, did not end up getting into any bother. When the balloon went up with the Drug Squad, Reid committed suicide.

In the police force, no one can resist a party, whether it's for the end of the shift or the end of the year. The St Kilda Police Station Christmas party was a ripper. Once again, everything was donated by grateful local traders and business people and/ or 'colourful identities', including Kranz and Mr Koppel JP. For weeks before the Christmas party the divvy van would ferry donated goods to the police station. Where were all these items stored prior to Christmas? Where else but in the exhibit room. Only one senior sergeant was supposed to have access to the exhibit room but in reality everybody did. As they returned to the station with a boot load of donations they grabbed the key, went into the exhibit room and stored the loot. No wonder so many drugs and other items went missing from the exhibit room.

TIME AND AGAIN I RECEIVED COMPLAINTS ABOUT THE ST KILDA coppers. One favourite scam was if the crook did not want to be arrested he could buy his own drugs back from the arresting officer. Problem solved, crook has his drugs back and the copper has made a nice little earn.

One of the cafés in Fitzroy Street was not only a well-known hamburger joint, but a great place to score smack. The proprietor was renowned for his hamburgers, especially the $250 hamburger, one with the 'lot'. This was a hamburger with a one gram foil of heroin inside. The proprietor kept slinging the cops so he was allowed to keep operating for years. Mind your fillings.

The stunt regularly pulled when issues arose was that the cop went on stress leave, then after a time was diagnosed as unfit for work and retired quietly on a full pension. Another tidy solution for the transgressor was for charges to disappear due to health reasons. This stunt has worked many times over the years, even up to today.

Recently Detective Sergeant Peter Lalor retired while being investigated in Operation Briars for his possible role in the murder of male prostitute Shane Chartres-Abbott. Peter Lalor is also famous for having his eye gouged by Jason Moran in a punch up many years ago at the Palace Night Club in St Kilda where the Major Crime Squad regularly drank.

ST KILDA THREW UP SOME RATHER INFAMOUS COPPERS BUT none more so than Constable Cliff Lockwood, later to be charged with the murder of Gary Abdullah. Even later again, in 2010, *The Age* newspaper reported that a warrant was issued for Lockwood's arrest on drug charges in the Northern Territory when he failed to appear in court. Rumour has it he had left the country.

I first came across Lockwood when he had been in the job a few months. His jaw was broken in a New Year's Eve blue at Regine's Nightclub in Moonee Ponds with a king hit from an old client of mine, Ricky Kapaufs.

While at St Kilda, Cliffy arrested some clients at the Zorro Club, an illegal gambling establishment in Acland Street. I attended at St Kilda to see my client and Cliffy came to the foyer to talk about bail. While chatting to him I saw a couple of uniformed constables drag in two Rastafarian types who were strenuously protesting their innocence and were taken just out of sight to the charge desk. I could hear the sergeant becoming more strident and the two blokes likewise. All of a sudden I heard one almighty whack and there was no more noise. Cliff looked at me, laughed and said: 'At least you can't blame me for that one.'

LIFE AT ST KILDA WAS NOT ALL RORTS AND FUNNY BUSINESS, IT was and still is one of the busiest police stations in Victoria and anything could happen at any time without warning and often did. There was never a dull moment. By the time Malcolm arrived at St Kilda he had many years experience as a detective and was able to put the skills gained in the CIB to good use on the streets on a regular basis.

Any type of case could crop up at any time. Like the night he was on nightshift when they received a callout to the Elwood Canal, in which a young bloke was found floating face down. He was in a bad way and they retrieved him from the water and commenced CPR. Malcolm could see this was serious, so he followed crime scene protocol and sealed the area off. He directed a search of the area and as other cops arrived directed them to various duties, searching the surrounding area, interviewing witnesses and door knocking for any other evidence. The weapon was located, a butterfly knife, and luckily some people out walking had seen the attack. He was getting somewhere. Armed with a description of the assailants the police began to trace their retreat.

In the meantime the ambulance arrived but paramedics were unable to revive the youth, who died at the scene. Malcolm now had a homicide on his hands but the Homicide Squad would not be there for ages so he had no time to lose in tracking down the assailants. The team worked throughout the night and by early morning had sufficient evidence to identify them. They found their address in St Kilda and by the time the Homicide Squad arrived on the scene that morning they were greeted by a perfectly preserved crime scene and two blokes in custody remanded on a charge of murder. A very satisfying night's work that later brought a commissioner's commendation to top it off.

On another occasion they received a tip off about a bloke on their patch selling heroin. Malcolm knew the punter by sight from being out and about in the area so they commenced watching him and yes, he was selling heroin on the street. While they watched and followed him it became apparent he was buying pharmacy drugs of a suspicious nature. The evidence pointed to a drug lab at his house so they raided the premises and sure enough it was a heroin laboratory. Heroin can be extracted from Panadeine tablets provided you have sufficient tablets, and he had plenty.

This little lab was turning out about one gram of pure heroin a day, not huge, but a very nice little earner. They arrested the bloke, but because a lab was involved, they had to call in the Drug Squad. Detective Sergeant Wayne Strawhorn turned up very pissed off. It transpired that the Drug Squad had been watching this bloke at the same time as Malcolm's team but couldn't catch him. Here they were, the local cops, landing a good pinch before the Drug Squad, who were not happy. Little did Malcolm know that their paths were destined to cross again. He was just happy to have properly investigated a crime, done a good job and obtained a top result.

The advent of the video recorder brought with it a whole new field of dishonesty in terms of theft of video recorders and of the videos themselves. At that time videos were a big ticket item and out of the reach of the average punter to purchase. If you can't afford to buy what do you do? Pinch one or accidentally on purpose forget to return the one you rented, which is what many punters did, much to the annoyance of the video shop proprietors. The bloke that ran the only video store in St Kilda at that time was in Barkly Street. His shop was huge and he was losing a lot of videos, a matter he was not happy about.

The store owner approached the coppers at St Kilda to repossess his missing videos. Because the coppers were always raiding houses he asked them to keep an eye out for his stock. The kicker was he offered twenty dollars for every video returned by the coppers and for good measure, once a month, upstairs at his shop, he held a beer, pizza and porno night. How good was this? The coppers executed a legitimate warrant, recovered a couple of overdue videos and copped a sling for it. What a ripper.

The practice of slinging the coppers at St Kilda was legendary. One story goes that a young constable pinched one of the St Kilda publicans for drink driving. Unfortunately for the constable the pub concerned was where the sergeants drank. Next morning he was hauled over the coals by one of the sergeants. 'What can we do?' asked the sergeant. 'Up to you,' said the youngster. 'It's your call.' 'I'll pull the ticket and try and get you a dozen bottles of beer for your trouble,' said the sergeant. The ticket went away but the constable never saw his dozen bottles.

Years later the same constable bumped into the publican and he gave him quite a spray. The constable asked, 'What's your problem? The ticket went away.' 'Yeah,' said the publican, 'but you charged me $500 for the trouble!'

Chapter Seven

SECRET SQUIRRELS

'Yesterday upon the stair
I met a man who wasn't there
He wasn't there again today
Oh, how I wish he'd go away.'

Antigonish—William Hughes Mearns

Malcolm tried to make the most of every opportunity that came his way. Looking back over those days he knows that his desire for success in the Force was related to his ongoing and ever present desire to be accepted, to belong. The more he achieved, the more likely he would be accepted as one of the Brotherhood.

He applied for and gained a promotion to Detective Sergeant which meant another move. When a vacancy arose in the Crime Surveillance Unit in 1988 (known in the Force as the 'Secret Squirrels' or the 'Shadowers') he applied. For Malcolm this was probably the best policing he ever did. The Squirrels were responsible for covert surveillance work carried out on behalf of other squads and they operated from a secret location in Richmond. Squirrels didn't get involved in arrests or giving evidence because obviously, if they did, their cover would be blown and they could never work in surveillance again.

A classic example of staying away from arrests, irrespective of how significant an arrest might be, arose after the murder of the pre-eminent Sydney heart surgeon Victor Chang. Chang was murdered in cold blood in Sydney and the police had very few leads. However, it turned out that one of the murderers had dropped his wallet at the scene. The NSW coppers kept that fact in the dark for operational reasons.

Police regularly keep significant facts away from the public and the media. These are usually facts that only someone involved intimately with the case knows. This can be crucial.

The New South Wales Police had tracked the murderer via his wallet to Victoria and the case was handed over to the Squirrels to try and locate the suspect. Malcolm was in charge of the operation and managed to identify one of the two Asian people suspected of being involved at a Chinese Restaurant in Toorak Road, South Yarra. They followed him to an address within walking distance of Toorak Road. They kept the flat under observation around the clock while gathering evidence establishing the suspect's identity. The surveillance operation lasted several weeks before they got lucky.

One Saturday afternoon Malcolm spotted the target with a small carry bag in Victoria Street, Abbotsford, an area known as Little Saigon. They had the target's car under constant observation. A short time later another male returned to the car and drove off. The penny dropped and Malcolm realised that this was the same male and that since he had been out of sight he had had a haircut, changed his hair colouring and was wearing different clothing. All of a sudden it was obvious something significant was afoot. Being Saturday afternoon, with fewer police available, along with the fact that they had been watching this bloke for weeks; they were on their own in keeping his car in sight. He started to head towards the CBD. When he reached the city he left his car and jumped on a bus to the airport. Malcolm tried to alert the Homicide Squad because chances were he was fleeing the country. Add to that the fact he had drastically changed his appearance and Malcolm was certain he was about to do a runner. He followed the bus to the international terminal at Tullamarine Airport, desperately trying to alert the Homicide Squad to get to the airport to arrest him before he left the country. By the time the bus arrived at the airport, the Homicide Squad had still not arrived and it looked as though Malcolm would have to make the arrest as he alighted from the bus. It was a very close call, but just as the bus arrived he saw the Homicide Squad pulling up behind it and he didn't have to intervene, merely point out the man as he came off the bus. Even though the Squirrels were told that under no circumstances were they to get involved in an arrest, if the Homicide Squad hadn't made it in time Malcolm would have had no choice.

The target was charged and convicted of the murder of Victor Chang. Malcolm considers the work that he did on obtaining a conviction against this man for the murder of one of Australia's greats to be one of the highlights of his career. He received a Chief Commissioner's commendation. This was very rare in the Squirrels because even though you might do an outstanding job, you were supposed to be out of the public eye, the reason not many were handed out.

Another occasion on which Malcolm received a Chief Commissioner's commendation was for his contribution to the arrest of George Gerard Kaufman, the infamous Armadale Rapist, as he was nicknamed by the media. Remember that he had been in the orphanage with Kaufman from a very early age, and knew him inside out—his drug use and his perverted attitudes to sex. He was one weird unit. Before Kaufman was even in the frame for these awful crimes, the Armadale Rapist had been on the job for some years. In the four and a half years prior to his arrest, Kaufman had raped three women and committed several aggravated burglaries, that is burglaries in which he was armed and used violence in either entering the property or once inside. There were a total of fifteen female victims of these, making a total of eighteen rapes and/or burglaries that he was ultimately convicted of over the period.

His addiction to heroin made him a burglar first and foremost. How he chose his victims was particularly insidious. When he broke into a house, he would work out if the resident was a single woman and, at a later date, return and violently attack and/or rape them. He was sentenced in 1989 to twenty-one years, three months, with a minimum of eighteen years.

There is a disturbing postscript to this case. Kaufman was convicted by a jury on overwhelming evidence but while in prison he refused to undergo any sex offenders' courses whatsoever and was released after fourteen years of a twenty-one year sentence. He was released straight back into the community subject to no supervision apart from parole and no one had any control over him whatsoever.

I should explain what may have happened in this case, as it did in many others. Prior to changes to the Sentencing Act there was no what the politicians call 'truth in sentencing'. In other words a convicted person did not serve the entirety of his sentence provided he was of good behaviour. The rule of thumb was that you served two thirds of your minimum before being eligible for parole. But Kaufman's sentence included a non parole period of eighteen years. Why he was released before his minimum sentence had expired is beyond me and has never been adequately explained.

After the government introduced truth in sentencing Kaufman would have served a minimum of eighteen years and upon release would have been placed on the sex offenders' register, meaning his every move would be monitored for the period he was on the register. These reforms were long overdue.

After spending time locked up with some of these monsters I wonder whether life behind bars or castration is not the answer. In my experience these blokes have no remorse, brag about their exploits and plot their next attack, no matter how many years away that may be. They are incorrigible and are, in my opinion, beyond redemption.

THERE WAS A HUGE INVESTIGATION BEFORE KAUFMANN WAS identified as a possible suspect. It was because of his burglary background and where he was living at the time that he became a suspect. As Malcolm had been in the boys' home with him he was asked about his behaviour, his personality type and other particulars that only somebody who had lived with him for many years would understand. So Malcolm was asked to go out on surveillance in order to identify him positively so that a full-time operation could commence. He did this and then he was taken off the hands on surveillance—Kaufman knew he was a policeman and if he had recognised him the game would have been up. Instead a long, detailed and complex surveillance operation was launched on Kaufman and this continued for many months until finally he was arrested, convicted and sentenced. This arrest was another high point in Malcolm's career and something he was proud of as he felt he was really giving back to the community.

An interesting aspect of the Kaufman arrest was that this was the first case where DNA was used. Obviously, for there to be DNA testing, they needed a DNA sample to compare with forensic material that had been obtained from the rape victims.

When Kaufman was arrested he was to be given a belting so that a blood sample could be taken without his consent for a DNA sample. To the credit of the coppers who arrested Kaufman, they refused to do this and the DNA sample was gained legitimately.

For Malcolm, who was not the most forceful of personalities, the Squirrels' work suited him. After his commendations he thought that he might gain what he desired most, recognition from his fellow officers, but he was wrong. Cops look up to the heavy hitters (both figuratively and literally) and squirreling did not cut the mustard.

Domestic life was always a struggle financially and while in the Squirrels he did other jobs on the side such as gardening, painting and odd jobs for friends. Another way he made ends meet was fixing items he found such as old TVs or lawnmowers. He was good with his hands and enjoyed repairing things. Then about once a month he would have a garage sale, making a few extra bucks for the family. There was not a lot of dough around but life was good.

While in the Surveillance Unit, Malcolm worked with Detective Senior Sergeant Christopher 'Knuckles' Notman. As I said before his nickname came from the days when he was in the now disbanded Breakers Squad. The Breakers Squad dealt with the safe blowers and big commercial burglaries and they had a reputation as extremely hard men, both inside and outside the police force. While in the Surveillance Unit lots of police had part-time jobs, as all coppers did in those days, even though it was outlawed. You couldn't bring up a family on a policeman's wage. Notman knew a lot of former police officers, among them a copper by the name of Peter Spence, formerly in the Major Crime Squad. Spence had established his own private investigation company. There was always plenty of additional surveillance work, outside police hours, for the select few who were chosen by Spence. On one job some police were doing surveillance work for Spence using police surveillance vehicles and police radios, mobile phones, cameras, videos—everything supplied by Victoria Police. As with every good rort it usually ends in tears and this stunt was no exception. Somehow the surveillance they were carrying out crossed over into a homicide investigation and the police surveillance was undermined. Homicide were filthy and wanted to know who was behind it.

An investigation ensued which revealed that Spence's team of merry men had been conducting surveillance on the side for cash. Notwithstanding all the kerfuffle that ensued not one of the offending police were ever charged with an offence for the use of police equipment or moonlighting. The whole affair was put aside and they all kept their jobs.

Funnily enough at the same time as all this was going on in Victoria, the New South Wales Surveillance Unit was sacked en masse for similar behaviour. Insufficient supervision took the Unit to the point where members were all out playing golf or rorting the system while they were supposed to be working— nobody had a handle on things. Drastic measures were taken. In Victoria, rather than adopt such a robust approach, the response was always to sweep it under the carpet, try and keep a lid on things and don't let the media get wind of it whatever you do.

THE FIRST TIME CORRUPTION CAME MALCOLM'S WAY IN THE Surveillance Unit was after the 'Great Cigarette Heist' as it was known. A number of very well-known old school armed robbers had decided to change their preferred target from banks to semi-trailers full of cigarettes. Next to money, cigarettes are the best things for crooks to pinch. They are light, easy to transport and readily saleable, particularly in those days when most people smoked and all the crooks drank in inner city hotels so you didn't have far to travel doing the rounds flogging hot ciggies.

Better than that the rate for hot smokes was better than for other hot gear. The going rate for most gear even today is one third of the ticket so if the price tag on a stolen new Zegna suit is $1800, the shop lifters receive $600 for it. Not so for cigarettes. Stolen cigarettes can still sell for 75 or 80 per cent of the current retail so they became a very attractive soft target for armed robbers, particularly as this was at about the time when the banks were really starting to crank up their security.

On this particular occasion, some good old school crooks, led by a bloke called Bob Airey, stole a semi-trailer load of over a million dollars' worth of cigarettes, which back in those days was an even more impressive amount of money. For good measure they also pinched the truck and the driver, who was later found trussed up like the Christmas turkey in the back of the driver's cabin.

The gang were arrested in a warehouse in Flemington. The Squirrels had been watching the trucks for a while because they had intelligence that one of the trucks was going to be hijacked. Sure enough, while the Squirrels were watching, they saw the whole operation take place and observed where the truck was taken. It was then their job to withdraw and advise the Special Operations Group (SOG) and the Armed Robbery Squad of the location of the truck. Needless to say, when the perpetrators were arrested, the Sons of God (as the SOGs like to call themselves) and the Armed Robbery Squad went in for a good deal of gun-waving and screaming. The gang were all later convicted and given hefty jail sentences.

The Squirrels sat outside the warehouse while the arrests took place and then, after the crooks were arrested and removed, they wandered inside to have a look at what was going on. This is when Malcolm first saw corruption on a grand scale. One of the Armed Robbery Squad was walking around with outers of boxes of cigarettes taken from the truck. An outer contained about fifty cartons of cigarettes and in each carton was twenty boxes so an outer contained around 1,000 cigarettes. He was asking blokes, 'Do you smoke? Here,' and giving them ten or twenty cartons of cigarettes. Malcolm asked somebody what this was all about and they said, 'Well fuck 'em, the whole truck load is insured and the insurance company will be rapt to get a good proportion of the cigarettes back. A few thousand bucks of smokes being knocked off doesn't really matter. Don't say a word. Mind your own business.'

Welcome to the real world. These blokes were going for broke, grabbing as many packets of smokes as they were able. The brazen nature of the theft was amazing to Malcolm.

COPPERS AND GUNS ARE A TIME-HONOURED PAIRING. COPPERS are obsessed with guns to the extent that many cops purchase their own private weapons, legitimately or otherwise. At that stage everyone had their own five-shot Smith & Wesson revolvers which they carried twenty-four hours a day, unless they went on annual leave when they would return them to the gun safe. In the Surveillance Unit there was one copper whose five shot was reported missing and he had to submit a crime report that suggested where he thought it had gone. An investigation followed to try and locate it. It's a big deal for a copper to lose his weapon—and no laughing matter. If a crime is committed with a stolen police-issue weapon, it doesn't reflect well on the force. In the wash up of the investigation it was found that this copper had approached a sergeant (who had previously worked in the Ethical Standards Department) who he knew had a double-barrelled shot gun for sale, which he purchased from him. The gun was unregistered and unlicensed and this copper, it was found, had then sold this shotgun to a friend of his, all highly illegal and improper. During the course of this investigation the missing police-issue pistol was also located at the friend's house and was promptly returned to the Surveillance Unit.

Nothing happened to the friend, nothing happened to the copper and nothing happened to the sergeant who sold the unregistered shotgun. The internal investigation found no evidence of wrongdoing. Each time an officer got himself into hot water, the Brotherhood would close ranks around him and do whatever was required to make sure he wasn't censured or sacked. This was to become more obvious to Malcolm and with even greater implications.

On the subject of guns, in about 1979 a large burglary took place at Guthrie Trading's warehouse in South Melbourne, the significance being that Guthrie imported firearms and pistols in particular. A large number of Ruger Magnum .357 stainless steel handguns were stolen, a real Dirty Harry-style gun. From time to time over the ensuing years these pistols bobbed up for sale. A bloke at the Squirrels landed twelve of them and flogged them to other coppers. No, that is not a typo, a copper was selling twelve stolen handguns to other coppers. Malcolm bought one. He thought it was fantastic and he regularly carried it around. He kept the pistol for a few years until he became too nervous that he would be picked up with it and on-sold it, to a copper of course. On another occasion Malcolm purchased a machine gun complete with filed off serial numbers from another surveillance copper. He also kept that for a few years before on-selling it to— you guessed it—another copper.

THE SURVEILLANCE UNIT OPERATED FROM VARIOUS LOCATIONS and was obsessed with secrecy. As a result virtually no coppers not attached to the Squirrels ever knew where they were, and there was no turning up at the office for a social visit. When Malcolm first transferred to the Unit they operated from a secret location in Windsor, then some years later moved to another secret location in Richmond. These locations were always chosen for the anonymity of the building and also because they didn't have windows opening onto the street, so stickybeaks wandering past could not see what was going on inside. Comings and goings were kept to a minimum for the same reason. When returning to base the cars had to be parked in the backyard of the premises, never in the street, for fear of one of them being recognised.

On one particular day there was a huge armed robbery in Richmond. Men dressed as road-workers with all the official looking equipment—road signs and machinery—set up in Punt Road. When the Armaguard van they were after approached it was diverted down a couple of side streets until the van was stopped by the 'road-workers' and relieved of a very large sum of money. The exact amount was never disclosed but the van was on its way to deliver money, not pick it up.

Guess where the robbery took place, right outside the Squirrels' office. They were having morning tea and no window means no view of the street. They didn't see or hear a thing while all this excitement was taking place not twenty-five metres away. The first the Squirrels knew of the robbery was when they heard the emergency call over the radio, upon which they all raced outside. But it was too late. The Armaguard van had been diverted down a laneway and believe it or not, backed into the backyard of the building where their cars were parked. They could not go out the backdoor because it was a crime scene. Then the media got wind of the stick up and were swarming all over the place. The Squirrels became prisoners in their own office. Their faces couldn't appear in public under any circumstances so they were stuck in their offices until the media furore had died down. At the same time, an emergency order went out that no Surveillance Units were to return to base for precisely the same reason. The cars and the occupants could have been identified.

The Unit could see inside the Armaguard van from the back door of their office—that's how close it was. The robbery remains unsolved to this day.

LIFE IN THE SQUIRRELS WASN'T ALL DEADLY SERIOUS—A humorous incident often turned up when you least expected it. Dennis Allen, alias Mr Death, a huge, ruthless and gratuitously violent heroin dealer was running hot in Richmond, not far from that secret office. (I often wonder what Dennis's reaction would have been had he found out that the coppers were just around the corner from the seat of his empire.) An order was given to commence surveillance on Dennis. The Squirrels commenced a full-scale operation on him one hot summer's afternoon, following him from his house. It was unusual for him to leave Richmond so they thought they had stumbled onto something big as they followed him to St Kilda where for some hours he hung around on the St Kilda light rail station. You couldn't miss Dennis—he always wore white Dunlop Volley runners with the tongue cut out and bib and brace overalls. Today, because it was so hot, he wore nothing else except for the huge amount of jewellery he was never without.

The Squirrels sat there watching for ages with no result. Then all of a sudden he moved off the station into the toilets. Here we go, there's going to be a drug transaction. So a couple of Squirrels followed him into the toilets. The cubicle was locked so they had a bit of a look under the cubicle door and there are Dennis's bib and brace overalls on the floor. He was obviously using the toilet—and had actually taken his pants off. They looked at each other, gave a bit of a wink and nudge and one bloke leaned under the door and quick as a flash whipped Dennis's overalls and underpants out from under and bolted. Dennis was left there in nothing but his Dunlop Volleys and his jewellery. It was a huge joke. They all jumped back in the car and found his wallet in the front of his overalls and, being Dennis's wallet, there was a lot of money in it. Adding insult to injury, they pinched the money as well. They didn't wait around to see how Dennis got himself out of that one but it would have been worthwhile seeing a bloke wandering off the station dressed in runners and jewellery.

Because the Squirrels were secret no one much in the way of brass came near, as it would blow their cover. The only supervision was in the form of the senior sergeant and a detective inspector who were part of the gang anyway. As in all police stations they worked rotating twenty-four hour shifts. Most surveillance was carried out on the day or afternoon shift, which finished at eleven. Nightshift went from 11 pm to 7 am. Virtually nothing took place in the wee small hours unless there was a big op on, in which case it was all hands on deck. Now, a lot of senior coppers became private detectives on retirement and a large portion of their business was process serving, i.e. serving summonses or debt collecting for finance companies. This meant these ex-coppers needed access to the police database to find out where people lived, where cars were registered or to do criminal background checks. To disclose this material to a non-copper is a serious offence but this didn't stop anyone. In the depths of nightshift there the Squirrels all were, sitting at their computers, checking information to give to private detectives. The pay was a ripper: ten dollars for a motor registration check and fifteen for more confidential stuff. Have you any idea how many of these checks you can carry out in an eight-hour shift? Nightshift was a very lucrative time to be a Squirrel.

As per every squad that Malcolm was ever in, the Christmas party was a big deal that they all looked forward to. In the Surveillance Unit they had become accustomed to having their Christmas party at the Cumberland Resort in Lorne and this was paid for through various raffles and other 'fundraisers' throughout the year. The idea for holding the party out of Melbourne was fed by the officers' fear of blowing cover; it was highly unlikely that any of them would be recognised in Lorne. They were able to take their spouses, boyfriends, girlfriends, whoever, and enjoy a weekend away in luxury. On arrival, there was plenty of free alcohol, and then as the afternoon wore on into the night there was a dance with a band, a three-course meal and as much grog as you wanted. As you entered the reception area, you were met by members of the Social Club who gave each member of the squad an envelope which contained a couple of hundred dollars. This was the amount each squad member would have been paid for the weekend. This meant it was a free weekend. And the tickets had been paid for from the proceeds of a poker machine, one of the old one-armed bandits. Because they were the Secret Squirrels and not many outsiders ever came to their office, it was easy to set it up in their meals area. Everybody played it, and all proceeds went towards the Christmas party. No one used their own cars to get to the party, and they didn't pay for petrol. Police vehicles were used to travel there and back. The entire weekend cost nothing.

During the time Malcolm was in the Squirrels and stationed at Richmond, parking was at a premium. One Friday afternoon, a bloke from the offices next door came knocking, Malcolm was the only bloke in the office at the time. He gave him an envelope and said, 'This is for the car parking'. Malcolm said, 'Thanks very much,' and closed the door. He looked in the envelope and there was money inside. You didn't need to be a genius to work out that it was payment for the car parks. The Squirrels had fourteen car parks available and some bright spark had come up with the brilliant idea that some of the car parks could be rented out to other surrounding offices for cash. It explained why they could never get a bloody car park in their own building when they needed one!

Just when Malcolm felt he was getting a handle on professional and family life Gillie announced that she was pregnant. Malcolm couldn't believe it. Their second son had only been born in April 1988 and when number three son arrived in July 1989 things became a real struggle financially. This would have to stop: no more kids, under any circumstances. The financial aspect of his life was getting him down, it didn't matter what he did they could not get in front and he started making crazy decisions for his rapidly growing family. Malcolm bought a new house for more than they could afford along with a new car. Talk about repent at leisure. He had a little enjoyment immediately after making new purchases but then severe buyer's remorse would set in and he worried himself sick until he had somehow got himself out of bother again, usually by selling the item at a loss. This did not do wonders for matrimonial harmony. Gillie had worked as much as she could but it was taking its toll on her.

Malcolm was becoming moody and his behaviour had a negative impact on everyone but there was nothing wrong as far as he was concerned. He was a detective and a hard bastard. To seek counselling would have been seen as a sign of weakness by the other coppers if it ever got out. And maybe they would not trust him in a rort or a tight spot. No, he had to hang tough and not let anyone see his vulnerability. Luckily for him Gillie stuck through all this when lesser people would have walked and taken the boys with her.

Chapter Eight

LET THE GAMES BEGIN: 'OPERATION NO NAME'

'If the facts don't fit the theory,
change the facts.'

—Albert Einstein

Armed Robberies have always been the go in Australia. From our earliest bushrangers and national icons like Ned Kelly, like it or not our folklore is scattered with armed robbers and their exploits. Cops chasing robbers is a story as old as this country and modern times are no different.

Before the banks started beefing up security with delay locks on safes, fly up screens and all sorts of electronic surveillance devices, if you were a good crook, you could make a lot of money very quickly for very little danger. By and large back in the eighties firearms were waved around and there was plenty of swearing and shouting but rarely was a gun discharged during a stick up, much less anyone getting plugged. There were a number of good armed robbery teams around; if you could pull off a stick up it was a good earn. Get pinched though and you copped a big whack.

Without today's technology the coppers were always playing catch-up footy, reacting to a stick up instead of trying to cut the robbers off before the robbery took place. So the Squirrels were brought in to try and identify the gangs and their potential targets. Some of the gangs got away with it for years, run by blokes such as Jimmy Samsonides, who was eventually charged with a violent armed robbery. His accomplice, a TV actor called Squires, was shot dead at the door of an Armaguard van in Melbourne's Western suburbs during a shootout with the armed guards. Jimmy was acquitted at committal because the Armed Robbery Squad had put together such a shoddy brief that his smart arse lawyers drove a bus through the holes in the case.

Bob Airey and 'Chocka' Rowley, old Painters and Dockers, committed many armed robberies and only got caught for a few, including the great cigarette heist mentioned earlier. The list goes on, indicating stick ups were certainly a 'good go' as the crooks say.

I even acted for a young kid who appeared in the Children's Court who came from one of the more infamous armed robber families. At twelve years of age, when asked about his aspirations, he proudly announced that he wanted to be an armed robber when he grew up, just like Uncle Bob. What an ambition.

Many years ago while the infamous Jika Jika division of the old Pentridge jail still existed I interviewed a client, Billy 'the Kid' Nolan, a good bloke but a mad armed robber—he loved doing them. Some blokes get off on doing stick ups, literally, like Ken Bone, the gentleman armed robber who would orgasm during the course of a robbery, but that was OK because he was wearing his specially-ordered large-size Huggies, one of Ken's little foibles.

Anyway, Billy was coming up for parole at the end of a lengthy whack for armed robbery and we were discussing the new-fangled security and how hard it would be to 'counter jump' (or get past the counter for a stick up). Billy looked at me, smiled and said with a grin; 'they all have to come out for a piss sooner or later'. He was out five minutes when he was pinched with another stick up. He had been lying in wait until a teller went to the toilet. Bill followed her and forced her to let him behind the counter. Easy!

For various reasons there was a period of a few years when there were virtually no big armed robberies committed. The likes of Victor Pierce, who was one of the great armed robbers, had gone on sabbatical. Victor was making a stack so he didn't need to run around doing armed robberies. Victor's half-brother Dennis 'the Menace' Allen was escalating his heroin business and he desperately needed muscle who could be trusted (sort of) with the money he wanted collected from customers who had suffered an attack of the forgets when it came time to pay. Dennis employed some of the armed robbers as standover men, such as Ross Franklin and Victor Geuroff, while both were on parole, so armed robbers became a bit thin on the ground. Dennis also employed 'Robbo' Robinson, on parole for murder, as muscle until he messed up with one of Dennis's shooters and was breached on his parole. Off Robbo went to the nick for another stint.

Dennis died prematurely from a fungal disease growing inside his heart and the wheels fell off his heroin empire almost overnight. No one had Dennis's brains when it came to running the business and they all started robbing each other. For instance Dennis hadn't even cooled off before the three hundred-odd grand's worth of jewellery he wore was stolen from his corpse by one of the family. When Victor needed to start getting an earn somehow, guess what, armed robberies cranked up again.

The Armed Robbery Squad could not initially identify the gang behind this new spate of robberies and, as a result, Detective

Sergeant Paul Mullett of the Armed Robbery Squad commenced 'Operation No Name' in an effort to try and identify them. The Squirrels were brought in to carry out the surveillance. They set up surveillance in the general inner metropolitan area and identified a couple of banks in the Melbourne suburbs as being highly likely prospects. One of these banks was in Boronia where they watched the Armaguard deliveries from nearby.

Sometimes these operations took a very long time before there was a result, and sometimes all the work counted for nothing. The Squirrels identified the first member of the team, Graeme Jensen, a robber who had been quiet for some time. The surveillance was cranked up a notch and over the next few months they managed to identify the remainder of the team: Victor Pierce, Peter McEvoy and 'Red Light'. Pierce was the most slippery and therefore the last to be ID'd. A man believed to be him was spotted parking his motorbike on the upper level of the rooftop car park in a shopping centre near the suspected target in Boronia. After a time the Squirrels also saw a car drive past the motorbike, before its driver got out and walked back towards it. They thought it was Pierce. Wrong—it was a tradesman pinching the motor bike helmet. He jumped in his car and drove off. One of the annoying things about surveillance was that you often saw crimes committed but you couldn't do anything for fear of compromising an important operation. So the helmet thief got away scot-free. After completing a stake-out of the bank, Victor returned some hours later to his motorbike where he realised his helmet was missing. He was unable to drive home because as a good law-abiding citizen he couldn't ride without a helmet. How's that for a contradiction. Pierce ran from the car park, waving the other conspirators down and was given a lift. He was dropped off at Chestnut Street, Richmond, so at last the Squirrels could positively identify him as Victor Pierce of that address. The Squirrels had another unexpected stroke of luck. Red Light's girlfriend came forward and started providing information about the gang's activities, which made the surveillance work much easier.

Departmental policy was to arrest armed robbers *after* they had committed the armed robbery, hoping to goodness that nothing went wrong during the stick up and some innocent bystander had been injured or worse. Therefore, if they were convicted, they were convicted of a very serious offence, namely armed robbery or, in some cases, using a firearm to resist, or worse still somebody getting killed, as with the tragedy of the murdered Armaguard Officer Hefti.

I don't know how many times I have cross-examined a copper who had allowed a serious crime to be committed while he sat and watched it all with a view to nabbing the offender after the fact. I was always staggered by the response that: 'We were waiting for the offence to be concluded before we arrested the defendant.' Numerous innocent bystanders suffered the consequences of this stupidity.

Jensen's gang was violent and unpredictable and as a result people were getting hurt during the course of the robberies. Hostages were being taken. Matters became a little too hot and the authorities, to say nothing of the media, started asking awkward questions that didn't appear to have occurred to Force Command like: 'Why not arrest the offender prior to the offence rather than risk public welfare?' In the face of public criticism an order from the top was issued that this procedure was to change. Instead, if it became apparent that an armed robbery was about to take place, the perpetrators were to be arrested prior to acting. This meant that at best the Armed Robbery Squad could bring a charge of conspiring to commit an armed robbery, but the policy clearly stated that even if all you got was possession of a firearm or a stolen motor vehicle that was enough. At least the crooks were in custody and the public was safe. Under no circumstances under the new regime was the armed robbery to be allowed to take place and the arrest made afterwards. This did not sit at all well with the Armed Robbery Squad as they were very gung ho.

Once the two banks that the criminals were staking out were identified, the instructions from the Armed Robbery Squad were for Surveillance to notify them when the robbers returned as they looked like they were tooling up in preparation for a stick up. The Armed Robbery Squad were nearby, but unbeknown to the Squirrels, so were the Special Operations Group (SOGs). In direct contravention of departmental policy and orders from above this armed robbery was to be allowed to proceed with the SOGs in position with the clear possibility of eliminating the four robbers once they had committed the armed robbery. Everyone was geared up for the armed robbery to take place. Surveillance was intense as the Unit waited for the gang to arrive. But for some reason, after months and months of these blokes travelling back and forwards to these two banks on an almost daily basis, all of a sudden, nothing happened. No appearance your worship.

The whole operation fell flat on its face. Malcolm has always wondered whether the gang wasn't tipped off by somebody on the take in the Armed Robbery Squad. It looked like some copper was prepared to cop a sling for information that the whole gang was 'off' and that if they had even started the armed robbery they were all going to be gunned down by the SOGs. The other theory was that Red Light's girlfriend was playing both sides of the fence and tipped the gang off that if they went ahead with the job that they would be bowled.

Whatever happened, they didn't turn up. The entire operation was aborted. The surveillance ended and everyone went about their other Squirrel duties. In the meantime, an armed robbery took place at a Coles supermarket in Brunswick, where Dominic Hefti was murdered. The Armed Robbery Squad put two and two together and as was more often than not the case came up with five. It was immediately suspected that Jensen and Pierce's gang were responsible, but as there had been no surveillance it was impossible to know. Serious surveillance recommenced of Jensen in particular as there was a piece of red hot information from a 'reliable source' that Jensen was about to do another stick up. As matters transpired, that information was wrong too.

In fact years later it was worked out that a crook by the name of Santo Mercuri was the one responsible for the Dominic Hefti armed robbery together with Mark Moran, one of the notorious Moran family. They had committed the armed robbery and had killed Hefti in the course of it. Mercuri was arrested, charged and convicted on DNA evidence. He was perhaps the second person after Kaufmann to be convicted on DNA evidence. Moran was never charged with this armed robbery and died in 2000. Mercuri died in jail from a heart condition.

Life in the Squirrels suited Malcolm and his personality type perfectly. He was very uneasy when placed in a confrontational situation and had an almost pathological fear of speaking in public, even giving evidence, which is not good if you are a copper and continually pinching blokes.

Chapter Nine

DIRTY WORK AT THE CROSS ROADS

'The end justifies the means.'

—*The Prince*, Niccolo Machiavelli

By 11 October 1988, Malcolm Rosenes was ensconced as a detective sergeant in the Surveillance Unit, going about his secret squirrel business. When he woke up that morning, little did he know he would witness an incredible incident that would result in a number of members of the Armed Robbery Squad being charged with murder. But that's only half the story of what he saw that day.

Malcolm's crew were working the afternoon shift. As the senior officer in charge of the surveillance operation, Malcolm had been briefed by the Armed Robbery Squad at Narre Warren about developments in the revived Operation No Name. The investigation of Graeme Jensen, Jed Horton, Victor Pierce and others who had been running red hot as an armed robbery gang throughout Melbourne had come to a screaming halt a few weeks earlier when the gang were a no show at the robbery they had been planning in Boronia. The Armed Robbery Squad was not happy that this crew were leading them a merry dance. And then, when Dominic Hefti was shot dead during the Brunswick robbery, the Squad were sure that it was Jensen's gang who were behind it. Not that there was a skerrick of evidence.

The operation was being run by the Armed Robbery Squad, and the afternoon briefing with Malcolm was held well away from Moray Court, Narre Warren, which was where Graeme Jensen, the afternoon's target lived. Malcolm's crew's job was to conduct surveillance of and if possible give a positive identification of the suspect, then to monitor his movements and report them to the Armed Robbery Squad. He was briefed that this was an intelligence-gathering operation only. Malcolm had spoken to the sergeant in charge of the morning shift and there had been no activity of any significance at the house.

Although it was an operation being run by Detective Sergeant Paul Mullett he wasn't at the scene. 'The Fish' (Mullett) had a reputation to be feared. He is a big bloke and to say he is aggressive or at best, brusque, is an understatement. Mullett later became secretary of the Police Association for many years, and is largely responsible for the combative nature of the Association's relationship with just about everyone except its own members.

There were five surveillance officers in four cars deployed to carry out covert surveillance on the suspect, Jensen. They took up positions in the immediate vicinity of Moray Court and commenced watching and waiting. They didn't have to wait long. An unidentified male left the house driving a blue Holden station wagon. Malcolm followed the car to a motor mower shop in a small shopping strip in Webb Street, Narre Warren. Even though he knew Jensen from previous surveillance he did not get a good enough look at the driver of the Holden to make a positive identification. When the driver got out of the car at the mower shop and went inside, the Squirrels still couldn't make the ID.

Malcolm ordered his crew to follow their usual procedure and take up observation positions north, south, east and west of the shop in order to cover the driver should he leave the shop and travel in any direction. Two other surveillance officers were also familiar with Jensen. So when the driver entered the shop, Malcolm sent them in after him to make a positive identification. He was pretty sure the bloke was Jensen but you always have to be 100 per cent certain. The two officers returned to their cars and radioed Malcolm that each had made a positive identification. It was Jensen.

Without warning, two other surveillance officers radioed to say Jensen was on the move. He had left the shop and was about to drive off. What came next was a bolt from the blue. All of a sudden one of Malcolm's crew, who was still on foot, radioed, reporting that Armed Robbery Squad cars had come from nowhere, accelerating flat out through the car park, fish-tailing on the gravel, and had pursued Jensen north at high speed. This was not only a huge shock but a dangerous and serious breach of all the protocols. Correct procedure was, and still is, that surveillance officers are always advised before there is to be an intercept. The Surveillance Unit in turn advise the Armed Robbery Squad, or Special Operations Group, the safest place to make the interception. This is because it is the Squirrels who have the target in sight and not the Armed Robbery Squad. They're well and truly out of sight for obvious reasons. If they barged in at an inappropriate time or location, members of the public or surveillance officers could be in danger. It is always the final call by the senior surveillance officer (on this day that was Malcolm) to make the interception call. But he had been told this was an intelligence gathering operation only.

The Armed Robbery Squad had no idea how many of Malcolm's crew were involved in the surveillance—they were all in plain clothes and driving unmarked cars. They had no way of knowing who were coppers and who were civilians or where any coppers were located.

Suddenly there was a volley of shots. Malcolm ducked for cover in his surveillance car not knowing where the shots were going or who was shooting at what or whom. When the shots stopped he quickly drove towards the car park where Jensen had been. The Holden had crashed into a pole and the Armed Robbery Squad were running towards it with their shotguns and handguns drawn. This was like nothing he had witnessed in his entire police career—it was like being in a movie scene.

The Armed Robbery Squad approached the car with their 12-gauge shotguns and .38 service pistols drawn and pointed at the car and Malcolm followed. When they reached the car, there was the deceased in his tracksuit pants, slumped over the steering wheel, some broken glass and that was it. It seemed that when the Armed Robbery Squad had come screaming into the car park, Jensen had thought something was up and had tried to get away. The Armed Robbery Squad members had fired at him from behind and hit him in the head. He had died instantly. There was no gun in the car. Jensen had been unarmed when shot.

Two Armed Robbery Squad cars had stopped to the south of the accident and two to the north to stop traffic entering the area. Malcolm's attention was drawn to three members of the Armed Robbery Squad who had been at the boot of their car and were now walking towards Jensen's car. One of them was carrying a rolled up beach towel. Malcolm thought they were going to cover the deceased with the towel. But on this day, nothing was turning out to be usual. He watched the officer unfurl the towel but instead of placing it over the deceased, a sawn off .22 rifle flipped out of the towel and fell through the car window to land next to Jensen. Then he draped the towel over the deceased. Malcolm was horrified. The Armed Robbery Squad were 'loading' Jensen with a gun. These blokes had just executed him in cold blood and now they were covering it up. No one said a word. No doubt they thought all was sweet; Malcolm was staunch with his fellow coppers as he had been taught since day one at the Police Academy.

The shooting had taken place in front of a number of office buildings. Christ knew who had seen what in those buildings so one of the Armed Robbery Squad detectives asked Malcolm to get his undercover operatives to go to all the offices in the vicinity and find out if there were any witnesses. They went to every office and extraordinarily no one had seen anything. The people in the offices only looked out of their windows after they heard shots and the car hit the pole. There had also been a bloke working on the roof of the mower shop at the time of the shooting. He would have had a bird's eye view of the car park and the route taken by Jensen. Where that witness went no one knows. But the real object of the witness search was to see if anyone had seen the towel unfurled and the gun being put in the car.

A number of matters have always concerned Malcolm about this incident. Why pursue Jensen at all? After all, they knew where he lived. They could knock on his door. If they wanted him to stop, why not shoot at the tyres? The police were armed with shotguns. Why shoot him in the head from behind? He was driving, and could not have been a threat at that point. Finally, why did the Armed Robbery Squad break all protocols and endanger civilians and surveillance cops? And then there was the planted gun. So many questions, so few answers.

Malcolm was busting to get away from the incident. He wanted nothing more to do with it. He said not a word to anyone at the Armed Robbery Squad about seeing the gun being chucked in the car. In fact he was shit scared. If they were capable of knocking off an unarmed bloke in the middle of the day in a quiet suburban street with potentially dozens of witnesses present, then they were well and truly capable of bowling some copper they thought might bring them all unstuck by, heaven forbid, telling the truth. They knew he had been standing there and they would have assumed yeah, he's seen it all and he's staunch, he's not going to say anything.

Malcolm did tell someone officially in the end. He told the OPI and the Ombudsman, Doctor Perry, when he was debriefed, but it seems little of what he said has ever been acted on.

He did tell close colleagues at the time. This being before mobile phones, Malcolm used the phone in the mower shop to call into the Surveillance Unit to let them know what had transpired. The Armed Robbery Squad had just knocked Jensen and loaded him with a shooter after he was dead! What the fuck was going on? The owner of the shop was standing right next to him when he made that call and could have heard the entire conversation. He didn't care, he was shitting himself. He got his crew together and went back to the office not wanting to be around in case they all got copped for a murder blue. The Armed Robbery Squad clearly didn't want them to be there and were happy enough when Malcolm said he was withdrawing his unit from the scene. As this was a murder scene, or at best a death-in-custody scene, they were all material witnesses and should have been ordered by the senior to stay put to have their particulars and preliminary statements taken by either the Homicide Squad or Ethical Standards or both.

Back at the office everyone was pretty shaky, but OK. The question was, what the fuck were they to do? They were, through no fault of their own, unwittingly caught up in the cold-blooded execution of a man in broad daylight. Whether he was a suspected armed robber or not, there was no valid reason to bowl the bloke. Malcolm told them: 'We are going to have to get our stories straight as to where we were, what we saw and every particular and detail.' Everyone agreed.

They started compiling a log of the sequence and timing of events of the day. There weren't many particulars to be put in it because they had not been privy to what was going to happen to Jensen. But all their logs and statements had to be done correctly because everyone from Surveillance had played a different part in the day's events. Once the log of events was complete they all stayed together and stuck around at the office and watched the news commentaries and the interviews of the people at the scene. Malcolm had an awful feeling they hadn't heard the last of this and he was right.

After they compiled their official log of the day's events, they then commenced compiling their statements. A first draft is done, usually by hand. This is compiled in consultation with all of the other coppers who had been at the scene and this statement was no exception. Being the senior officer in charge of the crew, Malcolm became the collating officer which is cop speak for the bloke who collects everything relevant and makes sure it is kept in a safe place. The documents that were generated that day also included a profile of the target with as much police material as was needed to do surveillance: a photograph of the target, known particulars such as height, weight etc and details of associates and vehicles. Add to this the surveillance log and there were five handwritten statements, one made by each officer present on the day.

As collating officer and a senior officer, the documents were Malcolm's responsibility, and he took that job seriously, particularly bearing in mind what he had witnessed that fateful afternoon. He placed them in a secure correspondence locker at the Squirrels' office pending further orders.

The very next morning all the Squirrels who had been at Narre Warren were contacted by the Armed Robbery Squad advising that there was to be a video re-enactment of the previous day's events and that they were all required to return to Webb Street and report to the Homicide Squad. Where the hell was Ethical Standards Malcolm wondered?

Malcolm went to Webb Street with enormous trepidation; what was he to do if he was told to tell a few porky pies in order to cover the Armed Robbery Squad's arses? The matter didn't bear thinking about. As luck would have it, when they arrived at Webb Street they did nothing but hang around before being told that they were not required. They were actively excluded from whatever was being said to Homicide, which suited Malcolm as he just wanted out of the whole mess. But he knew that was wishful thinking and that the game was a long way from over.

Malcolm never knew whether any of the other Surveillance officers had seen the load. Two of the officers who had a bird's eye view of everything said that they didn't see anything, because a truck was going across the highway in front of them at that precise moment.

Looking back down the years that day was the beginning of the end for Malcolm. He was frightened not only for himself but for his family. If the 'Robbers' had carte blanche to knock whoever they thought deserved it, then bowling someone who may be a threat, real or imagined, would not be a problem and he knew it.

Later he was diagnosed with a post-traumatic stress disorder clearly related to this event.

Chapter Ten

TRAGEDY STRIKES

'Criminals do not die by the
hands of the law.
They die by the hands of other men.'

—George Bernard Shaw

In the early hours of the day after Graeme Jensen was murdered in cold blood by the Armed Robbery Squad, two young constables, Tynan and Eyre, were gunned down in an ambush by unknown assassins. They had been called to what appeared to be an abandoned car with its doors open and lights on in the middle of Walsh Street, South Yarra, in inner Melbourne. When they arrived they were ambushed and killed. It was one of this country's most callous and notorious murders. Jensen's armed robbery gang were immediately under suspicion.

During the ensuing investigation into Walsh Street Jed Horton, of Jensen's gang, was also killed by the 'Sons of God' in what can only be described as suspicious circumstances.

Victor Pierce, who was my client at the time, was convinced he was going to be the next to be knocked by the coppers and surrendered himself to the Armed Robbery Squad over the murder of Dominic Hefti, even though it is now clear he had nothing to do with it. Once in custody the police could not get at him. He did not have to speak to or even see police on the grounds he was a prisoner and no prisoner can be forced to accept a police visit if he doesn't wish to.

FOLLOWING THE WALSH STREET MURDERS THERE WAS A MASSIVE input of police power to find the perpetrators. The Squirrels were given specific orders by the Chief Commissioner that all surveillance work on cases other than the Walsh Street murders was to cease. They immediately swung their resources behind surveillance of every suspect and there were plenty at that point. It was on for young and old. They didn't have enough coppers to mount all the surveillance that was being requested.

Malcolm had a dreadful feeling of foreboding, knowing what he did. He had a dreadful secret that could have short-circuited the whole sorry mess but he was terrified to let out a squeak to anyone, his wife included. He became very much on edge. He had to stay staunch; he was one of the Brotherhood. On the other side of the coin he didn't have the slightest doubt that if he had said a word about the death of Jensen his life would have been in grave peril.

Victoria Police declared war on the crooks that day and all the old rules went sailing out the window. There was to be a reign of terror until someone cracked. Instead all the crooks went to ground. Doors were kicked in in the middle of the night and gratuitous violence by the coppers became the norm in the hope of a quick breakthrough.

Inside the Force, Jensen's death was immediately nominated as a possible link to the murders. If the full truth of what happened the day before had been made public the link would have been more obvious to everyone else as well. All hell had broken loose in the press but they hadn't twigged that there was a connection between Jensen's death and the killing of Tynan and Eyre.

All Jensen's associates were of course immediately the subject of heavy surveillance. The coppers were watching Pierce, McEvoy, the Farrells from Port Melbourne, Gary Abdullah, and Jed Horton in Bendigo. Absolutely anybody who knew these blokes at all had coppers hanging all over them. McEvoy and Abdullah were part of the Flemington Crew at that stage and everybody involved in that crew was also subjected to heavy surveillance. All likely suspects had electronic surveillance in their house and in their motor vehicles.

McEvoy was very difficult to watch because his paranoia had well and truly kicked in and he was jumping at shadows. He rode a motorbike and when a tracking device was placed on his bike he found it. Then everyone around him became jumpy as well.

The coppers were playing for keeps and the crooks knew it. The crime rate plummeted. Better to stay home and not get an earn than end up plugged by some mad copper on a crusade, and there were plenty of them around.

The Squirrels were after solid evidence. In particular they were after the guns that had been used. One day they were following McEvoy through Flemington when he fell off his motorbike. There were four surveillance cars working on this one suspect and, in accordance with protocol, they just kept driving. They were subsequently reprimanded from above with the question; 'Why didn't you run over and kill the cunt when you had the chance?' This was the all-pervading attitude in the police force at the time.

The surveillance operation went on for some months and it was a bit like Operation No Name, extremely boring because the targets knew that the coppers were watching them and, as a result, pulled their heads right in. So they were watching people doing nothing. The operation was going nowhere in a big hurry. Then the orders came from above to execute a number of warrants and arrest all the blokes they were watching.

Raids were conducted over the ensuing days and the various suspects were arrested. Anthony Farrell was the first one arrested and the view was that he would be the weak link. I was in court when Farrell was taken up for remand and I was later famously recorded giving legal advice to Farrell to keep his mouth shut in the cells at the City Watch house. Not exactly endearing myself to the coppers.

The Squirrels had been watching and listening to Jed Horton for some time and listened to him talking, compliments of the listening device they had secreted in his caravan. But Horton had found one of the listening devices they had installed and was in a state of high anxiety. He knew that the coppers were onto him and his arrest was imminent. On the listening device tapes he was heard worrying that the coppers would knock him, a prescient observation indeed.

When it came time to arrest Jed Horton, the Squirrels who had been watching him were in Bendigo, where he lived, to positively identify him so that he could be arrested. The SOGs went to the door of the caravan to arrest him. It's hard to believe what they said happened next: that he pulled a gun on them and was shot dead where he stood in the doorway. It beggars belief that he would be stupid enough to answer the door and try to shoot his way out. He knew and had stated on the covert tape recordings that he was going to be arrested.

Malcolm got the wobbles and was having trouble coping at work. Then one night on the way home his car was hit from behind by another car. This seems to be a catalyst for what followed; he started suffering blinding headaches and had some sort of brain fade where he lost the use of his legs for a period of time. He sought treatment immediately and was diagnosed with severe depression and post-traumatic stress disorder. He was hospitalised for a couple of months in a rehabilitation hospital. Because he was able to say he was in hospital as a result of a car accident everything was OK at work—no suggestions, thankfully, of his being a weak bastard—and after he was discharged from hospital he returned to the Squirrels, driving a desk, with the sympathy of his colleagues. He could not display any weakness to his mates.

THE CROWN CASE AT THE WALSH STREET MURDER TRIAL WAS brought against Victor Pierce, Peter McAvoy, Anthony Farrell and Trevor Pettingill. It alleged that Pierce was beside himself with rage at the news of Jensen's death and vowed to get even. What nobody knew was that Pierce had been having an affair with Jensen's de facto. Pierce's wife Wendy didn't have the faintest idea. The Squirrels knew from their surveillance of Jensen's house. They had observed Victor coming and going while his mate Jensen was not about. This juicy little snippet would have made matters interesting indeed if Jensen had got wind of it. One wonders whether the gang would have stuck together.

The Crown alleged that Pierce, McAvoy and Jed Horton were the three killers of the two young coppers and the others had assisted them. After a long and bitterly fought trial, all four of the Walsh Street accused were acquitted by the jury. There were many reasons for this, but the main one was bad policing. The best way to catch a crook is to watch and gather evidence and when you have enough; you whittle down all the available material until it points to a likely suspect or suspects. Then you arrest, interrogate and charge them and if the evidence stacks up submit them to due process. Conversely you do not nominate likely suspects in the heat of the moment and then go about building a case around them. That course of conduct is precisely what the Tynan and Eyre Task Force adopted and it backfired on them monumentally and tragically.

This case was probably the high watermark of the 'old school' knock 'em down, drag 'em out policing. Many years later, two more police were tragically gunned down in the line of duty, Detectives Silk and Miller. The difference in the investigation to Walsh Street was chalk and cheese. Instead of the police kicking doors down and presiding over a reign of terror, it appeared that nothing was going on. In fact, behind the scenes, there was a very substantial surveillance operation in progress and the police worked on it for a long time until they were positive that they had not only identified the suspects but had sufficient evidence, out of the suspects' own mouths, that they were the people involved in the crime. When the time came and all the ducks were lined up, the police moved in and arrested Bandali Debs, who was subsequently convicted of the double murder. Debs has since been convicted of another murder. This is how policing should work.

Chapter Eleven

A DREADFUL ACCIDENT!

> ' "Curiouser and Curiouser!" cried Alice
> (she was so much surprised, that for the
> moment she quite forgot how to speak
> good English).'
>
> —*Alice in Wonderland*, Lewis Carroll

On 9 April 1989, six months after the death of Jensen, Garry Abdullah, member of the Flemington Crew, lout and associate of Jed Horton and Graeme Jensen, was shot dead by Senior Detective Cliff Lockwood from the City West CIB at the ripe old age of twenty-four. With Lockwood on that afternoon was Senior Detective Dermott Avon. Lockwood and Avon had been sent to 'arrest' Abdullah. What subsequently happened was not just a direct departure from the official company line, but in fact a dastardly deed.

First the lead up. It had always been asserted by the police that Abdullah, being a car thief, was the one who had most likely stolen the white Commodore sedan that was used as the decoy to lure Tynan and Eyre to their death in Walsh Street.

This evidence had come from Jason Ryan who was at that stage the prosecution's key witness. The only problem with Jason Ryan's evidence was that he was a pathological liar and this was demonstrated in court to the degree that his evidence was finally disregarded. Unfortunately the coppers were prepared to run with anything at that time in order to nail a quick result— they were desperate for arrests. In the cold hard light of day this 'evidence' was not worth a cold pie and never had been.

A number of significant aspects of Jason Ryan's evidence need to be looked at. First off it was well accepted within the Pettingill/Allen family that young Jason was a bullshit artist extraordinaire. But the coppers turned a blind eye to this. Jason had many and varied versions of what allegedly took place: every time he turned around his story changed. Also, the circumstances of his arrest left grave doubts about the voluntary nature of anything he had to say. When young Jason was arrested, he was seen being dragged, face bloodied to a waiting police car, past my former legal partner Charlie Nikakis, and was not seen again until after the trial.

Once the trial concluded, and Jason Ryan had outlived his role as star witness for the prosecution, he was thrown to the wolves. The prosecution had failed in spectacular circumstances and Jason had passed his use-by date. No more witness protection for him—a cynical and callous use of a very young person.

In those days of madness that followed Jensen's death and the Walsh Street killings the underworld grapevine was wild with rumours, mostly inaccurate. One was that Abdullah had been given the mail that he was 'off' (a dead man). Following the death of Graeme Jensen at the hands of the Armed Robbery Squad on 10 October 1988 and the shooting of Jed Horton at his caravan on 17 November 1988, Abdullah was beside himself with fear. And it turned out Abdullah's mail was correct.

An impartial addition to this story is from an old JP and bail justice by the name of Leo Musgrave. Old Leo had been a Justice of the Peace in the inner suburban areas of Melbourne for forever and a day and over the years I had appeared before him for many a client's bail applications in police stations, even over the phone at night. He was a tough old coot but a very fair man and Musgrave always had his ear very close to the ground on his patch. When he saw Abdullah's name on police bulletin boards he became most concerned for his wellbeing. Musgrave tried to convey that fear to Abdullah, indicating that it was his very firm view that 'the bastards' would kill him if they got half a chance. Musgrave approached Abdullah twice through intermediaries, imploring him to give himself up to police and promising him that he would make sure that he got into custody in one piece.

Abdullah went to ground for a couple of months, then with his lawyer he went to meet the Tynan–Eyre Task Force and told them that he hadn't come in earlier because he had been told in no uncertain terms that he was going to be knocked. In the meantime the Squirrels had bugged his flat and his car and set up a permanent surveillance post in a building opposite Abdullah's flat. For good measure they had installed listening devices in Abdullah's mum's house and his girlfriend's flat. Their orders were to leave no stone unturned in watching him and they didn't. There was that much surveillance on Abdullah that he could not have taken a breath without them knowing.

This is where things became interesting. On the day of Abdullah's death, the surveillance crew saw him leaving his flat. He was being followed by Detectives Lockwood and Avon in plain clothes in an unmarked police car. They pulled him over and searched him by the side of the road and drove him back to his flat. So far nothing out of the ordinary, but what followed has always bothered Malcolm, particularly as he had already witnessed the death of Jensen.

The sequence of events took a very strange turn. The Squirrels working on the Abdullah surveillance operation and Malcolm's crew were ordered to break all contact and return to base. In other words, stop listening, stop watching and come back to the Squirrels office in Richmond. Malcolm had an awful premonition of what was heading Abdullah's way. Why else would they be ordered to break all contact after spending so much time and effort bugging the bloke and just about everyone he ever knew? The usual order is to make sure everything is bloody well working perfectly so that every last syllable uttered is properly recorded for potential evidence.

Half an hour later Abdullah was dead, shot seven times by Lockwood. Nobody has ever asked why the order to abandon surveillance was given, or by whom. It is as plain as day that it was to ensure no loose ends—like inconvenient recordings of an innocent man being executed in his flat—were left hanging.

Lockwood's defence always was that Abdullah had pulled an imitation pistol on him when they got back to his flat and in self defence Lockwood shot him six times, emptying his own pistol, before grabbing Dermott Avon's pistol and putting another one into him just for good measure. Abdullah had been shot seven times while allegedly holding an imitation firearm which was later specifically denied by others in the flat.

It's interesting to note that the police defence for the murders of Jensen, Horton and Abdullah was the same for each. The story was that these were violent men who produced firearms to stop their lawful apprehension, leaving the police no alternative but to fire.

The Deputy Ombudsman commenced an investigation into Abdullah's death. The two officers under a cloud, Lockwood and Avon, with the support of the Police Association-funded legal team, refused to co-operate with the investigation on the grounds that they could incriminate themselves. This objection was allowed to stand but they were charged with Abdullah's murder anyway.

At the Supreme Court trial the Police Association were to the forefront, leading the charge. The jury was chosen from a jury pool—that is ordinary citizens called upon to serve as jurors. A pool list contains the full names, addresses and occupations of the potential jurors. The information on the list is kept secret, all an accused, or for that matter the prosecution knows about the identity of a juror, is when in court 'Joe Blow, Plumber' is called as a potential juror.

The day after the jury for the Lockwood trial was appointed personal particulars of each juror were in the hands of the police.

In the trial, Lockwood admitted discharging his gun 'accidentally' six times until it was empty and that he then grabbed Avon's and shot him one more time. The defence was 'self defence and accidental discharge'.

The prosecution failed and the two policemen were acquitted by the jury. They only had Lockwood and Avon's word for what happened. If the surveillance had been in place everyone would have known what really took place.

The only difference between Cliff Lockwood and the Walsh Street killers was that Lockwood wore a blue uniform.

Chapter Twelve

STICKING TOGETHER

'All for one and one for all!'

—*The Three Musketeers*, Alexandre Dumas

In the two years from April 1987 to April 1989 Victoria Police had managed to bowl a total of eleven members of Joe Public, precisely those they were sworn to protect. From two in 1985 and one in 1986 deaths rose to five in 1987 and the same in 1988.

As the bodies mounted so did public cynicism surrounding the behaviour of our finest. All one had to do to blow a hole in the absurd line the police were spruiking was compare Victoria's tally of deaths with other states. They were so far in front it was daylight to second place. Ordinary people were becoming jumpy about police behaviour. Something had to be done.

The State Coroner at the time, His Worship Mr Hal Hallenstein, announced that he would investigate the seven fatal shootings which had previously not been the subject of a coronial inquiry and also decided to look into previous findings made by other coroners in relation to fatal police shootings. The coronial inquiry which became more generally known as the

'Police Shootings Inquiry' opened in Melbourne in July of 1989. Malcolm was deeply concerned that the Armed Robbers thought Malcolm had the wobbles and might tell the truth. Then who knows what would befall him.

Things had got back to normal and nothing further was said about what happened at Webb Street until, out of the blue, the Squirrels including Malcolm, as the senior officer on surveillance on that day, were ordered to attend the Armed Robbery Squad offices for a conference. Malcolm didn't like the sound of this one little bit.

The Squirrels arrived at the Squad offices where they were ushered into a large conference room. Malcolm had the distinct feeling that they were about to be treated like the proverbial mushroom—kept in the dark and fed on bullshit. Seated around the conference table were a large number of Armed Robbery Squad coppers who had been at Webb Street, as well as Malcolm and his Squirrels. There weren't too many niceties and the Squirrels were left in no uncertainty as to the state of play. The conference was a list of orders that 'we' the Armed Robbery Squad, are going to say this and all you blokes are going to say the same. No ifs or buts. We are all in this together, like it or not.

The line that was to be followed was that the Armed Robbery Squad had set up Operation No Name to identify and apprehend Graeme Jensen, who was a known violent armed robber and the only suspect for the armed robbery and murder of Armaguard officer Dominic Hefti. Jensen was armed at the time of his apprehension and had produced that firearm in an attempt to evade arrest. Jensen was shot while trying to avoid apprehension. If that was what had happened at Webb Street, Narre Warren on 11 October 1988, then Malcolm must have been somewhere else. This story fell at the first hurdle because even Malcolm knew that Hefti had wounded his attacker prior to being killed. There was a substantial amount of blood at the scene from the wound Hefti inflicted on his killer. Yet everyone knew that Jensen had no wounds other than those inflicted by the Armed Robbery Squad.

This fantastic piece of conclusion jumping was before the days of DNA testing. When it was finally introduced Santo Mercuri was arrested in rural Victoria living the life of a hermit in a caravan in the bush. He had an old wound on his hand. Profiling technology proved beyond doubt that Mercuri was the killer. It had been a robbery that Mark Moran had organised. Mercuri died in jail years later.

All the surveillance members were well and truly intimidated by the Armed Robbery Squad—each of them was called before the Squad one at a time and told that none of them had seen anything. Not long after the original meeting with the Armed Robbery Squad the squirrels were called into their office again and told, not asked, that new statements were needed, in which they would confirm that no one had seen anything and accordingly Malcolm made what is known as a 'nil statement'. Like the three wise monkeys!

The whole reason for having experienced surveillance officers present in operations such as this was for the simple reason that they were trained to position themselves in the best vantage points, thereby enabling them to see things that others might miss. Off the back of their training and taking into account the care with which officers had been placed on the day, for not *one* person to have seen anything simply beggared belief.

As collating officer for the statements made on the day of the shooting, Malcolm found himself in the awkward position of holding the original detailed handwritten statements at the office, knowing that a second 'nil' statement had been made to the Armed Robbery Squad which was at odds with the original statements. Needless to say he was concerned. What if some lawyer got hold of this? They would have a birthday party over the statements being at odds one with the other. But as matters transpired salvation was at hand.

The Armed Robbery Squad called for all the original handwritten statements and guess what? When Malcolm went to the locker to deliver them to the Armed Robbery Squad, everything to do with the Jensen case was gone. The handwritten original statements made that afternoon and the original surveillance log were all gone. Missing, the locker was empty. Malcolm was dumbfounded, the Squirrels were in a secret location that was not known or accessed by ordinary police.

It was his job to tell the Armed Robbery Squad that all the documents they had called for had disappeared. When he relayed this news not one bloke in the Armed Robbery Squad seemed the least bit surprised and not another word was said about the missing documents. Malcolm has always thought the Robbers had an inside man at the Squirrels and stole what could have been very embarrassing documents for them.

Each was held with numerous Armed Robbery Squad members present. All designed to intimidate—mission accomplished.

There was a bloke named McBride who was a copper from the Ethical Standards Department assisting the police at the inquiry. And so everyone was interviewed again, this time by ESD. Finally they were taken out to the scene with maps and told to draft statements again. They all made 'nil' statements. The Squirrels told McBride where they had been stationed at the time of the shootings and the various reasons why no one had seen a thing.

When the subject of the Jensen shooting was broached at the Coronial Inquiry all the Squirrels involved were called to give evidence. They were told prior to going into court what the state of play was.

Malcolm swore on the contents of his nil statement and was in the witness box a very short time. The safest evidence to offer is always that you cannot recall or, as a surveillance officer, that you had managed to get yourself so badly positioned that it was impossible to see anything. It is misleading by deliberate omission, but at the same time, almost impossible to disprove. The minute you give a yes or no answer you eliminate the thousands of other possibilities that may exist and you are stuck with your answer for better or worse.

As Malcolm was the one who had seen it all he was waiting for the big grenade to be lobbed in his direction, the unanswerable question: why are there two conflicting statements bearing your signature? Luckily the question didn't come and he left the box a very relieved man. End of round one, as it turned out to be.

The conclusion of the inquest was not the end of the matter, as everyone had hoped. In a blaze of hysterical publicity the Armed Robbery Squad members involved in the death of Jensen on that fatal day were charged with murder. Malcolm was not happy about this because he was going to end up in the witness box again, only this time everyone was playing for keeps.

Chapter Thirteen

STARING THE BASTARDS DOWN

'An event has happened upon which, it is difficult to speak and impossible to be silent!'

—Edmund Burke

The Victoria Police Association is a union and an extremely militant one at that. If one looks at the website for the Victoria Police Association it makes no bones about the fact that it exists for one sole purpose, that is the welfare of its members, namely, the police. Two of its main objectives are to lobby the Government for the purposes of increasing policing numbers and to provide legal defence to police officers that the Police Association consider have been wrongly charged.

Once the Armed Robbers were charged with murder, the Police Association went into overdrive. The Police Association has a very substantial fighting fund for the defence of those accused of transgressing the law and is willing to pay for top barristers and solicitors. It swung into action in order to mount a watertight defence on behalf of those poorly accused, hard-working coppers.

After the coppers were charged with the 'Big M' McBride from Ethical Standards interviewed all of the Squirrels again and they became Crown witnesses (in theory) against the Armed Robbery Squad. Their brothers-in-arms had nothing to worry about; Malcolm was staunch. You stuck with their colleagues through thick and thin. After all who knows when your turn might come and you would need to be able to rely on your fellow coppers to get you out of the shit. You stick together no matter what.

There was an additional incentive to tow the company line and that was the danger of being charged with, at the very least, being an accessory after the fact to murder, a prospect that did not exactly thrill Malcolm. What made him particularly nervous was the fact that throughout the entire debacle no one had exonerated the surveillance coppers present and they didn't know if or when their lucky number might come up. They'd been at Narre Warren, hand in glove with the Armed Robbery Squad, and could have been in on the rort. They hadn't been cleared and yet they weren't treated as suspects. Malcolm couldn't understand why they didn't get a run for it. How did the prosecution know they weren't all part and parcel of the same conspiracy to murder Jensen? Surely someone would investigate them?

Malcolm didn't know how close he was to the truth. Douglas Meagher QC held the brief for the prosecution at the time the Armed Robbery officers were charged. Upon examining the evidence he reached the same conclusion as Malcolm had dreaded, namely that the Squirrels were involved in Jensen's death, and he fully intended to charge each of the Surveillance Unit coppers with a count of conspiracy to murder.

Doug Meagher had made his name as counsel assisting the Costigan Royal Commission into the Painters and Dockers Union back in the late 1970s and early '80s. He gained a reputation as being a dogged zealot and if he had been allowed to maintain the brief in this prosecution there would have been blood in the streets. Instead after Meagher stated that he thought the Squirrels were in on the giggle and that it was his intention to go back for some years and re-examine each and every Armed Robbery Squad prosecution and conviction the brief went elsewhere. Not that they gave the brief to anybody friendlier because Peter Farris QC, a fearless prosecutor, ended up with it.

Eventually, Malcolm's turn came to give evidence in the Supreme Court before the judge and a jury of twelve. Normal procedure is that all other witnesses are ordered out of court when a witness gives evidence. The practice of ordering witnesses out of court is to make sure that the witness in the dock can't hear the evidence that is currently being given and tailor their evidence to suit. This rule also prevents witnesses from warning each other of what surprises may be in store for them in the witness box. Each witness gives his or her evidence in a vacuum, uninfluenced by what others that have gone before may or may not have said. Trial judges invariably direct witnesses not to discuss their evidence with others and if you are caught doing so, you may be charged with contempt of court.

But the communication line between court and the police witnesses was simple to maintain because they did not have to sit outside court like ordinary witnesses; rather they sat in the police room, out of sight, out of mind. The coppers have the drop on the general public in a situation like this because it is police personnel on security duty, keeping a look out for people that may be acting improperly or intent on upsetting proceedings. Security invariably goes to young and inexperienced coppers, who wouldn't think of accusing police of wrongdoing, and in any case, you never knew when your number might come up and you needed the power of the Police Association on your side.

The trial was a tough one and the witnesses were advised that they could expect to be giving evidence for some days. But when Malcolm's turn came, he duly swore that he saw nothing, as was in his nil statement, and he was in the witness box less than an hour. His part of the job done. No witnesses, no evidence.

The final verdict was not guilty. Not entirely unexpected, with the arsenal the Police Association had provided and the fact that everyone remained staunch to the cause.

THIS EXERCISE TOOK A REAL TOLL IN TERMS OF STRESS ON THE Squirrels, and two officers who had been present at Narre Warren resigned from the job.

As for Malcolm, he was just glad to get the whole thing over and done with and out of the way with his arse still intact. Additionally he had demonstrated in the most profound manner possible that he was staunch. He could be relied upon to stand shoulder to shoulder when the whips were cracking.

After the trial and the verdict of acquittal on all counts was returned, the Squirrels didn't even get a 'thank you' from the Armed Robbery Squad, nor were they invited to the huge piss up that was thrown for the acquitted officers by their mates in the Armed Robbery Squad. They never ever heard another word about it. As the coppers say, it was all 'done and dusted'.

However, the rumour mill was grinding away among the coppers producing plenty of theories about the role of Detective Inspector John Hill of the Homicide Squad. He'd been in charge of the Homicide Squad investigation and subsequent charging of the Armed Robbery Squad coppers. He was a hardworking, honourable bloke who copped it from both sides for investigating other coppers, and he was clearly monstered by the Robbers.

One rumour said that before taking the gun from Jensens' car to forensics Hill placed some slivers of glass, from around Jensen, down the barrel of the firearm thereby creating the impression the firearm had already been in the car when Jensen was shot. Malcolm was told this on good authority by a copper who was present and says he saw him do it. Another former Armed Robbery Squad copper said that the gun came from another raid on a different crook altogether and the Robbers used this to load Jensen. Other police officers said Hill had not done his job properly and charged innocent coppers, putting them through hell unnecessarily. The pressure that was applied to this bloke was unrelenting, so much so, that about a year after the trial, Hill took his own life. Had he gone over to the dark side? No one knows. Only that Hill saw no other way out of his torments.

At the funeral, in a show of solidarity, the police lined Collins Street from the church on both sides while the cortege passed. This was an awesome display of solidarity by the union and the collective strength of its members.

In the writing of this book I spoke to other police, some still in the job. One thing is clear from all that I spoke to and that is that Jensen was loaded after his demise. This allegation is so serious that it's very posing demands a Royal Commission. I was also told Hill left a suicide note and that a recently retired officer holds the original. I wonder what it contains.

PART 2
BARBARIANS AT THE GATE

'Such was the public consternation when the Barbarians were hourly expected at the gates of Rome.'

—*Decline and Fall of the Roman Empire*, Edward Gibbon

Chapter Fourteen

LEAVING THE MONKEYS IN CHARGE OF THE BANANAS

'Double, double toil and trouble;
Fire burn, and cauldron bubble'

—*Macbeth*, William Shakespeare

You know what's going to happen: everybody with an axe to grind, an agenda to push or a backside to cover will come out swinging when they reach this point. I can hear the squawk: 'Rosenes and Fraser are dirty on the world in general and the Drug Squad and Strawhorn in particular.' That is not so. This is not about kicking Strawhorn or the Drug Squad, so before jumping to any hasty conclusions consider the following: this is the story of one officer's journey through the police force and is not intended to be a learned or definitive treatise on police corruption. It follows Malcolm's experiences through his years in the job and into his corrupt activities, culminating with his ultimate fall from grace and incarceration. Malcolm has pulled no punches in relating his tale to me so if anyone has their noses out of joint then frankly that's bad luck!

In this second part of Malcolm's story, we will see that Detective Senior Sergeant Wayne Strawhorn was the architect, instigator and executioner of the now infamous 'Controlled Delivery Scheme' and supervised the running of the 'Chemical Diversion Desk'. Therefore, if Strawhorn is continually mentioned it is because he is the person directly responsible in one form or another for this unmitigated disaster. To discuss the Controlled Delivery Scheme without discussing Strawhorn regularly and in detail is akin to discussing a Ponzi scheme without mentioning Bernard Madoff.

When Malcolm was promoted into the Drug Squad he was assigned to work directly under Strawhorn administering the aptly named 'Chemical Diversion Desk', aptly named because the drugs and the money had a habit of disappearing. Strawhorn was Malcolm's immediate superior. They worked hand in glove and he was bound to follow Strawhorn's orders.

I want to take the opportunity to emphasise that I do not consider all police to be corrupt; in fact, quite the opposite. Most police are honest, conscientious, hardworking members of our community, horrified at the goings on among corrupt officers. Not only do they erode public confidence in the Force but good officers are often hit by friendly fire and end up wearing some of the opprobrium that belongs elsewhere.

None of what I'm saying is new. In fact, there have been numerous reports tabled in Parliament during the last decade which disclose corruption on a massive scale, particularly within the Drug Squad.

Let's have a quick look at some of these reports and their contents, tabled over the last ten years.

Ceja Task Force was set up specifically to investigate corrupt activity in the Drug Squad. In May 2003 the first interim report of Ceja was tabled in Parliament. It makes interesting reading indeed. Specific incidents investigated by Ceja were:

1. October 1981: theft of 1.3 kilograms of pure methamphetamine from a locked and alarmed store room at the Drug Squad's office in Russell Street. Disciplinary action was taken against some members for poor management and procedural deficiencies that may have contributed to the theft. The theft itself remains unsolved. Due to the fact that the safe was locked and alarmed the inescapable conclusion is the theft was an inside job.

2. June 1992: theft of drugs and pre-cursor chemicals from the Attwood storage facility. This involved substitution of drugs which then went to methamphetamine manufacturers. As a result of this incident an officer, Kevin Hicks, was imprisoned.

3. August 1996: allegations of further theft of a large amount of precursor chemicals and drugs from Attwood storage facility. This remains unsolved.

4. December 1996, January 1997: burglary and theft of documents and tapes relating to 'Operation Phalanx' from the Drug Squad offices, now at St Kilda Road. This was a major investigation targeting some of the highest level amphetamine manufacturers in Victoria. The people responsible remain at large.

5. October 1999: firearm missing from a safe at the Drug Squad. A Barretta 9 mm pistol was stolen from a four-drawer safe in an office occupied by Detective Inspector Reid at the Drug Squad. Reid was in charge of Unit 2 at the Drug Squad and the pistol was later miraculously located in his office in July 2000. He has since resigned with his superannuation intact.

The first interim report of Ceja alone details substantial corruption, virtually none of which has been solved. It was followed by a further interim report by the Ombudsman, Mr George Brower, in June 2004. I don't propose to go through all of the matters raised in the report but will merely quote from the introduction, which should have sent the alarm bells ringing through the corridors of power.

Work on a number of these corruption investigations has progressed but many have also bought forward new and more alarming revelations. Some investigations have stalled or been given lower priority because of lack of co-operation from witnesses, or the necessary diversion of resources to other more pressing investigations.

Ceja's notable success has been overshadowed by a number of things:

1. The succession of the so-called Gangland killings and speculation about connection to police corruption.
2. Serious criminal charges against two members of the New Major Drug Investigation Division [these were the incorruptible police who replaced the Drug Squad] and an accomplice concerning the theft of drugs from an East Oakleigh house on 27 December 2003.
3. 15 May 2004 killing at their home in East Kew of the accomplice charged with the above theft and his wife.
4. Recent revelations of threats against Ceja investigators.
5. The persistent lack of a system of police accountability to detect serious misconduct and corruption would certainly invite questions about its effectiveness. The paradox of successful investigations such as Ceja in the exposure of corruption also tends to generate alarm based on fears that the corruption exposed is simply the 'tip of the iceberg'.

Mr Brower further noted that integrity is not negotiable. How true. However, he also quotes Dr Perry who in 1998 presented a report on Operation Bart, an inquiry into the infamous window shutter rort (in which police received secret commissions from window repair companies):

> It is a serious and continuing concern that while some
> of the supervisors have admitted their involvement
> in the scam and co-operated with Bart investigators,
> a large number of Sergeants, and Senior Sergeants in
> particular, had actively obstructed the investigation and
> encouraged subordinates to do the same. Furthermore
> there is evidence that some supervisors had colluded with
> or pressured subordinates to make statements which
> minimised the supervisors' involvement. A number of
> supervisors I believe have escaped disciplinary actions.

Note this report was made in 1998, before any of the Drug Squad problems came to light. The alarm bells were ringing everywhere except in the police force and government. The citizens of this state continue to pay a price as a result.

In July 2007 Ceja's final report was tabled in Parliament. It disclosed that at least 87 per cent of chemicals purchased under the Controlled Delivery Scheme had been lost or were unaccounted for and, as a result, had found their way into criminal hands, been made into amphetamine and had thereafter found their way into the community. Eighty-seven per cent is a mind-boggling figure and reeks not of inefficiencies or maladministration but of corruption leading to a flood of drugs onto Australia's streets. Using the same figures that the Drug Squad use these drugs could be worth well in excess of one hundred million dollars on the street.

Another report was ordered in February 2007, entitled 'Past Patterns—Future Directions: Victoria Police and the problem of corruption and serious misconduct'. This is a substantial document which effectively provides a definitive history of the *known* corrupt activities in the Force and suggests how to deal with them. It observes that the very nature of the job exposes officers to the temptation of corruption: 'Misplaced loyalty has allowed sections of the Force to decline into predators rather than servers of their community.'

One amazing defence often used by corrupt police and discussed in this report is the question of 'noble cause'. In short it is where police commit criminal offences in order to catch crooks, i.e. if the cause is noble, it is justifiable for police to act illegally in order to catch other crooks. This defence is dismissed in the report.

It continues:

> ... the challenge for individual Victoria Police is how
> do we raise a culture committed to professionalism and
> high integrity that can maintain solidarity but admit
> mistakes and learn from them. Accepting and admitting
> mistakes is fundamental to any reform in the Police force
> and if it takes a Royal Commission and thereafter the
> establishment of a corruptions commission, then that is
> what must be done.

For many years reports to Parliament have had a common theme: the existence of endemic corruption. This is a problem that has been discussed in numerous contexts and I commend reading all of the above reports to the reader; they are readily available on the internet and all make interesting, if not horrifying, reading.

But wasn't there a major clean out of the Drug Squad? It has been disbanded and the new Major Drug Investigation Division established. Corrupt police have gone to jail—problem solved. Right? Not so. Officers from the new Major Drug Investigation

Division, not long after its inception, were charged with corrupt activities and are serving their sentence. The proposition that the problem is solved doesn't hold water. Further, to suggest that pinching a few blokes clears the decks and corruption is eliminated is clearly absurd. Let's have a look at the police who have been charged:

- Wayne Strawhorn: Detective Senior Sergeant, Drug Squad
  Pleaded not guilty and was convicted by a jury of one count of trafficking a commercial quantity of pseudoephedrine (two kilos) to Mark Moran. Sentenced to imprisonment for seven years with a four-year minimum. Now on parole. The judge found that the trafficking was 'opportunistic' and lasted no more than a week. Malcolm's evidence says otherwise.
- Glenn Sadler: Senior Detective, Drug Squad
  Pleaded not guilty to one count of conspiring to traffic not less than a commercial quantity of heroin. Total heroin alleged: 4.5 kilos. Convicted and sentenced to ten years with a six-year minimum.
- Stephen Cox: Detective Sergeant, Drug Squad
  Pleaded not guilty to one count of conspiring to traffic not less then a commercial quantity of heroin. Total heroin alleged: 4.5 kilos. Convicted and sentenced to seven years with a four-year minimum.
- Ian Ferguson: Detective Senior Constable Drug Squad
  Pleaded not guilty to one count of conspiring to traffic not less than a commercial quantity of heroin. Total heroin alleged: 4.5 kilos, together with one count of money-laundering. Convicted and sentenced to twelve years with a minimum of eight. He is still in jail.

- Bradley Ferguson: Detective Senior Constable, Drug Squad
  Pleaded not guilty to one count each of trafficking amphetamine and cocaine. Convicted and sentenced to three and a half years with a minimum of two and a half.
- Steven Paton: Detective Senior Constable, Drug Squad
  Pleaded guilty to trafficking a commercial quantity of a drug of dependence. Sentenced to six years with a minimum of three.
- Malcolm Rosenes: Detective Sergeant, Drug Squad
  Pleaded guilty to one count of trafficking a commercial quantity of a drug of dependence. Sentenced to six years, three months with a minimum of three and a half years.
- Kellianne Gorrison: Senior Constable
  Pleaded guilty to one count each of trafficking cocaine and ecstasy. Received a two-year good behaviour bond (believe it or not) and paid a $1,500-contribution to the court fund.
- Matthew Bunning: Detective Senior Constable, Drug Squad
  Pleaded guilty to two counts of operating an account in a false name, four counts of theft and obtaining financial advantage by deception, eight counts of dealing with the proceeds of crime, eight counts of possessing a drug of dependence and altering a prescription, twelve counts of misconduct in public office and also possessing ammunition without a licence and possessing a regulated weapon. He was also a morphine addict. Sentenced to six years and ten months with a minimum of three years.

- David Miechel: Detective Senior Constable, Major
  Drug Investigation Unit
  Pleaded not guilty to one count of burglary, one
  count of theft, two counts of trafficking a large
  commercial quantity of a drug of dependence, one
  count of trafficking a commercial quantity of a
  drug of dependence and two counts of trafficking
  a drug of dependence. Convicted on all counts and
  sentenced to fifteen years with a minimum of twelve.
  He is still in jail.

There is something unusual about this list of offenders in that there is not one accused above the rank of Senior Sergeant. I have thought long and hard about this and the only options are that those more senior were either asleep at the wheel and failed to carry out their duty, cleverly deceived, or they were in on the rort. I can't think of any other alternatives.

By way of example, the Controlled Delivery Scheme was administered and supervised by senior police officers, some from outside the Drug Squad. Have any of these officers been questioned or subjected to scrutiny?

In addition to the reports mentioned here there is the fact that Malcolm conducted his debrief to Ethical Standards in 2001, nearly ten years ago now. Yet in those ten years you will see that little or nothing has been done to fix the problem.

Chapter Fifteen

A NICE LITTLE EARNER

'Sex and drugs and rock and roll'

—'Sex & Drugs & Rock 'n' Roll', Ian Dury and the Blockheads

Detective Sergeant Malcolm Rosenes was intent on grabbing every promotion that came his way, which would result, he hoped, in him reaching the rarefied heights of officer. Another promotion beckoned, not in rank, but in what was considered to be quality of work. Maybe he should have allayed his ambitions and stayed where he was comfortable and suited to the squirrel work he was doing. Alas, he did not. Late in 1997 he took a promotion to the Drug Squad at the same rank. The Drug Squad was an elite squad whereas Surveillance was not. The move was considered advancement within the job and placed him at the coalface of operational policing, where he could be noticed, and if successful, gain that much-wanted promotion.

When Malcolm started looking around for promotions, he noticed that there were at least ten vacancies for sergeants alone in the Drug Squad. If all was right with the world, how come there were ten vacancies for sergeants? If he had been thinking clearly, alarm bells would have started ringing that not all was as shipshape as it appeared. But Malcolm was oblivious to any hints of monkey business and applied for, and received one of the gigs at the Drug Squad.

The Drug Squad was headed by a Superintendent and the general supervision fell to a Chief Inspector. The Squad comprised three units: Unit 1 was the Heroin Unit, targeting Asian heroin traffickers, and had its own Senior Sergeant and Inspector. Unit 2 was the Clandestine Laboratory Unit, and operated under its own Inspector and a Senior Sergeant. Strawhorn was a Detective Sergeant in Unit 2. Unit 3 investigated other drug-related activity—cocaine and the large marijuana crops that always seemed to surface around Mildura. Each Unit had about twenty coppers participating in the various operations at the same rank as Malcolm.

Unit 2, where Malcolm found himself, investigated the manufacture of amphetamine and ecstasy. In the drug trade, the people who make these drugs are known as 'cooks'. The Unit's work entailed liaising with legitimate chemical manufacturers and suppliers, working with informers and following up on intelligence with a view to finding as many laboratories and exposing as many supply lines as possible. Life was busy and they were pinching plenty but never seemed to be able to nail the legendary Mr Bigs.

It wasn't until Malcolm had been in the Drug Squad for some time that the penny dropped as to why there had been so many vacancies when he applied. There had been a big clean out of anybody even remotely suspect after an infamous Drug Squad break-in, in which a brief relating to the Black Uhlan Motor Cycle Club was stolen. This brief contained the identity of a registered police informer, and its theft was a very serious matter indeed. The informer registration process is a strict protocol controlled by superintendents. To register an informer, his or her name is placed on a registration document and a number allocated. Once that number is allocated the sheet with all the personal details is locked away where only one person has access to it, the superintendent, who is the head of the Unit. Thereafter the informer is referred to by number only. Protecting an informer's identity is top priority for obvious reasons.

There were two ways to enter the Drug Squad premises: the correct way and a naughty, unauthorised way, if you had inside knowledge. Once you were out of the lift you turned left towards the toilets and went down a corridor to the rear of the Drug Squad and through a door that was supposedly kept locked but, in reality, was always open. You were then at the rear of the Drug Squad. Once through the door, interview rooms were on the left and there was an area that was partitioned off that nobody could see. This led to a storage room, which was always left open. In the room were police lockers, not only for changes of clothing but, unbelievably, to store briefs of evidence. Malcolm tells me the briefs were never kept under lock and key even though that was the directive. It was from this unlocked room, from an unlocked locker, out of view of anyone, that the Higgs brief was stolen.

It was hardly a break-in; it was the easiest thing in the world for somebody familiar with the layout of the Drug Squad to access this room unnoticed. The burning question is why the brief contained the name of a registered informer and why it was in this room, unless there was an ulterior motive. Such an occurrence was a breach of every protocol to protect informers. To compromise an informer's identity is to place that informer in mortal danger and whoever committed the breach would have known full well that this was so. The informer is potentially revealed far and wide as a 'dog' and any crook who has a reason to knock them now knows their identity. This business is life and death, as has been tragically revealed on more than one occasion.

In this case, discovering the identity of the informer would be of particular benefit to the Black Uhlan Motorcycle Club. The investigation had dragged on for ages with no result. The lack of progress meant the Black Uhlan Motorcycle Club was running rings around the Drug Squad and they didn't take kindly to being made fools of. Extensive surveillance was in place at a property near Shepparton, where two teams had been in place for several months. It became such a joke that each surveillance unit referred to it as 'Club Shep'. Half the crew stayed at the hotel sunbaking and hanging around the pool while the others played golf. The one poor bugger who had drawn the short straw spent his shift watching a semi-trailer sitting in a paddock, waiting for it to be moved. It supposedly contained pre-cursor chemicals. It never moved. No drug investigation in the history of the Drug Squad had run for so long, utilising so many resources, for so little result. There was intense pressure to get a result or wind up the operation.

There was a Melbourne Cup field of suspects for the 'break-in'. Malcolm's views on it are simple. The theft of the highly sensitive information justified the continuity of the operation. This is precisely what happened: the operation was expanded and given greater resources, still for no result, I hasten to add.

Ever since the break-in speculation has continued, both within the Force and the legal profession, as to who carried it out. The suspicion was that it had to be an inside job and that whoever did it must have been paid off. A former Drug Squad detective was, and remains, the prime suspect. He left the Drug Squad and later applied to return as Detective Sergeant. His application was refused. I should add that there has never been any finding of guilt against anyone. The matter remains unsolved to this day.

After the burglary a substantial cloud hung over the Drug Squad. Ethical Standards got a tip off and raided Strawhorn's house, where they located a substantial amount of cash, around $20,000. The question was: what was a copper of this rank doing with a heap of cash if he wasn't up to no good. The excuse he gave to ESD was he was saving the money for kitchen renovations. One might still ask, why did a lowly ranking Detective Sergeant, as he then was, with a family, have twenty-plus gorillas in cold hard cash? Why wouldn't he put his money in the bank like everyone else? Perhaps if ESD had investigated the incident thoroughly Strawhorn might have been out of business years ago. The final twist was that Strawhorn didn't pay cash for the new kitchen; it was paid for with another Drug Squad copper's American Express card. Why? Who knows? None of this has ever seen the light of day.

MALCOLM'S LIFE IN THE DRUG SQUAD INVOLVED THE USUAL long hours and pressure. With the explosion of the manufacture and use of drugs in the community there was an ever-increasing workload with a number of prime targets, prominent among them the three Reading Brothers: Joe, Jeff (who is now deceased) and Lenny—known sometimes as the 'Three Stooges'.

Malcolm's first job in the Drug Squad was to raid Lenny's house in Melbourne's Western Suburbs. Prior to the raid, Strawhorn pulled him aside and told him he would find three lots of pre-cursor chemicals for speed, using a new recipe, at Reading's house. The Readings enjoyed reputations throughout the underworld as speed cooks extraordinaire. This was a big raid and Malcolm was very excited. The search commenced and the house was tipped upside down—nothing was located. Malcolm rang Strawhorn, who instructed him to search the backyard. It is interesting to note that Strawhorn always remained at arm's length. Instead it was usually the youngest and most inexperienced, or a copper on secondment, that became the informant and gave evidence if someone was pinched. They genuinely didn't know what was going on behind the scenes and therefore gave their evidence truthfully. This placed a buffer between the Drug Squad and any illegalities.

Malcolm rang Strawhorn again and told him he couldn't find anything, the place had been searched from front to back. Strawhorn directed Malcolm to look under some rocks near the back fence, which he did, and immediately uncovered a plastic bag containing a purple chemical. The search continued without further results. Another call to Strawhorn directed the search to an area between the back shed and fence, where another chemical was located. The search went on but still no third chemical. A final call and Strawhorn pointed them to another area in the backyard where the third bag of chemicals was found. This was the first unpalatable incident for Malcolm in the Drug Squad. He had been used as the bunny to load Lenny.

Later during another search of the house, a young secondee found an underground publication known as 'Uncle Fester's Cookbook'. This is an American publication on the manufacture of amphetamines containing numerous recipes. Folded inside the book was a typed single-A4 page with a short recipe for speed, utilising the exact three ingredients located in the backyard. Malcolm was sure the book was not in the second bedroom when he had first searched it. In any event this room was occupied by another bloke, not Reading, and he was one of the Drug Squad's fizzers (informers). Lenny was arrested and charged.

I've known Len for a long time and he doesn't take kindly to being arrested in general and being loaded in particular. He protested his innocence vigorously. The problem is lawyers hear these sorts of allegations every day of the week from crooks so you tend to take little notice unless there is some cogent evidence to back up their claims. Len was interviewed, processed, bailed and tried. After Len's conviction there was a celebration at the

Drug Squad. It was then that it was confirmed that the chemicals had been planted. Malcolm had been set up as the innocent copper who gave truthful evidence. He wasn't privy to what had happened behind the scenes.

I have subsequently spoken to Lenny and he is still dirty on the Drug Squad. He maintains, as he did at the time, that the chemicals were planted along with the recipe and that he was comprehensively not guilty—as he pleaded in court. One factor in Len's favour was that the trial judge, after hearing all the evidence, in particular that neither the drugs or the book were in Lenny's personal possession, charged the jury for an acquittal and when they convicted him, a wholly suspended jail sentence was imposed. This conviction should be quashed on the evidence that Malcolm is now prepared to provide.

Once Malcolm was introduced to the load it didn't take him long to get into the swing of things. Loading blokes is a cost-effective and efficient way of getting a pinch. If somebody was up to no good and they couldn't catch them, load them. Don't worry about due process. Don't worry about the law. Just get the bastards and that's all there is to it.

The 'Penguin' was a legendary cook and the coppers desperately wanted to nail him for a lab they were convinced he was running. Penguin was hanging around with another well-known drug dealer, 'American Dave'. A full-scale surveillance operation was launched on American Dave hoping he would lead them to the Penguin. It was like a red rag to a bull that they couldn't nail the Penguin; the dogs were barking he was back cooking. Strawhorn met Penguin, who was one of his informers, and noticed acid burns on his hands, proof positive in Strawhorn's mind that Penguin was cooking. Then the coppers ended up with a double negative. They couldn't catch Penguin and he suddenly refused to work as an informer. It was decided Penguin needed a message loud and clear to start cooperating.

In Strawhorn's office was a four-drawer lockable filing cabinet. In the top drawer he kept myriad drugs, which he said were used as training aids, so he could show samples of marijuana or heroin to people he might be lecturing, be they police or members of the community. Right from the outset Malcolm harboured doubts about this explanation because the filing cabinet was an Aladdin's cave of illicit substances in substantial quantities, far more than would ever be used in a lecture or as a teaching aid.

He was dumbfounded the first time he saw a load. A crook had been arrested with a relatively small amount of cocaine. At that time, a traffickable quantity was two grams and this amount was well under. Strawhorn was sure the bloke was trafficking so without further ado he took the bag of coke from Malcolm, went to his office, opened the top drawer, took a teaspoon and whacked a good heaped teaspoon of cocaine into the bag. By the time it came back from Strawhorn's office it was about five grams and they pinched him with trafficking. Needless to say the bloke was not happy with his treatment. Over the time Malcolm spent in the Drug Squad it became apparent there were actually two reasons for Strawhorn maintaining this cache of drugs: first to use as presents for informers for services rendered and secondly to load blokes if required.

On one occasion, a tip off was received that a visit from the toe cutters (ESD) was imminent. Strawhorn emerged from his office with a handful of various drugs from the filing cabinet and distributed them around the room saying, 'Hold onto this, I'm about to get a visit and I don't want it in my office.' He gave Malcolm a bag of rock heroin weighing about half an ounce. Rock heroin is the highest grade you can get and on the street could be cut up to twenty times before reaching the ultimate consumer. Malcolm was told to keep it in a safe place and Strawhorn would retrieve it later. The Drug Squad was so blasé about the treatment of drugs Malcolm left the smack in a pencil case in a drawer of his desk and promptly forgot about it. Two or three months later, Strawhorn asked for it back.

Later that day, half an ounce of heroin was given to two detectives to load American Dave. Surveillance dogged American Dave as part of the operation to locate the Penguin's laboratory. The two detectives met surveillance and followed in convoy as American Dave unsuspectingly drove east on Burwood Highway. An interception point was allocated and local uniformed coppers were called in for a routine traffic stop. On interception the two detectives, who just happened to be nearby, put the heroin in Dave's car. This was then found by the two young coppers doing the traffic stop. Dave was charged with possession and trafficking and sentenced to a term in prison. This was considered all well and good and at the same time sent a message to Penguin loud and clear.

When the detectives returned to the office with American Dave, Malcolm was appalled to see the half ounce of heroin 'located' in Dave's car was exactly the same heroin he had returned to Strawhorn some hours before. It was packaged in precisely the same manner it had been when returned to Strawhorn. Luckily nobody fingerprinted the bag!

On the one hand Malcolm was relishing the challenges and kudos of being in an elite squad, but on the other, this is when he started to realise he wasn't coping. He was still rattled from the Jensen incident and had taken to consuming prescription medication—addressing the symptoms, not the cause. Malcolm had sought medical help and had been prescribed valium and he overdid it. When the effect inevitably wore off with excessive consumption, he was prescribed another sedative, Ducene, overdoing this one as well and resulting in an addiction to both medications.

Malcolm had transferred to the Drug Squad in order to be accepted. He had remained an outsider throughout his career.

A significant aspect was Malcolm's religion, and while he did drink, he was first and foremost a family man. He didn't go out on the grog with all the coppers on a Friday afternoon as was the accepted practice. He liked to attend synagogue with his family rather than pissing on with a bunch of drunken detectives in some lowlife pub. Notes were left on his desk containing objectionable references to his religion and he was regularly referred to as 'you fucking Jew'.

IT WAS A STANDING JOKE THAT A SEARCH WARRANT WAS A licence to steal and that didn't just mean drugs or money. Whatever wasn't bolted down went free. Dave Miechel, whose hobby was mechanics, had the best equipped toolshed you'd ever seen.

One memorable story related the execution of a warrant in Hoppers Crossing, an outer suburban housing development. The street consisted of small blocks of land with small spec homes but at the end of the street was a double block with a huge McMansion. It had a six-car garage, a huge satellite dish and inside, the whole shooting match was furnished in the most ostentatious bad taste. Because this was a covert entry an inspector was called. While searching the house the Squad found drawers and cupboards containing stacks of $100 notes laid out everywhere. Everybody wondered whether this was an Ethical Standards integrity test with all the money marked and cameras trained on the coppers. The money was counted and handed to the inspector. As well, large volumes of heroin were found in the garage. After the money and drugs were properly accounted for the inspector left. This was when the fun started. The walk-in wardrobe looked like the Myer Emporium. The coppers were greeted with row upon row of brand new Zegna and Hugo Boss suits. One drawer contained only brand new Hugo Boss underwear. Another full of sunglasses, one for socks, and on and on it went. Everyone was searching through the suits, which is normal procedure, but then the detectives decided to try on the suits. How annoying that the bloke who owned them was a large unit and the suits were of no value to anybody. How dirty they were that there was nothing to steal. As matters transpired, the cash and drugs had not been an integrity test. Nobody made a quid that day.

This wasn't always the case, particularly with the first raid on Carl Williams' house in Broadmeadows. It was a double-storey unit and the neighbours had been complaining of a constant clunking noise. In an unrelated matter the Broadmeadows CIB were investigating the resident of that address for credit card fraud. Little did they realise the resident was Carl Williams, because the name on the card was false. Williams came unstuck when the CIB turned up to investigate, not having the faintest idea what was going on. Carl and George (his dad) were both present. The coppers lobbed and heard the same clunking noise; but thought it was a washing machine. On further investigation CIB found in the upstairs bedroom a one-stamp pill press (each stamp produced one pill at a time—some drug dealers have stamp presses that do up to sixteen). This machine Carl had running was pumping out 60 pills a minute, still a very good earn when you consider the bloody thing was clunking away twenty-four hours a day. Imagine the money he was making. The Broadmeadows coppers arrested Williams on the credit card fraud but they couldn't help themselves: one of the sergeants was charged and convicted of pinching Carl Williams' bank book and stealing $7,000 out of the account.

Because of the amount of drugs present, Unit 2 was called in and immediately sealed off the area. Nobody was allowed in because it was a crime scene and a potentially dangerous environment because of the chemicals. The great thing about a crime scene for the coppers is that you have to keep everyone out—no witnesses to lag. Next to the pill press was a 25-litre white plastic bucket overflowing with ecstasy. There were thousands of tablets in the room. Chemicals sat on plastic sheeting, measured and ready to go in the press. Different tablets were being made, mimicking imported ecstasy brands. In the hallway were shoe boxes full of pre-packed orders, sandwich bags containing 500, 1,000, or 2,000 tablets, all with customers' names on them. This was the easiest of pinches, with blokes' names plastered all over the bags, easy to track down if the coppers so desired. All up there were maybe 50,000 tablets, a shit-load in anyone's language.

They left all of the pre-packaged tablets in the shoe boxes for their fantastic evidentiary value. However it was open season on the thousands of tablets in the bucket next to the press. Everyone was wearing Drug Squad overalls so they couldn't fit many pills in their pockets. There was no shortage of plastic bags in the house though and a couple of bags at a time were filled, stuck in overalls, and taken out to the car. Straight under the nose of other coppers, with no questions asked—after all, they were the elite drug squad.

When they returned to the Drug Squad Malcolm counted the tablets, there were in excess of 1,000. Strawhorn then announced to all present that the tabs were going to be used to load Jason Moran. Malcolm wasn't remotely surprised at this because the Morans had been in their cross-hairs for some time without any joy. This little effort might tip the scales comprehensively in their favour.

Pinching drugs wasn't the only way to make a quid. Informers were sometimes paid living expenses or given cash rewards, and this opened up other opportunities. There was a Geelong businessman informing who was guaranteed a $500,000 reward for his assistance. A dispute broke out between the coppers and the Government over payment. The reward was finally whittled down to $350,000, with Strawhorn fighting very hard for it. On the day payment was made, Strawhorn came dancing into the office waving the cheque over his head, jubilantly telling everyone he had a cheque for $350,000. It was common knowledge Strawhorn was getting a substantial whack from the reward. Ethical Standards got hold of the businessman and tried to extract a statement from him against Strawhorn but he refused. Not being a police officer he could not be compelled to answer their questions. We will probably never know the truth of what happened because the bloke is recently deceased.

The usual argument trotted out by the police in defence of loading crooks is that they're bad eggs anyway. It doesn't matter if they are convicted for one they didn't do; it goes some way to balance up for other crimes they got away with. This argument displays a breathtaking disregard for the rule of law.

Chapter Sixteen

ELDORADO

'"Over the Mountains
Of the Moon,
Down the Valley of the Shadow,
Ride, boldly ride"
The shade replied—
"If you seek for Eldorado!"'

— 'Eldorado', Edgar Allan Poe

Malcolm continued to wear the stereotypes attributed to the Jewish faith until he was given control of the Chemical Diversion Desk, which meant working directly outside Strawhorn's office door. He was finally accepted. Four coppers ran the Chemical Diversion Scheme: Malcolm, Steve Paton, Paul Firth and later David Miechel. What a great team. The only one not charged was Firth.

Strawhorn was considered the gun investigator because he always nailed the big pinches. He was the golden-haired boy who could do no wrong. An example. The strict, and I mean strict, protocol when taking promotion was that you returned to uniform. This applied even to the rank of Inspector. You returned from CIB to uniform and usually after six months applied through normal channels for a posting to the CIB. In the recent history of the Victorian Police Force there has been one exception to that rule and that was Wayne Strawhorn. The whole idea of moving police around is to minimise opportunities for corruption. If kept on the move an officer has less chance of establishing corrupt connections. When Malcolm first joined the Drug Squad Strawhorn had managed to work his way into a position where he was considered indispensable, hence the exception to the rule, allowing him to take promotion from within. This was the only such example Malcolm had seen in all his years in the police.

In the 2007 report, 'Past Patterns—Future Directions' by Ombudsman, George Brower, a telling observation was made about the so-called 'high achievers': 'These police used the processes of the Force and their intimate knowledge of Force procedures as shields to conceal and expand their illicit business. Lastly these people were generally above average performers; they got results, they had established "operational" credibility; they were not the kinds of people who would be suspected of illegality.' Mr Brower went on to say: 'Another clear lesson from this analysis is that for effective personnel management and supervision "high fliers" must be scrutinised just as closely as the under achievers.'

Strawhorn was one of those high fliers and was awarded a Churchill Fellowship to study in the UK. He learned about the Controlled Delivery Scheme of pre-cursor chemicals and drugs from legitimate sources to criminals, following the production and distribution network from end to end with the idea of ultimately catching all concerned. On his return he lobbied hard for the Controlled Delivery Scheme to be implemented. In Europe the success rates were high, with many arrests. The scheme wasn't implemented overnight and there was much arguing for and against before the scheme was finally introduced, supposedly subject to such stringent supervision and constraints as to render it incorruptible. To say this was a controversial scheme is an understatement.

The Chemical Diversion Desk was established to implement the Controlled Delivery Scheme. The mechanics were simple. Precursor chemicals on the black market are hideously expensive and difficult to source but if purchased legitimately by the police from chemical companies like Sigma at normal retail prices, these drugs could then be onsold through the police informer and undercover network to the crooks at the going black market rate. The police would follow the distribution network to the street. When all the ducks were lined up, the theory was, they would strike, wiping out the whole network in one hit. All great in theory but as we will see, woeful in practice. It was far too vulnerable to corruption and boy did the Drug Squad ever make a meal of it.

The problem was that those charged with supervising didn't do so, to the eternal detriment of the public. And the very police whose job was to stop drugs hitting the street became up to their eyeballs in drug trafficking. It is significant that no other state in Australia ran with this concept on the grounds that it was too open to abuse, irrespective of safeguards. How right they were.

A kilo of pseudoephedrine in its pure form, sold on a legitimate wholesale basis, was about $220 a kilo. In turn, sold on the black market, it returned about $20,000. Yes those numbers are correct—they are not typos. One point two kilograms of pseudoephedrine, properly processed, returns one kilo of pure amphetamine. Once amphetamine leaves the cook, it is cut every step of the way down the supply chain, resulting in product that is often less than four per cent pure on the street. It isn't hard to do the numbers and be seduced by the unimaginable riches that flow from that kind of deal. Frankly it's no wonder crooks go for amphetamine cooking like chicken into hot gravy.

For example, if one extrapolates from the numbers provided in sworn evidence by Detective Sergeant McIntyre in the case of Bob Slusarczyk in the County Court, by the time it hit the street every kilo of pure amphetamine was worth two and a half million dollars!

By the time Malcolm arrived at the Drug Squad the scheme had been up and running for some time. It was supposedly stringently overseen and administered by a committee comprising officers from the Drug Squad and other intelligence groups together with no less than three superintendents. It was the committee's job to select targets and decide the amounts of pre-cursors to be sold. There was a bank account set up at the Drug Squad where any monies coming in, and there was substantial profit made, would be paid. It had several hundred thousand dollars in it. Nobody appears to know how this money was used or what was done with it after it was lodged in the trust account other than to say that it did go to police use, either for equipment, or back to the Government. At the outset we have an unacceptable situation in which the police force is profiting from the sale of illicit drugs. The dough was also used for lunches for officers and booze ups. When the Drug Squad was disbanded the shit really hit the fan, with stacks of dough unaccounted for.

Someone administered this account. Where was the bloody money? No one has ever been brought to account, charged or even disciplined. A huge amount of money disappeared and the public (whose money it is) have a right to know what really took place.

The Controlled Delivery Scheme also provided potential for informers to get drugs to on-sell for profit. This was a common occurrence. The informer was given drugs as part of his 'package' for informing and then he would on-sell them, theoretically for a pre-arranged price. The problem was most informers refused to wear a wire when they met their criminal mates and the Drug Squad had no idea of the price the chemicals were on-sold for. They knew the informers were making profits and they turned a blind eye.

The lax administration permitted *uncontrolled* deliveries in order to keep informers sweet. After all, it didn't cost the coppers anything—there was plenty more where that came from. Giving the informers the 'green light' had been accepted practice for some time when Malcolm arrived. It made it impossible for any cop or crook to keep track of how much of what went where. That dealings were impossible to keep track of only reinforced the feeling of invincibility in the Drug Squad. If they muddied the waters sufficiently, nobody would ever be able to work out what had happened.

One thing that struck Malcolm when he arrived at the Drug Squad was that everybody from the most junior member up appeared to be renovating his house, buying a new car or going on an expensive holiday. He kept asking himself how they all did it on a copper's wage. After all, he was a copper with a family, and he couldn't afford that lifestyle. He soon learnt how they did it.

It became clear that the Drug Squad had worked out how to purchase chemicals *outside* the scheme. It was simple—all the coppers were so well known at the chemical companies they didn't need documentation signed by Force Command or the Controlled Delivery Committee, as was the protocol. Instead, coppers merely rang the companies and said, 'We need another kilo of pseudo.' Then they rocked up to the chemical company, paid cash and collected the chemicals.

As soon as Malcolm took over the Chemical Diversion Desk, at his first meeting with a chemical company, there was a discrepancy involving a quantity of chemicals picked up by the

Drug Squad that hadn't been paid for, to the tune of $2,400. There was no record at the Drug Squad of what was ordered, who ordered it or which investigation the chemicals were used in. When Malcolm asked the officer who had picked up the chemicals how he would pay the chemical company and where the money was coming from, he was told the amount wouldn't be paid as the coppers had no record of the purchase and that he would have to remedy it. Detective Senior Constable Steve Paton came to the rescue, pulling him aside to tell him how to fix the problem. Fictitious purchases would be generated to cover the loss of the unaccounted for transaction and once authorisation was given for payment for the fictitious purchases the debt that was still outstanding to the chemical company was paid. There were many anomalies at the Diversion Desk.

Initially Malcolm was appalled at these goings on. It was obvious the entire system was being abused. Even worse, Strawhorn and Paton regularly ordered Malcolm to double up on an order. Therefore half a kilogram of pseudoephedrine became one kilogram but the second half had no paper work. This order was given so often that it became the norm that virtually every order 'doubled up'.

Pre-cursor chemicals were good but the best earner was Sudafed tablets. Sudafed were purchased regularly in large quantities by cooks because they contained an easily extracted source of pseudoephedrine and amphetamine could be cooked from the extract. Accordingly, Sudafed was much sought after and often cooks had gangs trotting around the countryside purchasing as many packets as they could get their hands on. This practice has been stopped to a large degree. Now if you purchase Sudafed, you must produce your driver's licence and the purchase automatically enters a central register. If you purchase too many you come unstuck. In those days it didn't matter. Sudafed retailed for $13 a box of 60 tablets and you could buy as many as you liked, no questions asked. The Drug Squad purchased wholesale at about $5 and on-sold on the black market for $30. A nice little earner indeed!

Malcolm was the bloke who was supposed to know exactly what chemicals were purchased and where they were going. One afternoon he went to the locked storeroom where the firearms were kept and to which in theory only the Inspector had the key and access. He obtained the key and went to the room to retrieve something, but he couldn't get in the door—blocking it was a wall of packers of Sudafed (containers of 100 boxes). There must have been hundreds of packers. The pile was over six feet high, four packers wide and two deep. Malcolm stood there dumbfounded, not having the remotest idea where they had come from or how they got there. He relocked the storeroom, went back to the office and asked, 'Where the fuck did all those Sudafed come from?' No answer, was the stern reply, meaning: mind your own business. Nothing else was said. Later, when Malcolm returned to the storeroom for another reason, guess what? All the Sudafed had disappeared without a trace, gone as quickly as it had arrived.

Not surprising then that Ceja Task Force's Report into drug-related corruption found that 87 per cent of drugs purchased legitimately by the Drug Squad and then on-sold were unaccounted for. By the way, this figure doesn't include the illegal purchases, which are open-ended in value. Somewhere there is a very large hole with a huge amount of money in it and there are coppers who know all about it.

The system was out of hand. Huge amounts of chemicals were heading to all points of the compass, rendering them impossible to track. It was a dog's breakfast.

The Victoria Police Chemical Diversion Desk was also used by interstate police to set up controlled deliveries interstate. Queensland, New South Wales and South Australia had all previously considered and rejected controlled deliveries. But it was a regular occurrence for interstate coppers to contact the Drug Squad with a view to steering a crook to Victoria to purchase chemicals. A suspect arriving in Victoria would be watched on behalf of the other state. The Drug Squad notified chemical companies that a target was coming and to allow the purchase to take place. The crook was then tracked back over the border, in theory. This was disastrous because a lot of these purchases disappeared off into the Mulga without a trace. One exception was when the Drug Squad followed some bikies into New South Wales. The local coppers were tipped off and a number of laboratories were located. In that raid an arsenal of weapons was also found for good measure.

If police are following somebody up the bush where laboratories are often located, if you don't have a tracker on their car it's easy to lose the crook and you are left with the prospect of searching for a needle in a haystack. Usually by the time the coppers track the car down, it's days later, the cook is finished and the birds have flown the coop. That's how manufacturers operate: do a cook, pack up and shoot through like a Bondi tram, usually leaving the equipment behind—after all it's highly incriminating to be sprung with it.

For every one good bust there were a dozen that were a complete and utter waste of time, the drugs were lost and no result. All the Drug Squad was doing was putting chemicals in the hands of criminals and as a logical progression into the community.

One of these stuff ups happened when bikies from South Australia purchased a huge quantity of Sudafed. They were followed through Mildura and then to the South Australian border, where the Drug Squad stopped surveillance. The bikies disappeared off into the Mallee night. The coppers turned off their lights for fear of exposing themselves and by the time the

South Australian coppers had the faintest idea of what was going on the blokes had disappeared into thin air with a large amount of chemicals and all the glassware required, never to be found.

The former National Crime Authority and Victorian Police Ethical Standards Unit are both supposed to be totally independent of the police force. However, it happened regularly that police went on secondment from the Drug Squad to NCA or Ethical Standards. This meant the Drug Squad received prior warning of any visit that might be potentially embarrassing. This was all highly irregular. Most probably the coppers thought they were just looking out for their mates by tipping them off, but they unwittingly enabled corruption to continue.

Malcolm reckons he hadn't smelt a rat at the Drug Squad until two new detectives arrived. They were formerly undercovers and sat about four desks away from Malcolm and Paton. On arrival, Paton swung back on his chair and greeted them by yelling out and holding up his hands, saying, 'I've made twenty large this year!' ($20,000). The other two smiled and made some comment back which Malcolm didn't hear. Paton replied, 'Yeah, and there's plenty more where that came from.' Four or five months later Paton visited him at home one night, unannounced, and asked him to come outside. Malcolm didn't think anything of this until Paton then told him on Strawhorn's behalf that there were opportunities to sell legitimately purchased chemicals to informers to run unauthorised operations. How would he feel about being involved? This was it. Finally he had been admitted to the inner sanctum, something he had craved all his life. He replied, 'No problem.' Malcolm is adamant that he did not turn his mind to the legal ramifications of this move. His naivety was astounding.

Paton emphasised that there would be a good earn in it for everybody. Unauthorised purchases would take place and the chemicals would be on-sold to crooks for full black market price.

The mark ups were astonishing. Malcolm was now in the know. He was even given a price list of drugs that might be requested by crooks and the price he was to sell them for. Even in the Drug Squad there was retail price maintenance!

This moment was the beginning of the end and to this day Malcolm can't give a credible explanation as to why he unhesitatingly made such a stupid move. He asked himself later time and again how he ended up corrupt and in jail, his career ruined, all by his own hand. It wasn't a considered decision, rather a gradual blurring of the lines between right and wrong. It sounds lame and he can see now that it is, but that was the way it was.

This, in short, is how the wheels started to fall off for Malcolm. He was battling anxiety, receiving treatment, yet inappropriately self-medicating. The pressure was really getting to him, but on the other hand he had been accepted into the gang. His entire life was at a crossroads. Unfortunately, he took the wrong turn, headed for oblivion.

Here's the sort of thing he was letting himself in for. There was a buy/bust in Elwood of one kilo of cocaine for $160,000. The $160,000 came out of the safe at the Drug Squad, not a bank account. The sting was set up, the kilo of cocaine was to be purchased and the $160,000 recovered. As a matter of protocol each raid is supposed to be accompanied by a senior officer, but this rarely happened unless it was a high profile pinch.

When a raid occurs, the crook is supposed to be taken from room to room with a searching officer so they can view the search and make sure it is kosher. As a matter of policy this never happened in the Drug Squad. A warrant was taken out and the raid conducted. Ten or more officers would race in the door, grab the crook and remove him from the scene without further ado. He would not see one second of the search if they could possibly help it. Coppers would fan out through the house searching. Who knows what blokes were doing in the other rooms? At this particular raid Malcolm was searching a wardrobe when he found a handful of $500 and $1,000 Crown Casino gambling chips. The next day Malcolm gave some of the chips away, keeping the others for himself. Malcolm later gave Strawhorn another Casino chip for $500 to be used for a Unit barbeque for those who had attended the raid. There were about $5,000 worth of chips at that raid and Malcolm later cashed his share at Crown.

There was another unexpected bonus that day; in the garage the coppers stumbled over a hydroponic set up. It was huge and sophisticated. Bags of harvested cannabis heads were lying around. Malcolm estimates they weighed about five kilograms each. There was also a large number of plants of top quality. Because the Drug Squad warrant excluded everyone else from the property, Malcolm promptly pinched three bags of heads. He gave one to Paton the next day and the other two to informers as payment for information. He didn't keep any for himself.

Malcolm has gone to great lengths to emphasise that he did not take illegal substances as a serving copper and for the entire period of time in the Drug Squad he saw nobody else indulge in drug taking either. Whether this was because of the chance of being drug tested or whether they just didn't like the concept of taking drugs themselves, nobody knows. It doesn't paint the Drug Squad in a very good light. If they had been committing offences due to an addiction—that would at least be an explanation, if not an excuse. The only other conclusion is that they were dealing out of avarice, the ultimate betrayal of their oath.

While on the topic of paying informers, one practice that has never had the light shone on it was the reimbursement of informer's fees. This involved a note in your official diary that you had paid an informer an amount of money (generally fictitious). The informer's requisition fee was taken to an Inspector who would sign off on it. The reason for paying the informer was stated on the requisition, together with how much was being requested. The amounts were always small to avoid detection, usually between $200 and $300, because the Police Department wouldn't as a general rule pay more for informers. The false claim was submitted to the officer and the money handed to the claimant. An intelligence report (again fictitious) was lodged to verify what information had been obtained from the informer and the copper made a note in his official diary, which would be signed off by the Inspector after the money was handed over. Mostly these documents were deliberately falsified. There was no informer or money expended. This stunt was pulled purely for the coppers to have money for lunch. Each week a couple of coppers pulled this rort on a rotational basis so a pattern wouldn't emerge. On lunch day, the gang would be off to Dan Murphy's to buy grog and then to a restaurant for a big lunch—compliments of the non-existent informers.

Chapter Seventeen

IT'S NOT WHAT YOU KNOW, IT'S WHO YOU KNOW

'The greater the power, the more dangerous the abuse'

—Edmund Burke, eighteenth-century British politician

It always pays to have friends in high places. One Friday Malcolm and another detective were called into the office of a senior officer, who was in a state of agitation. He sat both sergeants down and announced that a friend of his from the golf club had got himself 'into the shit' and that 'we need to make it go away without further ado'. He added that this was highly confidential. He didn't care how they dealt with the problem, they just had to do it.

It seemed that his mate was the subject of a tip off from one of the chemical companies: he had been purchasing pre-cursor chemicals without authorisation.

Without further ado, the two sergeants headed off to the chemical company. On checking the purchase records they found that this bloke hadn't bothered to try and disguise his identity at all. Like a dill the purchaser had used his own driver's licence as ID. The sales manager provided the cops with all they needed: the bloke's name and address and the registration number of his car, which made tracking him down the simplest of tasks. The two sergeants scurried back to St Kilda Road, took out a search warrant for the bloke's house and car and headed off.

By now it was past close of business on Friday afternoon and the bloke was already home—and shocked by the arrival of the two coppers. Malcolm and the other sergeant searched the car, finding no drugs, but when they conducted a swab test, which indicates whether drugs have been present, sure enough in the boot there was evidence of drug residue. The house was searched to no avail. He was arrested, cautioned, handcuffed and conveyed back to St Kilda Road, where he was taken to an interview room and questioned. He couldn't help himself. He tipped in one hundred per cent, making a full and frank admission. Malcolm had his orders and was not to be deterred so instead of accepting the bloke's mea culpa, which in other circumstances would be considered a coup, the two sergeants sat the bloke down and read him chapter and verse on the way it was going to be. They told him he was to say nothing and when they started taping the record of interview, which was a legal requirement, he was to make no comment. If he mucked up the interview they would repeat the effort until they had a word perfect denial, just as they had been ordered. As the police had no drugs and the swabs had by now been thrown away, there was no other evidence against him.

The bloke was looking completely bamboozled by now and in accordance with directions he didn't ask for a lawyer. He had been told in no uncertain terms that nobody outside the interview room was to know what was going on. Duly the taped record of interview commenced and a number of questions were put. He went along with the script provided by the coppers, answering 'no comment' to every question. After a few minutes of this the coppers concluded the interview. Entries were made in their respective diaries that no offence had been detected and he was put through the interview register, in which an independent officer records complaints about treatment by police. The bloke told them he was very pleased with his treatment and was released: 'no offence detected' equals no charges laid. The senior officer was extremely pleased with the result when he was told later that night. The man was very lucky in his choice of friends.

It turned out that the man concerned had been the chauffeur for a now deceased businessman who used the Hells Angels Motor Cycle Club to conduct some of his company business. No prizes for guessing where the chemicals were headed.

Perverting the course of justice is probably the most serious of the forms of corruption. It strikes at the very heart of the administration of the criminal justice system and when police of senior rank commit these types of offences what hope has Joe Public got of having any confidence whatsoever in the police force?

Chapter Eighteen

A PARALLEL UNIVERSE

'Oh what a tangled web we weave
when first we practise to deceive'

—'Marmion', Sir Walter Scott

To give the reader a feel for how the Drug Squad operated it is interesting to follow how they went about turning crooks into informers and for their part how treacherous and duplicitous the informers were. From a lawyer's point of view, informers are interesting characters in the criminal justice system. Like the Secret Squirrels, rarely does an informer end up in the witness box. It is crucial not to blow their cover. For an informer, he/she is out in the open with nowhere to hide, with potentially fatal results, as we shall see a little later on. A surprising fact about informers is how often they are very close to the person being informed on. Wives, girlfriends and close mates of many years' standing often turn out to be the snake in the grass.

Never forget the old saying: keep your friends close and your enemies closer. Here's an example. The Morans—Lewis and his sons Mark and Jason—were dominant players in Melbourne's cocaine, speed and ecstasy industry. Lewis had been around the traps for years as an SP bookmaker, receiver and standover man but resisted the lure of drugs for a long time until his sons demonstrated the untold wealth drugs can generate. The career move to the drug industry turned out to be a fatal decision for the family. All the Morans are dead as a result of the gangland wars.

The Morans always figured in any Drug Squad discussion but try as they may the cops couldn't get near Lewis; he was an old dog to a hard road and as cagey as hell. Everyone knew the family was up to their ears in drugs but couldn't get a handle on them. The Squad decided to nail the Morans once and for all and so commenced the first real Moran investigation, codenamed 'Operation Vere'. Vere kicked off with blanket surveillance on Mark, and the Drug Squad set up controlled deliveries of Sudafed to him via informers Country Ken and another known by the nicknames 'the Sudafed King' or 'G-String'.

During Vere, Mark was seen on numerous occasions around Melbourne's inner suburbs with an unidentified male, and also with Lewis and Jason. No one had any idea who this bloke was; he had kept well and truly under the radar. It became clear this bloke had Mark's ear and every time he was spotted he was driving a different new car. Boy, were the coppers ever keen to find out his true identity. Their interest was further piqued when motor registration searches came up with false names and addresses. The only identifying feature was that he had long blond hair in a ponytail. Surveillance was conducted on him to no avail. Eventually a breakthrough came when surveillance followed him to an address in Abbotsford. Mr No Name was also followed to a self-storage facility in Thomastown. At long last the cops had a starting point. The fact that this man was unidentified was driving the police mad. He was clearly in the swim with some of Melbourne's most serious crooks and yet the police couldn't get a sniff of his identity. He must be good.

Then, with Vere in full swing, Mark Moran was murdered and the controlled deliveries to G-String and Country Ken concluded abruptly. Mark Moran died at the front of his house when an assassin ambushed him, shooting him at point blank range. Carl Williams, another substantial underworld player and rival drug manufacturer, pleaded guilty to his murder and as a result was sentenced to a life sentence with a minimum of thirty-five years.

I don't know why Williams pleaded guilty to this murder. Lewis was a client of mine for almost the entirety of my legal career. Shortly after his son Mark's death Lewis came to my office and told me he knew Mark's killer, a bloke named Dino Dibra, also recently deceased in the Melbourne Gangland war. I asked Lewis how he knew this; he only replied he did. He went on to say he also knew who killed Dibra. I asked who? Lewis looked me in the eye and said, 'Me.' I nearly fell off my chair; that was the first time in over twenty-five years in the law that somebody had admitted a murder to me. Lewis went on to say that if he was pinched for the killing he would plead guilty to it as it was a payback for Dibra killing his son Mark.

By the way, I am not the only person who shares this belief. There are very senior coppers who don't think Williams was the killer, because he was elsewhere in Victoria prior to the killing and didn't have enough time to travel back to Melbourne and do the deed. The other reason is that Carl Williams didn't have the ticker to pull the trigger himself. He has since been murdered at Barwon 'Supermax' Prison.

By the time detectives from Purana Taskforce (set up to solve the murders) visited me where I was, by now, in jail, all the above players with the exception of Williams were brown bread, so I was able to relay my info to them. The coppers were unimpressed and said the suggestion that Dibra had killed Mark was bullshit and nothing further was done about it. All I know is that for all the years I knew Lewis Moran he did not lie to me.

But back to our mystery man. The police had become so obsessed with Mr No Name that blanket surveillance was employed, but still they couldn't locate a residence. By his actions it was clear he was used to surveillance. He continually employed counter-surveillance techniques and was adept at giving the Squirrels the slip when it mattered. He alway parked his car away from wherever he lived and headed off on foot, with the result that no residence was located.

Vere dragged on without success and everyone was anxious about results. Eventually two houses, in Abbotsford and Brunswick, were identified as the homes of No Name. Search warrants were taken out and simultaneous raids occurred. No Name was arrested at the front door in his underpants in Brunswick by Paton, Firth and other police. It was finally ascertained what the bloke's name was: Jack Cheeseman, hallelujah!

Unfortunately for Cheeseman the drug squad also discovered six kilos of cocaine still in compressed block form which means that it was freshly imported and hadn't been cut. A large quantity of ecstasy and other drugs were found to boot. To complicate matters at this early stage of the pinch $265,000 cash was located and promptly taken by the Drug Squad. Cheeseman spewed and made a lot of noise after his arrest about the stolen money because it was Lewis Moran's for deals done on his behalf. Lewis got very nasty indeed if he thought he was being short changed by anybody.

Turning a crook into an informer is simplicity itself when it is all boiled down. A crook is arrested on serious charges that carry a big whack if convicted. Police capitalise on the fact the crook is not in a position to bargain—do it the police way or cop the consequences. Usually senior cops such as a senior sergeant read the crook the riot act. 'We have you cold on nasty charges but if you cross over to our side and start informing for us we will look after you and no court appearances. If you don't become an informer and cooperate there will be no mercy: you'll cop a huge whack.' In other words, they put the fear of God into them, terrifying the crook into turning. Once they have been turned they invariably get the 'green light' to traffic drugs. This scenario is often complicated by police making promises they can't honour in a million years, such as guaranteeing large rewards, new identities, anonymity and on it goes. The coppers get so carried away at the prospect of a new informer they overstep the mark.

Back at the Drug Squad, Cheeseman was delivered the final ultimatum by Strawhorn and Paton: the only way to save himself from the full ramifications of being found with six kilos of Peruvian marching powder was to tip in as an informer or he would be staring down the barrel of twelve to fourteen years in the nick. At the same time, unbeknown to Cheeseman, his other house at Abbotsford was also being searched. Police located more drugs there, so all his property was seized. The entire house was cleaned out.

Malcolm had been on leave when Cheeseman was arrested but he returned to find the investigation ongoing and Mr No Name identified and on remand. To Malcolm's amazement, he found a huge haul of drugs of all types sitting in the Drug Squad office that hadn't been sent to Forensics. He asked Paton why they hadn't been sent and was told that the drugs had to be sorted through.

The drugs were not even in the safe, for the simple reason that there was such a huge volume they couldn't physically fit inside. Instead, Malcolm obtained a key to the Drug Squad conference room and all the Cheeseman drugs were laid out on the conference room table and the door locked. None of the drugs had been itemised or listed so there was no official version of what was present. Over the next few days Malcolm noticed, on a daily basis, the amount of drugs was diminishing—the mice were clearly nibbling at the haul. So much for security.

It took about three weeks to sort through the property seized. Among the loot was a black leather bag discovered at Thomastown. It was so heavy the drug squad didn't have facilities to weigh it, so Malcolm took the bag to the police gym and weighed it there. Over thirty-five kilos of powders and ecstasy tablets of all different colours and patterns. This was turning out to be one hell of a bust. The coppers couldn't for the life of them work out how a player of this magnitude had ducked their intelligence for what must have been a considerable time.

Cheeseman's speciality was repairing tablet presses and supplying the dies to criminals throughout Australia. He was in partnership in this venture with Mark Moran and had a die-maker in Glen Iris manufacturing the punches for them. Police discovered approximately thirty different punches for ecstasy tablets with various logos. There was also a vast array of different ecstasy tablets. Cheeseman confessed that he kept a book of all the ecstasy formulas and samples of the resulting tabs. The better ones he replicated later. The samples were packaged in press seal bags, each containing between one and twenty tabs. There were literally thousands and thousands of tablets.

None of this haul should have been touched by the Drug Squad. The drugs should have been taken straight to Forensics to let them do the sorting and weighing. It's meant to work like this: drugs that are found during a raid should immediately be handed to a designated exhibit officer who logs the time, date and location of the discovery with a short description like 'small clear press seal plastic bag of white powder suspected of being heroin'. Upon return to the police station the drugs are receipted, labelled with an exhibit number corresponding with the number in the exhibit log and lodged in a safe awaiting transfer to Forensics for analysis. There is often a wait until there are a number of exhibits and a designated officer gives the exhibits to a property officer who officially takes control of the drugs. Another receipt is issued and the exhibits are transferred to Forensics for formal analysis. At Forensics the analyst keeps the original exhibit bag and examines the contents. Whatever is not destroyed during analysis is replaced in the original bag and the whole exhibit is then given a number for cross referencing with the original exhibit log number, thereby ensuring the same item is accounted for every step of the way, from crook to court. As I've mentioned, in court, demonstrating continuity of an exhibit is vital, otherwise it can't be proved beyond reasonable doubt the substance in court as an exhibit is one and the same as was seized from the crook. If continuity is faulty then a jury could not be satisfied beyond reasonable doubt that the exhibit in court came from the crook on trial and he walks.

Malcolm recalls during this period going to the police storage facility in Collingwood where large items were stored. He was delegated to check and itemise all the furniture, TVs and other electrical equipment seized from Cheeseman's house. He was also ordered to return a rental van used to transport all the household items to storage. Not having been present during the week of Cheeseman's arrest, he jumped into the van and was amazed to see thirty or forty red ecstasy tablets scattered around the van. It was not even a police van. Malcolm suspected the coppers at the pinch had ripped open a packet of tablets to help themselves and in their haste dropped some. It must have been night time and they hadn't noticed.

Cheeseman had been on remand for a month or so and as the reality of his predicament dawned he was desperate to assist the Drug Squad, wanting out of jail, pronto. He was granted bail after being assessed by the police as not being at risk of reoffending. This was so he could get the 'green light' from the Drug Squad to operate as an informer, meaning open slather in the trafficking department.

After bail was granted a meeting took place at the Drug Squad between Cheeseman, his barrister, Malcolm, Paton and Strawhorn. During the meeting Cheeseman rattled off a list of Australia's top crooks, whom he was currently dealing with, and was willing to give up to ensure he didn't cop the twelve years threatened. A deal was struck and he was registered as an informer. What a fantastic night's work—here was literally a who's who of the cream of the country's crooks and this bloke was going to deliver their heads on a platter. The coppers couldn't wait. Once Cheeseman turned informer he told Malcolm he turned over in excess of thirty million dollars in his drug business. On the available evidence that claim was plausible. The $260,000 found in the raid would be small change indeed for such a high-volume drug trafficker.

Cheeseman was allocated a registered informer number and was thereafter referred to only as informer 230. After the deal, numerous meetings with 230 occurred but the police hit a hurdle early on because the cocaine that had been seized belonged to Lewis Moran. 230 was to cut the coke (doubling the weight) with a baby laxative known as 'Manitol'. This substance is used because it is of similar consistency to cocaine and has a slightly bitter taste. It also recompresses well to assume the look of pure coke. The only catch from the consumer's point of view was the purity was now less than fifty per cent.

Lewis Moran had given Cheeseman strict instructions never to keep any of Lewis's drugs at his house in case of a visit from the coppers. Already 230 was in the shit because he had ignored Lewis's instructions and you do that at your peril. 230 had to lie to him after Lewis heard he had been visited by the cops, telling him the cocaine was safe in a storage facility. To cover the theft of the $260,000, 230 told Lewis the coppers had robbed him and Strawhorn had his money.

Naturally enough, Lewis didn't want to know about it and told 230 in no uncertain terms he had to repay the money. If it really was stolen by the coppers it was his bad luck. When it came to money Lewis was not to be fucked with—he was ruthless in pursuit of debts. 230 was worried sick because Lewis wanted his money repaid and his cocaine back and he was sure Lewis would knock him if he didn't cough up, quickly. At the Drug Squad, Strawhorn and Paton agreed 230 should be allowed to keep trafficking, enabling him to pay the debt that he owed Lewis.

So the new informer, who was a very major trafficker, was on bail as a result of police intervention and was given the 'green light' by senior coppers to traffic large quantities of drugs and profit from his dealings, not just a breach of his bail conditions, but an ethical nightmare.

Chapter Nineteen

DESTRUCTION

'The golden rule is that there are no golden rules'

—George Bernard Shaw

A character called Kevin Hicks, who Malcolm knew at the Drug Squad, first became known to me during his days in the Major Crime Squad, which was disbanded for corrupt activities back in the early 1990s. I'll tell you a story that will give you an idea of what went on there. Some time after the Major Crime Squad had moved from St Kilda Road, the decorators were in their old offices, doing some work. When they tried to replace a loose ceiling tile, thirteen pistols fell out of the ceiling onto the decorators' heads. Of course there was a hue and cry but as per usual with Victoria Police, everything quietly went away with no satisfactory explanation ever proffered for the presence of the pistols. What were they doing there? The answer came my way recently when I caught up with retired Major Crime Squad Detective Senior Sergeant and old fashioned hard nut, Mark (Wild Boy) Wiley. I don't know how many times I have cross-examined Wild Boy—we locked horns regularly. We discussed the guns in the ceiling and I asked the obvious question: 'What where they doing there?' His answer was, 'It is considered very bad manners to attend a party and not take a present.' We laughed. The message was loud and clear. They were there for loading, an integral component of your corrupt copper's arsenal of tricks.

Yet another of those mysteries arose when McEwans hardware went from conducting its own payroll, with officers licensed to carry pistols, to outsourcing this function. In the early 1980s with the arrival of Armaguard and other payroll companies, McEwans decided to use a security company and its pistols were handed back into Russell Street Headquarters. What a surprise when some time later Dennis Allen, the notorious heroin dealer and murderer, was found in possession of one of those pistols. There is only one conclusion to be drawn: Dennis the Menace was given one of the McEwans pistols by a corrupt police officer.

But back to our friend Hicks. Kevin Hicks was a lazy copper, always looking for the shortcut. I should have realised that he was always motivated by money. In one particular case, I appeared for a dairy farmer from Mt Beauty in Victoria's north east, who was charged with growing marijuana. Hicks by now was at the Drug Squad, after the disbandment of the Major Crime Squad. The following story was related to me by four members of the family, all eye witnesses. Hicks led the raid on the farm and he raced in the door, grabbed hold of the old farmer, smashed him to the ground and screamed out, 'Where's the fucking money?' The farmer had migrated to Australia after the Second World War and had never been in any trouble. Nor had any member of his family. He had worked hard to build up his dairy farm at Mt Beauty. I was instructed to act and saw the farmer the day after his 'arrest'. His eyes were blackened and all the poor old bloke could say to me through his split lips was, 'Why does Mr Hicks hit me so much?' I did not have an answer.

This is the Kevin Hicks who, while in the Drug Squad, was placed in charge of the supposedly secure Chemical Storage facility at Attwood near Tullamarine in Melbourne's outer Northern Suburbs. Hicks had become embroiled with a career criminal by the name of Peter Pilarinos. Over the years that Hicks ran the 'secure facility', he sold Crown exhibits in the form of drugs and chemicals to Pilarinos. Components of drugs would be replaced so that at first glance nothing was amiss. The classic example was when a client of mine was charged with possession of a commercial quantity of red phosphorus, a necessary pre-cursor to the manufacture of amphetamine. It was often my practice in those days to have the drugs independently analysed which, by sheer coincidence, we did on this occasion. Guess what? The analysis came back not as red phosphorus but as tile grout. Hicks had substituted it for the chemical, which he had on-sold to Pilarinos. This little rort had been going on for years and Hicks was subsequently sentenced in May of 2000 to five years' imprisonment.

When Malcolm joined the Drug Squad he tells of a similar scam. One of his first jobs was in charge of all exhibits and property held at Cleanaway's, a secure location in Dandenong. At Cleanaway there was a yard covering several acres and in it were four or five shipping containers, supposedly securely locked, containing hundreds of exhibits seized in drug busts and from clandestine laboratories. Each time a court case was concluded, his job was to check property off in a property book and make sure it was destroyed or returned to its owner. Malcolm attended Cleanaway on numerous occasions with other Drug Squad members to work out what property related to which case. When he opened the containers he could not believe the sight that greeted him. It was clear others had been there before him and the property stored in the containers was in total disarray. It was impossible to distinguish one pile from another or figure out what related to which property book entry. To add insult to injury rain had got inside the containers and condensation had caused handwriting on exhibit notes to disappear. It was a complete and utter dog's breakfast.

It was such a disgrace that Malcolm returned to the Drug Squad to report his findings. While waiting for some firm order from his superiors, Malcolm appropriately destroyed property from completed cases that he had been able to identify including glassware, books and other paraphernalia. One day he was destroying glassware in a forty-four-gallon drum with a hammer when Paton turned up and asked what he was doing. He told him he was destroying exhibits as per instructions. Paton said, 'No, no, we don't do that,' and Malcolm watched as Paton retrieved the items of glassware that would be of value to speed cooks. Malcolm was staggered by this but pursuant to the instructions stopped destroying the glassware. Instead it was boxed up and taken back to the Drug Squad for future sale to criminals and informers.

The question of exhibit storage has been raised recently in the media. Allegations have been aired that exhibits have evaporated, been 'recycled to crooks' and tampered with or contaminated. A great number of cases may never be able to be prosecuted in the courts. Nothing appears to have changed since Malcolm's day.

All Malcolm's training impressed upon him that immediately after an arrest he was to complete a detailed property statement including the approximate weight of drugs or number of items seized. Not long after joining the Drug Squad Malcolm was sitting at his desk counting ecstasy tablets. He had already completed some of the property slip with approximate weights of other drugs seized on the same raid. Strawhorn asked him what he was doing, so he told him. Strawhorn said, 'You don't do that here.' Malcolm replied, 'But I have to fill out an accurate property slip.' Strawhorn told him that in the Drug Squad the practice was that everything was recorded as 'a quantity' and not to be specified under any circumstances. This flew in the face of every other order and protocol Malcolm had received in relation to dealing with exhibits. Strawhorn went on, 'It's up to Forensics to specify quantities and weights. For instance here on the table in front of us is a quantity of ecstasy tablets.' There were a few hundred. With that he leant over, took a handful and put them in his pocket. 'See,' he said. 'There is still a quantity of ecstasy tablets there.' Malcolm was amazed at this performance but Strawhorn was his senior officer and Malcolm followed his orders thereafter.

Often when cross-examining Drug Squad coppers, one is drawn to the exhibit book which specifies exhibits, just as Malcolm says. When I have asked what 'a quantity' might represent, the answer was as specific as could be provided, pending forensic examination. I have never appeared in a case where detailed evidence of quantities was not expected. Each one of those Drug Squad cases must have a very large cloud hanging over it.

To return to the fiasco at Cleanaway, the hierarchy finally decided an audit of every item ought to be conducted to the best of Malcolm's ability, with a Forensic team to accompany him. The plan was ultimately to destroy the lot because exhibits were contaminated and it was impossible to make any matches with outstanding cases. All chemicals were separated as best they could be and quantification was attempted. Once that task was completed, everything was photographed. I don't know why because once the exhibit itself is destroyed the photographs have no evidentiary value.

Everything was to be destroyed in the large secure furnace at Cleanaway. Some chemicals had been mislabelled and something was chucked into the incinerator that shouldn't have been. There was a God almighty explosion which blew the side out of the incinerator, putting it out of action for several weeks. Cleanaway was most unhappy with the coppers' ineptitude. As usual, the incident was hushed up and later, when the furnace was repaired, the coppers returned to conclude their work. The operation was a massive task which took weeks, with four detectives and three or four members from Forensics sifting through everything and destroying it.

One wonders how the outstanding court cases fared after that but it appears that the coppers bumbled their way through the minefield of giving evidence and to this day I don't know of one defence counsel who ever tumbled to the disaster that was Forensic storage, such was the coppers' ability to cover their arses convincingly in the witness box. Should any cold case need reopening they will have Buckley's.

After the big clean up it was decided to start again with a clean slate. Orders were given for all chemicals and other materials seized to be taken to the Forensic Science Centre and to be kept in a secure location in which chemicals could be safely stored. That was all well and good but it did not necessarily solve the problem of pilfering.

A new procedure was introduced that still provided a smorgasbord of opportunity for theft and pilfering by whichever coppers drove the drugs from Forensics to Cleanaway. There was nothing to preclude them helping themselves. Malcolm was in cars with officers doing exactly that. There were clearly more holes than Swiss cheese in this procedure and it continued until some time after 2001.

Malcolm particularly recalls a raid on the house of the cook for Mark Moran. After Moran's murder a search warrant had been executed on the cook's bungalow. It was a large haul; in several rooms there were drugs scattered on the floor in shoe boxes, each containing five to ten ziplock plastic bags holding 500 or so ecstasy tablets. In other rooms there were stacks of boxes of Sudafed. The coppers stumbled on 2.5 kilos of pseudoephedrine and several kilos of ketamine, also known as Special K. At this raid Malcolm saw three members of the Drug Squad helping themselves to tablets before the evidence was photographed or catalogued in the property book. He estimates that on that raid alone between three and four thousand tablets were stolen by Drug Squad members. The current market value of an ecstasy tablet is about $50. Do the numbers; it's certainly a nice supplement to a humble senior detective's wage.

ONE WOULD HAVE THOUGHT THAT AFTER HICKS' DEMISE AND all the goings on at the Drug Squad back in the '90s things would have changed, but it appears not. In late 2009 the Victorian Ombudsman launched a scathing report about the goings on at the Forensic Science Laboratory: the pilfering of drugs, lack of supervision, poor handling and labelling and most importantly from a court's point of view, the failure to establish continuity of the handling of drugs.

I hasten to say that the many problems appear to be a result of under-resourcing and ineffective administration. It is a very real problem that continues notwithstanding the fact that there are now three tiers of culpability as far as storage, cataloguing, continuity and destruction of exhibits are concerned. I wonder how many cases have been abandoned when it turns out there are no exhibits available to be produced in court.

Chapter Twenty

WRESTLING AN OCTOPUS

'If you want to tell people the
truth make them laugh, otherwise they'll
kill you.'

—Oscar Wilde

Mark Moran's mate, Informer 230, turned out to be a past master at playing both sides off against the middle. It emerged eventually that he had been an informer elsewhere on several occasions, using various aliases, and had been arrested by the AFP during major operations on more than one occasion. He well and truly knew the ropes and used his experience to his advantage.

230 had two lists of crooks: one list he was prepared to give up and another of close associates he was not. It was these mates he continued trafficking to and from in large volumes for the duration of his relationship with the police. This became obvious when some of 230's friends were raided and large volumes of cash and drugs were seized. The coppers suspected 230 wasn't giving them the whole story and they were right. It goes to show

what a mess the informer system was. Major trafficking by a registered informer was allowed and yet the coppers weren't really sure who he was dealing with until after they were pinched. Talk about trying to unscramble an egg. And 230's deals were always big, never less than multiple kilos of cocaine. The coppers hadn't the faintest idea what and how much he was trafficking or who he was trafficking to.

After 230 compiled the list of major criminals and gangs he had contact with, it was submitted to a committee comprising Drug Squad and Crime Department officers. Without doubt this bloke was capable of delivering some serious scalps and everyone was very excited at the prospect. His information was top priority and all the operations at the Drug Squad were using it.

Right from the outset 230 displayed an extraordinary arrogance. He thought he could remain in control of his own world, keep going the way he always had. Having been in partnership with Mark Moran, he was in good standing with the Melbourne underworld. He believed himself to be a master criminal. A significant development arose almost immediately after Mark Moran was murdered. Lewis and Jason told 230 that whatever partnership he'd had with Mark was now a three-way split between them, no argument. 230 relayed this to the coppers and resisted police pressure for him to continue dealing with Lewis. The police were desperate to arrest Lewis so 230 was ordered to meet Lewis and continue to traffic with him, or else. But 230 wouldn't wear a wire when meeting Lewis because Lewis was very cagey and occasionally asked whoever he was talking to without warning to remove their shirt. If that happened he would be a dead duck, literally. So no conversations were ever recorded, leaving everyone in the dark about what had been said. The cops only had 230's word to go on.

Regarding meetings with other criminals on his list, 230 was told to introduce undercovers into the deal, that way he didn't have to worry about dealing direct with the crook and it was the undercover cop who would wear the listening devices and gather evidence. This tactic is regularly used by police to quarantine an informer from the fallout that inevitably follows the disclosure that an undercover is responsible for a bust. By then the informer has faded from the picture long before the axe falls and can deny any knowledge the undercover was a copper. This didn't sit at all well with 230. He didn't want to let go of the reins of his little empire; nor did he want police listening to him and his criminal mates. It was obvious 230 was only relaying back what suited him. By no means were the Drug Squad getting the full story.

Operations commenced on smaller targets with huge success. Drugs were bought and sold on an evidentiary basis. Everything was running like a dream. A special task force was set up to specifically target those 230 was shelving. Strawhorn was in charge of Task Force Kayak, with Malcolm leading the investigations with Paton and Firth. Later, Detective Miechel and three other detectives came on board. Kayak operated out of a separate office, away from the Drug Squad. Controlled deliveries to criminals via 230 continued and in return he purchased ecstasy, cocaine and amphetamine from crooks the police were tracking.

230 was keeping his end of the bargain with the police on catching run of the mill crooks. He had no problem setting up smaller crims but was more and more reluctant to deal with the Morans. He was under intense pressure from Lewis to return his coke and $260,000. Though 230 was trafficking with police knowledge, he lied to them about having repaid the debt to Lewis. If you're going to lie that outrageously you had better be smart because one slip up or inconsistency can bring you undone in a big hurry.

Like many in the drug game, 230 was using cocaine heavily and the paranoia that accompanied heavy use was obvious. With some justification he was terrified that Lewis Moran would turn nasty and kill him. One morning he was at home in Brunswick when Lewis turned up unexpectedly. 230 had no money or coke to give Lewis so he locked himself in the bathroom and hid while Lewis banged on the front door until finally he gave up and left.

Again 230 told the coppers he was not prepared to work on Lewis. But Strawhorn wasn't to be deterred and threatened him that he must deliver crooks to the police or twelve years' imprisonment was on the cards. Malcolm thought that Strawhorn's tactic of ramping up the pressure on 230 while he was vulnerable was dangerous. At one point during Kayak 230 went to ground without a trace. Strawhorn directed Malcolm and Firth to visit his house and leave calling cards from the Drug Squad knowing full well Lewis and other crims visited regularly. This was an intimidation tactic and it worked. It was a message to let him know they could ring him at any time and say, 'You're off.' As anticipated, 230 was terrified and suddenly enthusiastic to resume work as an informer. It was back to business as usual and Operation Kayak managed to graduate to medium-level crooks. The pinches were racking up, making everyone look good, but the major targets still evaded them.

During this time 230 started meeting Terence and Christine Hodson, and Kayak started buying and selling virtually every type of drug from them. These meetings were documented. Evidence was being gathered for a pinch.

230 continually resisted having a police operative take over on any deal, even though it was a core condition imposed by Force Command. He kept all the work to himself and maintained control of the deals. The reason for this became blindingly obvious after a particular deal. 230 was to get $70,000 for the deal and asked for the cash to be wrapped in bundles of $10,000. Malcolm didn't find anything unusual in this; he assumed it made it easier for the money to be counted. The deal took

place: another controlled buy of substantial proportions. After it went down 230 shouted Malcolm, Paton, Firth and Detective Anastasiadis dinner at the Hogg's Breath café in Chadstone. When 230 went to pay Malcolm noticed he had two wads of $50 notes, one in his wallet and another that he had pulled out to pay with. Malcolm grabbed the notes and asked where he had got them. He had told them he was broke and Malcolm's immediate suspicion was that this was some of the money given to him earlier for the deal. Malcolm made a note of the serial numbers, then gave them back and continued drinking.

The following day Malcolm checked the serial numbers against the $70,000 given to 230 and discovered the twenty or so notes he'd recorded were from the same batch of notes. Paton and Malcolm raised the issue with Strawhorn, who only rebuked them for socialising with him and ordered them not to in future. His only worry was that they were socialising with informers. Malcolm confronted 230, accusing him of stealing some of the cash destined for the controlled buy. He brushed it aside, never giving a credible explanation.

Several weeks later Malcolm visited Paton at home, where out of the blue he copped $1,000 from him. Paton told Malcolm it was from 230. Malcolm didn't enquire where or how, just stuck it in his pocket. A short time later 230 approached him and asked whether Paton had given him a couple of thousand dollars. He told him that it was $1,000 and that Paton had said it was something to do with him. 230 explained that he had overcharged for some ecstasy tablets he had purchased by the tidy sum of $20,000 and had given $5,000 to Paton, with Malcolm's whack supposedly being $2,000. Malcolm had been short-sheeted by his colleague.

Chapter Twenty-one

IVAN THE TERRIBLE

'This is the way the world ends,
This is the way the world ends,
This is the way the world ends,
Not with a bang, but a whimper.'

—'The Hollow Men', TS Eliot

One of the biggest speed dealers around at the time 230 was informing was a man called Ivan. He came to notice when a house he owned in Brunswick caught fire during a cook. Cooking speed is a very dangerous occupation. The recipes used often combine inappropriate mixtures of highly volatile chemicals and if you put a foot wrong the result is disastrous. Houses where cooks are going on often blow up or burn down. This happens largely when you have an inexperienced cook already off his face from inhaling the fumes and in a hurry to boot. Nothing like a good head full of the Lou Reed to make you nice and paranoid. No workplace health and safety at a cook.

Have you ever noticed how often an innocuous-looking suburban house blows up for no apparent reason? Rather than spook the horses by letting on that a cook has been going on in some leafy suburb the coppers merely blame a gas leak. Think again next time it happens.

This cook was burnt severely in the fire and arrested at the scene. A huge amount of amphetamines was recovered from the operation and the cook was sentenced to a lengthy term of imprisonment. After this Ivan went very quiet but he was always of interest to the Drug Squad; he was too big a fish to ignore.

Close to the time the cook was to be released the Drug Squad received intelligence that Ivan, a convicted criminal, had visited Fulham Correctional Centre and picked up a prisoner—the cook—for day release. This was totally forbidden. Getting leave from prison is difficult enough without requesting to spend the day with somebody as notorious as Ivan. Surveillance followed them for the entire day after he had driven into the grounds at Fulham, as bold as brass, picked up the cook and taken him away for his outing. The cook and Ivan were watched at McDonalds in Sale enjoying their afternoon and probably organising the next cook. The cook returned to prison later in the day and Ivan went quiet again.

It was not until informer 230 was arrested and claimed he could purchase drugs from Ivan that the coppers realised the extent of Ivan's organisation. It turned out he was the biggest name 230 had given them, probably the biggest player in this country, as canny as Lewis and as difficult to nail. The Drug Squad was dying to nab him; it would be the ultimate feather in their cap.

The operation into Ivan gained impetus, with controlled deliveries via 230 of numerous chemicals, all in large quantities. 230 protested that he didn't know Ivan very well, but the police didn't believe him. He was covertly taped during meetings and the friendliness in their voices indicated they were old mates. 230 was the No 1 tablet man in the country, repairing presses and keeping them running. He even had the necessary mechanical skills to speed up the presses to punch out more tablets per minute. Ivan desperately needed his expertise and their relationship was a two-way street. 230 provided Ivan with tablet presses for ecstasy and in return Ivan sold 230 large quantities of cocaine.

The operation was huge and had grown underneath the police's very noses. Ivan was not only manufacturing amphetamines in enormous quantities, he was importing by the container load—not one, but three and four container loads at a time of ecstasy, pseudoephedrine, cocaine and numerous other drugs being used in the manufacture of tablets in Australia. The organisation conducted cooks in New South Wales as well as Victoria. It was all happening and the cops nearly missed it.

230 under police supervision commenced buying copious amounts of drugs on credit from Ivan. The drugs were always of the highest quality, with the highest grade purity of cocaine, in the 80–85 per cent range. The ecstasy was the best seen in Australia, imported from Amsterdam at about 40 per cent pure, and what's more he appeared to have a never-ending supply.

Ivan was importing five hundred thousand to a million tablets per container load and his resulting wealth was displayed in the buildings and businesses he owned in and around Melbourne and Sydney. For instance, he owned a building in Sydney, unencumbered, and wanted $12 million for it. An offer of $10 million was made which was promptly knocked on the head on the basis that he was receiving $1.8 million per annum rent, so he might as well keep it. The numbers are staggering.

230's story on Ivan was that he knew him but hadn't done business with him before. This was a bit hard to swallow in light of the fact that on 230's 'first visit' to Ivan he returned with 5,000 ecstasy tablets and a great deal of high quality cocaine, all on credit. Like prostitution, the drug industry is strictly cash only. Credit is scarce, particularly when dealing with transactions in the tens or hundreds of thousands of dollars. It is usually extended only in unusual circumstances or to trusted mates of long-standing and impeccable credentials, never a blow in, as 230 claimed he was.

When Kayak made its first purchase from Ivan everyone was very excited about the buy and the quantities involved. Apparently, orders came down instructing the police at Kayak not to send the drugs to Forensics, but instead to keep them in the Kayak office safe. Only 1,000 of the 5,000 tablets were to be kept as an exhibit and the other 4,000 went to 230 to on-sell. The idea was to allow the balance of the money to become a Drug Squad slush fund to purchase other drugs to on-sell to and entrap other crooks.

The tablets remained at the Drug Squad and each package was opened and two tabs were taken from each and sent for analysis. All packaging was removed and destroyed and the remaining tablets were counted and re-packed by the police into packets of 100 for easy counting and sale. If 230 was to be sent out with 500 he just took five packets and threw them into one large bag. The safe was unlocked all day and only locked at night when the office was unattended. Not locking the safe saved time and allowed every man and his dog unfettered access to it. These drug movements were supposed to be recorded in the continuity book that was supposed to carry a record of all drugs purchased through the Task Force.

The book detailed when drugs were removed from the safe, what was being done with them and by whom.

As Task Force Kayak rolled on, more and more drugs moved in and out of the safe. But disaster struck, and the book went missing. The police were left with no evidence of continuity and there were no back-up records kept. So they decided to reconstruct the chain of continuity of drugs in that book from day one. Malcolm, Paton, Strawhorn and Miechel had to chip in and lend a hand. They had to reconstruct (read fabricate) times and dates, and then they put their signatures in the book at the various locations where they guessed items had been taken or placed back in the safe.

At best, the reconstruction was an educated guess, but it certainly didn't provide evidence of continuity that would have a snow flake's chance in hell of standing up to courtroom scrutiny. The book had been running for approximately three months when it went missing. Whatever they couldn't remember they invented. One wonders how many people were convicted without proper evidence.

230 WAS SENT TO IVAN WITH TEN KILOS OF RED PHOSPHOROUS purchased for less than $1,700 in total from the chemical company Sigma. It was sold to Ivan for $1,000 per kilo. The profits went to the Drug Squad and funded further purchases from Ivan.

There was another upside to such deals for the coppers: there was a shit-load of cash in the slush fund so they often went to a slap-up lunch. This little 'bonus' was compliments of the slush fund—no questions asked.

Now Ivan it must be said was a very, very shrewd operator. It didn't matter how closely he was watched, the cops never saw or caught him with drugs or chemicals. He always had at least one layer of protection between him and the contraband. A trusted lieutenant handled the drugs and collected the cash. On every occasion that 230 met Ivan, he wore a wire and recorded Ivan's conversations. This was very unusual. He had steadfastly refused to do it for meetings with Lewis. The information coming back on the tapes made the Drug Squad's hearts race. The discussions were not just about drug trafficking, importation and manufacture but his criminal involvement generally, which cast a far wider net, reaching across the world. This bloke, out of his own mouth, was admitting to criminality on a scale rarely seen in this country. Fantastic—they couldn't wait for what was shaping up to be a huge pinch, but in the meantime they had to dance on eggshells. He was smart, and the slightest fuck up would ruin all their efforts.

Ivan purchased a $380,000 computer laser metal stamping machine to make fake $1 and $2 coins. He already had replica Deutsche marks and had tested them in Germany on trains and in various vending machines. His plan was to bring the machine to Australia and manufacture Aussie coins. This gives an insight into how Ivan operated. The plan was that Ivan would buy gambling venues with poker machine licences attached to them and pump in the fake coins, thereby inflating the turnover of each business, and then sell the businesses to an unsuspecting buyer for an inflated price based on the false turnover of the machines. This was an ingenious plan but, throughout the whole investigation, they never came across the coins or located the machine.

This was only one of Ivan's many plans. He also purchased the latest model tablet pressing machines. Remember Carl Williams' original machine was punching out one tablet per second? Ivan purchased the latest sixteen and thirty-two-station tablet-pressing machines which at a minimum run were able to punch out 700 tablets per minute. This output was phenomenal indeed considering that these machines ran around the clock. The quantity of drugs Ivan was producing in Melbourne and Sydney was astounding. He didn't just have one tablet-pressing machine operating; he had six that they knew of. The police were privy to this information because 230 was purchasing and maintaining the machines for him. He also supplied the punters with the various logos that were embossed on the tablets.

230 and Mark Moran had established a connection with a manufacturer of the stamps and dies and they had bribed this bloke early in proceedings by paying him four times the going rate for a legitimate stamp made for pharmaceutical companies. This business was a nice little earner for Moran and 230 while Moran was alive.

An order from Assistant Commissioner level was given allowing the police the green light to traffic. However one stipulation was imposed: it must always be an undercover doing the dealing, thereby ensuring all the money came back to the police. 230, the shifty bastard, flatly refused to work with every undercover introduced to him. It didn't matter which state the copper was from, 230 found a reason for the undercover to be unacceptable. Matters had reached the stage where the Drug Squad had to keep dealing if these operations were to remain on foot. Strawhorn told the others to disregard the order and continue trafficking through 230, who was clearly making huge profits on the side, compliments of the cops.

After 230's initial purchase from Ivan, things slowed down, as he had a number of importations on the go which hadn't yet landed. Anything potentially available was still on the water. The momentum of the operation started to flag so 230 was used in other areas, filling in gaps, waiting for Ivan's next offering. And his offerings were worth waiting for. They were huge in comparison to anything that Malcolm had seen previously in the Drug Squad. This bloke was massive. Malcolm couldn't believe the numbers. For instance, he had one container alone, allegedly containing over a million ecstasy tablets. Another container was on the way with half a million ecstasy tablets, plus cocaine, and yet another which had arrived containing several hundred kilos of pure pseudoephedrine.

Information from 230 disclosed Ivan was about to import bulk pseudoephedrine secreted in toilet cisterns in China.

Unfortunately, between the time surveillance commenced on the container arriving and it was filmed being unloaded, all the pseudoephedrine had disappeared. That's right, not a sausage, all gone. A mega amount of chemicals pinched from right under the Drug Squad's noses while the whole shooting match was being filmed.

If the media is to be believed (and I doubt that on any assessment) the amount of pseudo in the dunnies was sufficient to cook a billion dollars' worth. A billion dollars of speed and the coppers missed the lot! Why hasn't anyone been shot at dawn?

All that remained were traces sufficient to indicate there *had* been pseudo in every toilet. There must have been a very large amount indeed. How embarrassing for the cops: no drugs seized, notwithstanding the container being under heavy police surveillance from the moment it docked. What a fuck up. The coppers were not happy. Needless to say, 230 denied any double dealing, but to this day Malcolm reckons it has his name written all over it. Surveillance observed the container being unloaded outside a factory in Coburg during the night while Ivan sat in his Mercedes a half a kilometre away.

When thinking about the mind-boggling quantities of money being made from the sale of these drugs, we also need to consider the outlays prior to importation. A million ecstasy tablets would easily have cost Ivan three million dollars. And it didn't stop there. If he had three million tied up in one importation one wonders how much he had tied up in all his various schemes in total. But the risks were worth it. For an outlay of three million, plus importation costs, he stood to gross fifty million on the sale of the ecstasy alone. Not a bad day's work in anyone's book.

These ecstasy tablets were easily the best quality ever seen anywhere in Australia: from 40 to 60 per cent pure. Australian tablets were nowhere near this quality and 230 announced that

Ivan intended to crush the tablets, dilute them by 50 per cent and have them re-pressed with his own logos, doubling his return. They still would have been very pure tablets by Australian standards and his profits would have been stratospheric.

In addition to his domestic activities he had people travelling overseas purchasing cocaine. Two were arrested by the Mexican Police trying to import cocaine. Ivan hung them out to dry, so they evened up by giving evidence against him in a later trial.

Ivan also conducted numerous legitimate businesses that he put millions of dollars into. One of those businesses was a group of shops into which he had pumped over three million dollars. Ivan was paying the bills for these businesses, designed to launder money.

There are several bookmakers who would have some very uncomfortable questions to answer if the truth were known. He led what could only be described as a 'high flying' lifestyle. It was all one hell of a red light.

The coppers were hot to trot with Ivan and Task Force Kayak was going along very nicely. Stacks of drugs were purchased from him and he was sold loads of chemicals, capable of producing millions of dollars' worth of speed and ecstasy. The best part was the Drug Squad also made a bucket of money on-selling the differential between drugs kept as exhibits and the amounts actually purchased—and believe me the difference was big.

Intelligence from 230 came thick and fast about all the bits and pieces Ivan was up to but he was becoming increasingly worried about Lewis and fearful for his life. He wanted out, but the Drug Squad always wanted more, and were relentless in their threat of a lengthy jail term.

On one occasion on which 230 wore a wire when meeting Ivan he told him that he had been pinched and would need his bail varied. Ivan offered to sort the bail variation through his lawyer and to introduce 230 to 'Strawnie', who would be able to do something about the brief either being edited favourably or going missing. If Ivan had twigged 230 was taping him he'd have been in the poo well and truly. The tape was damning indeed, as it suggested Strawhorn had been on Ivan's payroll.

After this conversation 230 approached Paton and offered $50,000 for Paton to destroy the brief against him. He approached Malcolm with the same offer. They both refused. Never taking 'no' for an answer he went on to ask Malcolm that if he couldn't do anything with the brief could he help by giving dodgy evidence? Again he refused.

230 had had enough and evaporated, which made Malcolm genuinely fear for the informer's life. At a unit round table meeting at Kayak, Strawhorn said that if 230 didn't come back on board Strawhorn would go and kill him himself and put Malcolm's fingerprints on the knife. Whether this was in jest or not, Malcolm took it as a personal threat. He saw Strawhorn's malice showing through.

The investigation stopped dead in its tracks and it looked as though Kayak would be wound up there and then. But, in an amazing stroke of good luck, an unknown informer surfaced and the Task Force swung into a new operation called 'Operation Ski' investigating Dave McCullough. It became an operation dedicated to catching McCullough. Ivan, luckily for him, dropped completely off the scene for the time being.

Not surprisingly the Australian Federal Police had long taken an interest in the Ivan investigation and, off the back of what was provided by way of intelligence from 230, they were also able take out telephone intercepts and run several operations on Ivan.

Chapter Twenty-two

THE FIX IS IN

'There are three signs of a hypocrite:
When he speaks, he lies
When he makes a promise, he breaks it
When he is trusted, he betrays his trust'

—Prophet Mohammed

I regularly used to receive instructions from clients that they had been loaded by coppers generally and the Drug Squad in particular. My deceased client Bob Slusarczyk was loaded with drugs, as Malcolm has since admitted. He even told me that the speed used to load him came from another bust at Brick Kiln Road, Bendigo. The speed was analysed and was found to be chemically different to that the police alleged Bob was cooking at his farm at Beechworth. Luckily for the Drug Squad the day before Bob was due to give evidence to the Ombudsman about being loaded his ultralight plane fell out of the sky and he was killed. Investigating this extraordinary stroke of luck for the Drug Squad has not been taken further since Bob's timely (for the coppers) death.

In the early 1980s two blokes, Bruce Power and Dave McCullough, ran a caryard in the Western Suburbs called Powermac. The business bore the appearance of a legitimate caryard but was in fact a front for a huge heroin distribution business. As demonstration vehicles were driven around Melbourne, the real purpose was not to test drive them but to distribute high-grade heroin. Nobody twigged and the business went on for years. But ultimately Power and McCullough were caught, charged, convicted and received substantial jail sentences. Once McCullough was released he stayed under the radar for a number of years, until informer 230 came on the scene and he became a target for the police.

230 reckoned McCullough was back in business, only this time, the preferred drug was cocaine. 230 claimed he regularly purchased large quantities from McCullough and could help the Drug Squad nail him. When McCullough's name came up Strawhorn sent the Drug Squad after him like a shot. Hold the front page: here comes a red hot suspect—the Drug Squad had to drop virtually everything else. This appeared odd to Malcolm because McCullough was, and is, so high profile he was convinced the coppers would have got wind of his activities prior to 230's revelations if he had been up to his old tricks.

The operation (code-named Operation Ski) got into full swing when 230 offered to ID McCullough for the coppers by 'accidentally' bumping into him in the street in Port Melbourne where he knew McCullough lived. The Squirrels were immediately on the case and commenced heavy surveillance. They reported that McCullough had morning coffee in the same restaurant every day where he always sat looking into Bay Street. 230 was to stroll along Bay Street and bump into McCullough, positively identify him and strike up a conversation, potentially to purchase cocaine. All was in place, the joint was rotten with

Squirrels watching and filming every move, but something odd happened. 230 and McCullough passed one another without any hint of recognition. 230 reported back shortly afterwards, saying that he didn't know the bloke; that wasn't the McCullough he was talking about. Everybody thought McCullough must be selling cocaine to 230 on the side. That was why 230 changed his mind and decided against giving McCullough away.

McCullough was very good at keeping deals at arm's length. It was thought by the coppers that McCullough had been involved in a shipment of 400 kilos of cocaine into South Australia. Unfortunately for McCullough's bottom line the coke was intercepted. It was only one of a number of shipments the coppers thought McCullough was responsible for.

For whatever reason, Operation Ski fell apart, with nothing happening for months. Then out of the blue the coppers had a lucky break when an old time armed robber was released from prison. He had spent time with McCullough and even shared a cell with him. McCullough offered the old crook work if he wanted it. Upon release the old timer took up the offer. He had a contact point, a solicitor McCullough knew in Melbourne. At this point Malcolm's allegations become contentious, because the solicitor concerned denies the alleged conversations vehemently, and was never charged. According to Malcolm, the robber said that he visited the lawyer and a job offer was put to him to sell drugs for McCullough.

Apparently the prospect of jumping back into a life of crime along with staring down the barrel of another large sentence did not appeal to the crook. After all, this bloke was in his late fifties and the prospect of selling drugs didn't sit well—he was morally opposed to drug dealing.

Instead the crook went to the Drug Squad, which was a real turn up for the books. The coppers should have been more careful from the outset though, because the old crook was generally regarded as a bullshit artist of the first order. In any case he became an informer for Strawhorn with two detectives from the Drug Squad as his handlers. He was wired up and sent to the lawyer's officers for a second time, where it was alleged the offer had been put to him to work for McCullough. Under police instruction, the old crook accepted the offer. At that stage, police methodology kicked in and the old timer was gradually replaced by an undercover operative who began trafficking and buying drugs from a group supposedly run by McCullough.

Operation Ski was resurrected and rattled along with drugs being bought and sold at a great rate but not one meeting or purchase was with or from McCullough. If he was involved he was certainly keeping dealings at arm's length and in fact was never sighted.

Operation Ski continued until the coppers thought they had sufficient evidence and warrants were issued. They had all their ducks lined up and the operation was to conclude by recording a number of covert sales from McCullough's gang and McCullough personally via the undercover. As is often the way, each transaction became bigger until the final sale was to be huge and the bust would follow in a classic entrapment situation. The first transaction took place and a substantial amount was paid by the undercover via a sidekick to the syndicate, not to McCullough personally. More importantly, no McCullough at the deal—he was nowhere to be seen. This wasn't looking good as far as nailing McCullough was concerned. The coppers couldn't get anywhere near him and it was giving them the shits how clever he was turning out to be. Strawhorn was adamant the last deal should take place in McCullough's flat in Port Melbourne with him present. The money was to be left at the flat so that when the search warrants were executed the money would be located, leaving only one possible explanation: the money was from the drug deal and McCullough had been the dealer.

The big day arrived, the money had been marked and photocopied, and the undercover headed off to do the deal, supposedly at McCullough's. Don't forget so far in this operation McCullough had not been present once, nor had he been involved in one piece of negotiation with the undercover. As far as the coppers were concerned he was cold. They had to nail him this time or the whole operation was history.

But then, when the undercover headed off towards McCullough's he was contacted by a mate of McCullough's, with a change of destination. He was directed to Roden Street, North Melbourne, near a warehouse owned by another mate. The place was not within a bull's roar of Port Melbourne.

Malcolm's diary entries and his memories of the day set out the chain of events.

10.51 am: the deal is done with McCullough's mate in the car park of a block of flats in North Melbourne, nowhere near McCullough's place. Everyone is pissed off so the coppers continue to wait and watch. The Squirrels and Drug Squad are all on the case. The bloke jumps in his car with a black satchel, which is later found to contain a large quantity of hash, and drives off. Not to Port Melbourne, but to his house in Altona. No luck so far and this is not looking good.

11.21 am: Another unanticipated detour occurs when the bloke drops in at his brother's house in Altona, and is observed depositing the satchel in a back shed. He then drives to his own house in Altona, where he takes $7,000 from the money paid by the undercover and leaves it at his house.

11.30 am: The bloke phones McCullough and organises to meet him at McCullough's flat. There is no talk of a drug deal or money. The coppers are getting anxious.

11.45: McCullough is then seen leaving his flat in his Jaguar but there's a complication. He isn't alone; there are three other blokes in the car as well, each of whom has a shit-load of convictions.

11.51: Surveillance follows the Jag along Beach Road, where a decision is made to intercept and arrest the occupants. Malcolm is in one of the pursuing cars and he intercepts the Jag outside the Bleak House Hotel in Beaconsfield Parade and makes the arrests.

The passengers are pulled out of the car with the exception of McCullough, who refuses to budge from the driver's seat. Malcolm's colleague Miechel is yanking at his arm and another detective is helping. Malcolm joins in. McCullough is hanging onto the steering wheel for grim death with his left arm clenched over the centre console. When the coppers finally prise McCullough from the car, Miechel and Malcolm quickly search it and locate a large wad of money in the centre console, obviously from the drug transaction. This find and the arrest are relayed to Strawhorn in another car, along with the complication of the three other crooks. Strawhorn hits the roof. From an evidentiary point of view, this set of circumstances is worthless. If the money is in the car and there is more than one person present the coppers cannot demonstrate whose money it is. Any one or all of the passengers are in possession of the cash. There has been no transaction between McCullough and the undercover and, as matters stand, McCullough is arguably not in possession of the money. Any of the others could well have put it in the console. McCullough could walk away unscathed.

At this stage, if this was the extent of the evidence against McCullough, then it was so flimsy as to be almost non-existent. McCullough was not at the deal and on the face of it appeared to have nothing to do with it. It's all well and good for coppers to harbour suspicion but our system supposedly operates on the basis of evidence that proves a case beyond all reasonable doubt.

Back to the events of that day. Malcolm is standing near the Jag and overhears a conversation between Strawhorn and the other detectives. Strawhorn is spewing that the money is not in McCullough's flat so he tells the detectives to take McCullough back to his flat and search it. The last time Malcolm sees the money from the console is in Strawhorn's hands at the point of arrest. Malcolm is never asked to make a statement about the arrest and nor is David Miechel, yet they're the two coppers that physically hauled McCullough out of the car and arrested him. Clearly they're not in on the giggle. Strawhorn is blueing that the money is supposed to be in the shredder bin at McCullough's house and that this had better be fixed quick smart. The detectives take McCullough in handcuffs off to his house and guess what? $51,460 is found in the shredder bin. What a coincidence. There is also $340 of marked money in McCullough's wallet.

Thank goodness everyone finally got their acts together. They now had what they needed—proof of money in McCullough's house—and unless McCullough had a valid explanation for its presence he would be, at law, in possession of the money. They had his pinch. The story doesn't end there. Malcolm was placed in charge of searching the two Altona houses, he found money and hashish.

2.50 pm: Strawhorn arrives in Altona, counts the money, receipts it and takes possession of the hash. Meanwhile

Drug Squad detectives return to McCullough's flat with him reluctantly in tow.

At the door of the flat, McCullough gets a smack in the mouth and then detectives 'find' the proceeds of the drug deal where it's meant to be. The coppers are so busy belting McCullough they totally forget to search the rest of the flat, so a second search warrant is taken out for the next day.

Next day, 5.50 pm: McCullough's property is searched again. This time it's a proper search and McCullough's computer and other exhibits are seized.

This piece of deception that they searched his flat twice was not disclosed at McCullough's trial. Who knows who had been in the flat in the interim and what was put there? Cross-examining the coppers about this stuff-up would be fun indeed.

The case proceeded to trial; McCullough pleaded not guilty but was convicted and is now serving a lengthy sentence.

In the days of the Powermac operations I acted for McCullough's partner, Bruce Power, and as a result got to know McCullough well. Over the years I bumped into him from time to time and we chatted—we had an easy relationship. When I ended up in Port Phillip, who was there but Dave McCullough, still screaming blue murder over his arrest and the Drug Squad corruption that he said was behind his charges. Due to the seriousness of these allegations McCullough was released on bail prior to trial but was subsequently convicted. The troubling aspect of McCullough's conviction is that the circumstances of the conviction as he relates them fit exactly with Malcolm's version of events. McCullough may well have been a naughty boy but I don't think he is guilty of the charges that presently have him residing at Her Majesty's pleasure. His entire prosecution was based on a load, perpetrated in order to salvage a failed operation.

I spoke to McCullough's lawyer about the incident and asked him to repeat his instructions from McCullough. The reply was in lock-step with Malcolm's version. McCullough's defence to the jury was that he had been loaded but the jury accepted the police's version of events and McCullough is now paying the price.

Malcolm's daybook entry makes note of no injury to McCullough when he was arrested yet later back at the Drug Squad Malcolm personally noted a graze above McCullough's left eye and that his nose was off to the left, appearing broken. One of the detectives, by his own admission to Malcolm, bashed McCullough at the front door of his flat because he was giving a bit of cheek. Second and more significant was that Malcolm's daybook made no mention of the cash in the console. Why? He received a direct order not to mention any money in his statement as it was supposed to be at McCullough's house in order for charges to stick. By the way, there was no forensic evidence such as fingerprints or DNA to link this money to McCullough.

Loading blokes is not the only way of achieving a desired result. Sometimes you're required to give the crook a bit of a helping hand if you expect cooperation in the future in return, but those favours don't always achieve the desired result, as was the case with a bloke called Midas Conway, pinched with operating a speed lab from home. The Drug Squad took him back to St Kilda Road where they managed to turn Midas into an informer. The Drug Squad did not oppose bail even though the offences were serious. When released Midas went straight home and murdered his girlfriend.

I met Midas while I was at Fulham still enjoying Her Majesty's hospitality. He believed that his girlfriend had lagged about his lab to the coppers so when he was released on bail, he worked himself into a rage, before taking revenge. But he was wrong; she was not the lagger, someone else was.

Chapter Twenty-three

G-STRING AND COUNTRY KEN

'Life is not a matter of holding good
cards, but of playing a poor hand well'

—Robert Louis Stevenson

Operation Vere was targeting an alleged speed cook and after watching him for a while the penny dropped that his sister Antionella was married to Mark Moran. The Drug Squad became very excited at the prospect of one of the Morans bobbing up in their crosshairs so without missing a beat Vere moved to Moran. The operation, previously run by Steven McIntyre, now went to Malcolm and his crew.

During a briefing Strawhorn announced that he had two informers, who he would not name, that he would supply with Sudafed and that they in turn would sell it to Mark Moran. All the coppers were very excited because the mail around town was that Moran was a big-time cook and dealer; to pinch one of the Morans would be a huge feather in their collective cap.

Mark Moran was Vere's sole target; everyone else paled into insignificance once he'd popped up.

Vere was in full swing and Malcolm believed only Sudafed was being delivered via the Controlled Delivery Scheme. The tabs were delivered by Strawhorn personally to the informer Country Ken. Surveillance followed Ken as he took the Sudafed to G-String and then observed G-String delivering it to Mark Moran. These transactions went on for several weeks yet the cops couldn't get enough evidence for a pinch. Each time there was a delivery Moran was too slippery for surveillance and evaded the net. Once the Sudafed was delivered Moran drove it away to a secret location. This was starting to give everyone the shits. This bloke was wary, good at counter-surveillance. His father Lewis Moran had obviously taught him well.

The object was for surveillance to follow Moran, pinpointing his final location in order to carry out a covert entry to the premises to establish whether a laboratory was operating. But the operation was in a holding pattern, with Sudafed being delivered to Country Ken then on to G-String, then to Mark Moran, with the tabs finally evaporating before their very eyes. All the coppers were achieving was the ongoing supply of illicit drugs to Moran.

What was out of the ordinary about this operation was that normally after two or three deliveries in which drugs go astray and surveillance becomes impractical or unsupportable, the operation would be abandoned. Not so in this case, which should have rung alarm bells. Each time the Sudafed evaporated after delivery to Moran, more was ordered. As quick as it was lost another delivery would be organised. Normal procedure was that if a number of deliveries went astray, the powers that be would stop any further deliveries. Drugs were going astray, clearly being turned into amphetamines and sold onto the street. This was most assuredly not the aim of the Controlled Delivery Scheme.

Everyone knew the drugs were reaching Mark Moran but they couldn't catch him. The deliveries to Moran gave him sufficient pre-cursor chemicals to cook five or six kilos of pure amphetamine. Five or six kilos have a value at street level of about ten million-plus on Drug Squad figures. This was, from any viewpoint, a big earn.

During the surveillance the operatives had recognised G-String and Country Ken as ex-coppers and raised their concerns with the Drug Squad. G-String had been a copper for many years and retired to the bush. Country Ken had been in the Armed Robbery Squad and the Drug Squad and had also recently retired to the bush. When this intelligence was received it was decided Country Ken, although he had been recognised as a former Drug Squad member, was not to be written down in any official police logs by name. He was to be identified only as 'Unknown Informer A'. G-String was 'Unknown Informer B'. This was a direct order made ostensibly to protect the informers' anonymity. It was a gross departure from standard operating procedures relating to informers.

The troubling aspect of Strawhorn's relationship with his two mates from the country was that no one was ever allowed to be present nor surveillance in place when the Sudafed was handed over. Strawhorn insisted on handling the drugs alone, very odd indeed. The very fact a detective senior sergeant was dealing drugs directly with informers was unusual. Now everybody understands why Strawhorn behaved the way he did. He was not just handing Sudafed to Country Ken, but also pure pseudoephedrine, which in turn was being purchased by Paton illegally, using the company name: 'PAS Chemicals'. Malcolm later discovered that PAS stood for Paton and Strawhorn. They thought this was a huge joke. They had opened a covert account to deal with chemical companies with the name.

This backdoor dealing was possible because the two had established a great rapport with the chemical companies. All they need do was wander in, flash their official ID and purchase what they wanted, without paperwork.

The upshot was large quantities of chemicals were reaching Mark Moran, before going onto a cook to manufacture drugs in a bungalow in Airport West. It's clear to Malcolm the chain of supply ran from Strawhorn to Country Ken to G-String, then to Mark Moran and the cook and guess what, yet another batch of Lou Reed hit the streets undetected.

Chapter Twenty-four

ALL RABBITS' FRIENDS AND RELATIONS

'The only way to get rid of a temptation
is to yield to it.'

—*The Picture of Dorian Gray*, Oscar Wilde

As the years progressed the drug industry and culture exploded. The Drug Squad expanded with them. The sheer volume of drug investigations and prosecutions brought about the need on occasions for other police to be roped in on the big raids and it was common practice for Malcolm and others to give the heroin blokes a hand when the need arose. The Heroin Unit dealt almost exclusively with Asian heroin dealers for the simple reason it is the Asians by and large who are the major players in the heroin industry in Australia, just as it is those of Italian heritage who predominantly grow cannabis. This is not racial profiling, it is fact.

Even in jail the junkies know it is the Asians who have the smack to sell. While I was at Port Phillip Prison I met an Asian bloke in for his second heroin trafficking stint and he had a nice little business going. The purity of drugs in jail is much lower than on the street and is sold at many times the street price, exponentially increasing profit margins. By the time I reached minimum security at Fulham this bloke was already there, well established, and business was booming. Fulham is a privately run prison and renowned as being awash with drugs. When this bloke was released the business passed to his Vietnamese lieutenant, who had been groomed for the job over several months.

By the way, when I made a criticism about Fulham and its endemic drug culture on national radio recently I received a letter from the CEO of the company that operates Fulham containing a thinly veiled threat concerning what I should do with my criticism. I replied, inviting the CEO to a debate about the state of his company's facilities on the same radio station. I have never received the courtesy of a reply.

When I first went to jail I was sent to Port Phillip, where I was offered cocaine. Don't forget I had been placed in maximum security and protection, yet cocaine was still available. At that time a quarter of an ounce retailed on the street for about twelve to fifteen hundred dollars. When I enquired as to the price I was informed it was $4,000. Apart from the fact I had well and truly stopped using by this time, the price was outrageous. I relayed this item of intelligence, together with the handwritten banking instructions provided by the crook, to the authorities at Port Phillip and to Detective Inspector De Santo of Ethical Standards, yet nothing happened. The very same bloke was still in jail when I was released years later and he had not been given a tug over this incident. Amazing.

ON ONE OCCASION MALCOLM WAS SECONDED TO ADD manpower to a raid with Detectives Ferguson, Cox and Sadler of the Heroin Unit. David Miechel, Malcolm's colleague from Unit 2, was also seconded. On this particular night, a search warrant had been issued for a house in Footscray where heroin dealers were known to operate. During the briefing prior to the raid all present were instructed that a large amount of heroin would be located. This was a big operation. Surveillance had been dogging these dealers for a long time and ascertained that they had quite a distribution network going. The minute that one of their street dealers was arrested, they had another take their place at the same spot within the hour. Street-level dealers are the cannon fodder of the drug industry. These blokes were moving heaps and to have any impact on the whole gang Mr Big and his mate had to be arrested. That's what this raid was all about.

It is well known in the job that there are certain idiosyncrasies attached to virtually any group of drug dealers or criminals. These were Asians. They often kept their cash with them. Many of them come from politically unstable backgrounds and have an inherent mistrust of banks, so the dough is invariably secreted around their houses. There were about seven houses to be hit simultaneously in this raid. All targets were suspected heroin traffickers and the coppers were eager for a nice little earn that night. When raids took place there were no niceties, speed was of the essence, otherwise drugs might go down the toilet. It regularly happened. The first priority should always be to secure all persons in the house. Without warning doors were smashed down, with police racing in flat out. What happened next was a new chapter in Malcolm's Drug Squad education.

As the coppers tumbled through the front door, to the right was a lounge-room. Sitting there like a couple of stunned mullets were two Asian blokes at a table weighing up white powder. There were foils, scales and what appeared to be another big bag of white powder. Next to that was another large pile of powder, all of which was assumed to be heroin.

In anybody's book this was a big pinch. Did anybody secure and arrest the two blokes in accordance with normal protocol? No. All the coppers raced to different parts of the house and Malcolm was at a loss to know why until it was pointed out to him that the coppers were heading for the usual places in which Asians hide their cash. First cab off the rank was the freezer, second the fridge, then often the washing machine or in the rangehood in the kitchen. Money was often in the laundry powder and finally under beds or mattresses. There were blokes racing all over the house. One headed for the fridge and trashed it for no result.

All of a sudden there was a yell from the front of the house and everybody charged for the bedroom. What a sight greeted the coppers. Two police had lifted the queen-size mattress off the bed and between it and the base were tens of thousands of dollars in hundred and fifty dollar notes, just lying there. They weren't even bundled up—there was one hell of a lot of money. Following the location of the jackpot a feeding frenzy ensued. It was every man for himself. Blokes started grabbing fistfuls of money and stuffing it in their pockets. They were even stuffing money into their socks; there was that much cash there.

Malcolm couldn't believe what was going on. He who hesitates is lost, so he grabbed handfuls of dough and stuck it in his pockets. Once the jackpot was exhausted and it was obvious no more money was to be found, somebody said, 'By the way, has anybody arrested those two blokes in the lounge room?' In charge was Sergeant Cox. He said, 'Shit, somebody get out and arrest those blokes quick smart.' The targets of the raid were still sitting in the lounge, fifteen minutes after the raid had begun, totally nonplussed by the carrying on of the police. The blokes got such a surprise at the cop's behaviour that they were rooted to the spot. Lucky they hadn't done a runner. If they had booted off it would have taken some explaining indeed.

In order to prove trafficking you need drugs and proof of commercial dealing or transactions; this can comprise scales, the packaging of drugs into smaller deals and the presence of money or notes taken showing that there has been selling of drugs. The catch was now that the coppers had no money to produce as an exhibit. The two blokes in the lounge were in possession of a large amount of heroin so if the police could show evidence of any commercial dealing they were gone for a long time. The problem was that the coppers had gone berserk and stolen every last cent from under the mattress. Unbelievably, the hat was passed around and everybody present had to kick back in a few bob from the theft so that there was some money to stick back under the mattress to be photographed and produced as evidence. Apparently, you would not believe the whinging about having to kick back in a miserable few bob in order to secure such a good pinch.

Another example of how anything that wasn't nailed down was lifted came after the arrest of the two blokes in the lounge. When Malcolm went to search the toilet he couldn't get in because Ferguson had one of the defendants in there and as Malcolm tried to kick the door open he saw Ferguson steal the crook's mobile phone and stick it down his pants. He couldn't believe how petty this was. Why bother stealing a drug dealer's mobile phone?

IF YOU THINK THIS LITTLE EFFORT WAS AN ISOLATED INCIDENT, think again. Detective Sergeant Stephen Cox, together with senior detectives Glenn Sadler and Ian Ferguson, had managed to carve out quite a nice little heroin trafficking empire which as it turns out was running parallel to the Chemical Diversion Desk's illegal activities. This clearly demonstrates how off the air the squad was and not just Malcolm et al.

In early 1999 a heroin dealer was arrested on a charge of trafficking. Cox and Sadler used this opportunity to put the fear of God into him, pulling the old 'turning an informer' trick. The good old offer you can't refuse. He became an informer and the deal almost immediately paid off when he tipped in another heroin dealer by the name of Duy Le, who was arrested doing a drug deal in the car park at Kmart, Burwood in April 1999.

Prior to Le's arrest Cox and Sadler had approached the informer to sell heroin for them. The very fact that heroin was readily available and that they were confident enough to try such a brazen approach indicates this was not the first time this happened. Luckily for the informer he had enough brains to knock back the offer and he drifted out of the picture.

Le was made of different stuff and when a proposal to traffic heroin was put to him he was more than happy to go along with the deal. The very next day Le received his first delivery, an ounce from his own bust provided by Cox in the foyer of the St Kilda Road police headquarters.

The method of dealing was simplicity itself, not remotely sophisticated. It was an arrangement doomed to come unstuck sooner or later. The fatal flaw of these rorts is that the coppers believe they're bullet-proof. Their biggest mistake is to trust their informer. Being an informer requires a certain capacity for treachery and subterfuge, otherwise they would not last in the cut-throat world of drug dealing and informing.

To kick off, Le was supplied with a couple of ounces of heroin by the cops every second day or so, for which he paid between $4,200 and $4,700 cash. This is dealing on a substantial scale.

Heroin is sold differently to other drugs. The usual street measurement is a 'cap', short for capsule, which is how it was sold in the good old US of A years ago. As with everything else we adopted their measurement and the slang for it. A cap in Oz is about a quarter of a gram but the deals are imprecise and can weigh anywhere from an eighth to a quarter of a gram. The heroin Le was supplied by the cops was top quality and capable of being cut ten times; in other words one ounce from Cox et al becomes ten in Le's hands. This is then sold on the street at $50 per cap. Big money. The police usually met Le at a predetermined location: unbelievably, around the corner from the St Kilda Road police complex.

Cox retired at the end of 1999 but rather than his involvement causing the deals to drop off, they increased to the extent Ferguson supplied Le with a 350-gram (twelve and a half ounce) block of pure heroin that smelt of lemon. The price? A staggering $50,000 cash. This large-scale trafficking was extraordinary given the fact that the traffickers were police and the smack sold was pinched from raids legally conducted by Drug Squad officers. The charges brought against the three fall far short of what really went on.

From 6 November 2000 until 13 February 2001 Ferguson was seconded to the National Crime Authority (NCA), thereafter to the Crime Department of Victoria Police until October 2001, and finally to the Organised Crime Squad. These organisations are all top of the tree in law enforcement and supposedly only the impeccable and above reproach get a gig there. Makes you question the vetting processes. During November 2000, while at the NCA, Ferguson and an unnamed NCA colleague were ordered to take exhibits seized in drug raids to Forensics at McLeod. Instead Ferguson met Le nearby and sold him another 350-gram block of heroin, this time for $55,000 in cash.

Smack was usually delivered by one of the three stooges: Cox, Sadler or Ferguson, but on one occasion another cop (again unnamed) made the delivery of a number of ounces to Le at Maribyrnong. What happened to these two unnamed heroes?

When things became too hot for Le, with two trials listed for hearing, he failed to answer his bail in the County Court on two occasions. The first was in May 2000 on heroin trafficking charges (the charges Cox, Ferguson and Sadler had originally arrested him on), and then in June 2000 on charges of aggravated burglary from Detective Blakeley of the Asian squad. Aggravated burglary takes place when the burglar is armed and the occupants of the house are assaulted. On this occasion Le entered a house in Springvale, armed and assaulted a mother and daughter and subjected them to awful threats.

Blokes shooting through on bail are not all that unusual but doing so with the knowledge and consent of the very coppers who charged him and then trafficked to him is. Not wanting to miss out on their pocket money, the cops continued trafficking to Le while he was a fugitive and to add insult to injury gave him information about police intelligence that helped him stay one jump ahead of the law for a couple of years. Detective Blakeley made a number of enquiries about Le to Sadler and Ferguson and they failed to disclose his whereabouts. On one occasion Sadler told Le not to do a drug deal because the police had become involved. Ferguson also warned Le that the cops were closing in on him and that he had better leave the state.

This was a very profitable scam for the three cops. They accumulated plenty of cash, which they started spending indiscreetly on items they could not possibly justify on a copper's wage, such as luxury cars, renovations, travel, a swimming pool and a speed boat. Ferguson even bought a BMW from Le.

Nothing lasts forever and after a couple of years as a fugitive Le was finally run to ground in Sydney in December 2002. And guess what? He immediately tipped over and started talking to Ceja Taskforce, which came into existence to investigate certain corrupt cops. Add Le's evidence of trafficking to the large amount of inexplicable wealth in the vicinity of Ferguson, Sadler and Cox and they were in the shit up to their eyeballs.

The trial judge found the total amount of heroin trafficked amounted to approximately four and a half kilos. This was the amount proved in court and as is always the case only represents a fraction of the amount actually trafficked. The true amount will never be known but it was certainly huge.

Unbelievably all three pleaded not guilty, were put on trial and convicted. They all copped a huge whack for their efforts and forfeiture orders were made for their ill-gotten gains. Their penalties are set out in Chapter Fourteen.

Whenever the question of corruption is discussed you must have noticed how the National Crime Authority and the Australian Federal Police always sneak out from under, with the result Joe Public is of the opinion these two bodies are not corrupt. Wrong. The only reason the question of honesty in both these bodies is not dealt with in this book is because this is the story of Malcolm's journey through the Victoria Police and as he did not spend time at the NCA it is irrelevant for present purposes.

Chapter Twenty-five

OPERATION REGENT

'Three great forces rule the world:
stupidity, fear and greed'

—Albert Einstein

One of the coppers' biggest informers was John Brickell, a violent armed robber who was acquitted of a double murder charge in New South Wales. His co-accused, another career armed robber, also beat the charge. Immediately post-acquittal both moved to Melbourne to pursue their profession as armed robbers. Brickell also trafficked drugs in substantial quantities on the Mornington Peninsula but had managed to stay under the radar after arriving in Victoria. It turned out Brickell was also wanted for armed robberies in New South Wales and had done a runner before being caught.

A very keen young detective from Rosebud woke up to Brickell and commenced a limited operation on him from Rosebud CIB. He installed a listening device in Brickell's car and realised he had bitten off more than he could chew—this was going to be a big operation. Such operations require substantial resources in terms of manpower for physical and electronic surveillance, which only the Drug Squad or other major squads had access to. The young detective approached the Drug Squad with what he'd stumbled upon. A major operation was instigated and they seconded the young bloke to work on Brickell.

Armed robberies were also going off in the Rosebud and Mornington areas and Brickell was in the frame. Malcolm's view is that he probably did stick up the Rosebud Post Office, but other jobs, such as the one at McDonalds, were highly unlikely to have been him because they bore the hallmarks of gross amateurism. As per usual, that small fact didn't matter. He was going to wear them all in order to clear the books. A bloke is nabbed for a burglary in a particular suburb and ends up in the frame for every job in that area over the past six months.

The stuff coming over the airwaves on the listening devices was amazing. Brickell had teamed up with his mate from Sydney and they were seen staking out a potential target, a Safeway store in Burwood. During their conversations, the two were heard talking about being prepared to shoot it out with police, or even killing the Armaguard officers to get their hands on the money. It was shocking stuff. These were dangerous men prepared to kill innocent people.

Off the back of this information, the Armed Robbery Squad was brought into the picture and, as was usual with a potentially violent situation, they used the Special Operations Group as back up, as a shootout was well and truly on the cards. Things were getting pretty exciting as Brickell and his mate nominated the day for the stickup. Again they were seen by surveillance sitting near the supermarket. The Armed Robbery Squad, Drug Squad and the SOGs were all there, ready for anything. The Armaguard truck arrived and then, for some unaccountable reason, the crooks drove away. No stick up. No result.

The tape of them talking as they prepared for the robbery that day was hair-raising. They were talking about putting balaclavas on, and you could hear the slides of their pistols operating as they loaded them. Again they were talking about shooting it out with the coppers. Instead, they drove away. Everyone was dumbfounded. Malcolm thinks they got a tip off that the cops were ready for a shootout and they realised they would be bowled if they went ahead with the job.

After the no go with the armed robbery, Brickell was arrested for trafficking. He was brought to the Drug Squad and regaled with a litany of offences, which was shit-loads, even without the New South Wales stuff. He was looking down the barrel of conspiracy to commit armed robbery, conspiracy to murder plus drug trafficking, possession of a gun and a whole heap of other stuff that they just made up, like robberies around the peninsula. They hit him with everything but the kitchen sink, then made an offer he couldn't refuse. It was no contest, he had to turn informer.

By coincidence, it was me that Brickell briefed to appear on his bail application. Bail was granted. Brickell told the Drug Squad he would help them but he needed the green light to make a quid, and went on trafficking despite being on bail. He didn't know though that his house and his car were still being listened to. In the car, he was heard talking to Lewis Moran about buying a .45 automatic.

Before we continue with this aspect of the story we need to return to Operation Vere, the huge operation launched to bring in the notorious Moran family. The coppers had received plenty of intelligence that the Morans were red hot into the speed, cocaine and ecstasy business, but they were such outstanding crooks the cops had not been able to get near them. Their luck was about to change.

During Regent the cops employed surveillance teams to stay as close to Lewis Moran as possible. Bearing in mind how cautious Lewis was this was no easy task. At one meeting in a park near Flemington, Lewis was seen with an unidentified male handing over a small package. The Drug Squad wanted to ascertain who the bloke was. Later, when Brickell was arrested and the surveillance tape surfaced, they discovered that Brickell had been that unidentified male. A copy of the surveillance tape from Operation Vere went from the Surveillance Unit to the Armed Robbers, because of their involvement with Brickell.

And so intelligence surfaced that Lewis, while not personally involved in armed robberies, was the facilitator and organiser of some major stick ups. He identified targets then recruited the gang to do the job, receiving a percentage of the proceeds. This had been going on for years but no copper could ever get a crook to lag on Lewis; he would have been signing his own death warrant. Once Brickell turned, the Drug Squad had the potential, via Operation Regent, to make inroads into the investigation of the Morans. Brickell was shown the surveillance tape of the meeting with Lewis, and asked about the meeting and what was in the package. Brickell said it contained a pound of pure speed supplied by Moran. The coppers were very pleased with this information; here was a substantial breakthrough in the capture of Lewis Moran.

Brickell, like 230 before him, provided the Drug Squad with a list of criminals he could set up or supply with chemicals to give the Drug Squad a much-needed result. The first and most significant item on his list was the Moran clan. The next big-ticket item was the Bandidos Motorcycle Gang, in particular Kim Sloan, who Brickell maintained he was close to.

Brickell made a number of controlled deliveries, but claimed he had cooks in New South Wales who were always chasing chemicals. The New South Wales Police didn't allow controlled deliveries or any other deals allowing informers to run chemicals. In order to stymie that directive Brickell was supplied with chemicals in Melbourne, with surveillance following him to the border. Then New South Wales surveillance took over, following until the chemicals were delivered. This happened on at least two occasions, and Brickell was credited with shutting down laboratories run by the Hells Angels in New South Wales. In addition, one of the bikie labs produced an unexpected bonus: a large cache of firearms.

Brickell kept working for the police, knowing that at any given moment, on a whim, the plug could be pulled and he would be back in the nick. Do not pass go. Do not collect $200. Even more dangerous for Brickell was that the crooks would discover he was an informer.

The first major legitimate Brickell operation was to deliver chemicals to the Bandido bikies and a cook who lived near Brickell in Mornington. Over several months the Bandidos received numerous deliveries of pre-cursor chemicals and tablets via Brickell, delivered to the bikie clubhouse. Brickell received chemicals from the cops and was told the price he was to on-sell for. As is often the way with the Brickells of this world, police discovered discrepancies between the price Brickell was given to sell at and the price he actually charged via the listening devices in the clubhouse. The sneaky bugger was copping a very good earn on the run through. The cops didn't let on they were aware of the rort; instead they turned a blind eye. This was a typical informer situation. The police never enquired as to profit margin. It follows that on occasions profits were huge. It sounds foolish and naïve, but this was the way deals were done. The amazing illegalities condoned frankly didn't worry anyone. An informer was in place and that was all that mattered. Hopefully a big pinch was just around the corner.

Brickell widened his horizons and started supplying chemicals directly to the cook and, more significantly for the cops, Lewis Moran. There was one catch: Brickell was the type of crook who always needed to be tooled up and when he was pinched the police seized his shooter. Blokes like this don't feel safe unless they have a shooter on board; this was a problem which needed fixing.

On one hand surveillance was being maintained on Brickell and his criminal associates, on the other Strawhorn was cultivating him as an informer. Brickell was seen meeting with Moran to collect the .45 gun mentioned earlier. Once he picked up the firearm and got closer to his house, he was buckled by the local police. They stopped him, searched the car and located a loaded .45 pistol. Brickell was arrested.

Here's another intriguing aspect to how the police turned crooks into informers by the use of the 'double whammy'. After the initial arrest bail is arranged and the criminal is allowed out to commit further offences. The police then arrest the crim again and read him the riot act so now he'll do anything demanded of him, their freedom in their tormentors' hands. This tactic never failed. The police held all the cards and could revoke bail at any moment if cooperation ceased. Former US President Richard Nixon had a plaque on his desk which read: 'If you have your opponent by the balls his heart and mind will surely follow.' Doesn't that ever ring true here? The Drug Squad well and truly had Brickell by the balls.

He found himself rearrested and this time bail was refused. Off he trotted to the nick for three months. During this time Paton built a rapport with him, acting as his handler. Paton promised Brickell he would look after his wife while he was away and even used a false ID to visit him in prison. He would have easily been recognised at the prison yet he was still allowed to get away with it.

When Brickell had his bail refused on the pistol charge, Paton and another detective were ordered to go to Brickell's house to retrieve ten kilos of red phosphorus stored there for future deliveries. It was a surprise how such a large amount of chemicals had fallen through the cracks in the Controlled Delivery Scheme and now didn't officially exist. This meant the coppers could traffic it themselves—what a bonus! The red phosphorus was brought back to the office without further ado. The detectives were hardly back when Strawhorn ordered Malcolm to return to Brickell's because the Armed Robbers were planning to execute a warrant and there were more chemicals at Brickells that had been given to him by the coppers but outside the scheme. Malcolm didn't react; he just got on with the job. When they arrived at Brickell's house, they met his wife and told her they were there to remove something incriminating from the garage. The excuse given to his missus was that while Brickell was locked up other crooks had learned of the chemicals and there could be trouble.

A 20-kilo drum of phenylacetic acid, another speed precursor, was in the garage. Malcolm hadn't seen this chemical at the Drug Squad for at least two to three years. Supply had stopped because it was cumbersome and very, very smelly. It was last used in an operation into 'Smiley' Chris Vertkas and Malcolm was amazed when he saw the drum in the garage. Following orders he retrieved the drum, no problems, and more significantly, no paperwork. Malcolm wondered where the phenylacetic acid had came from as he hadn't seen it since the operation on Vertkas. A similar barrel was in the Drug Squad store room during that operation. It turned out the barrel was purchased by the Controlled Delivery Desk legitimately for the Vertkas Operation, but when the substance became too difficult to control because of its volatility, it was sidelined and never used again.

The naughty part of the story was that it had never been returned to Sigma; it was typically lost in the shuffle and ended up being on-sold to Brickell. A deal would begin as legitimate, but there was no tracking of the chemical, so it officially ceased to exist. On the way back to the office Malcolm asked Paton, 'Where are you going to store it?' and he replied, 'We're not going to store it; we're going to sell it.' Paton then asked if an informer Malcolm worked with, Jacob Schentzer, would be interested. Paton knew full well that Schentzer had contacts with a cook known as the 'Alien', who the Drug Squad often supplied with deliveries of phenylaceticanhydride.

By the way, a cop in the Drug Squad owned an investment property in Elwood. Guess who he leased that investment property to? None other than the Alien and his brother Porky. Incredible.

Paton put a proposition to Malcolm to offer the drum's contents, approximately eighteen kilos, to Schentzer for $1,000 per kilo. This was done. Malcolm gave Schentzer a sample and a couple of days later he confirmed he'd take the lot for $18,000. Paton organised it and collected the cash. Malcolm met Paton a couple of days later at a hotel in Heidelberg. Paton parked his car next to Malcolm's and as he opened the car door Paton showed him a large bundle of money and grinned, yelling out that it was the dough from Schentzer. He peeled off $6,000 and handed it to Malcolm, who took it gleefully. He announced that Brickell's wife was going to get $6,000 too. Malcolm agreed that it would be fine to give his wife something while he was in prison.

Brickell had repaid some of his debt to Strawhorn by doing what Strawhorn wanted but Strawhorn was not one to ever let go once he had you in his clutches so he sent Brickell back to Lewis. It was now common knowledge in the criminal community that Brickell had been pinched with a conspiracy to commit armed robbery, trafficking drugs and possessing a firearm. The bloke was red hot and somebody as smart as Lewis was highly unlikely to even talk to him until he cooled off. And when Brickell visited Lewis, he slammed the door in his face. What a surprise.

However, Strawhorn kept pushing Brickell, so Brickell got to know Jason Moran. When Lewis Moran wouldn't do business,

Strawhorn directed Brickell to load Jason Moran with 1,000 ecstasy tablets—the same 1,000 tablets Malcolm stole from Carl Williams.

Brickell knew where Jason hid his drugs, so while Jason was out, Brickell broke into his garage and planted the tablets in Jason's stash. The idea was that the Drug Squad would race through and get a big pinch on Jason. There was one problem with this bright idea: at the time that the drugs were hidden in Jason's garage, he was standing trial with Alphonse Gangitano for serious assaults on a number of tourists at the Sports Bar in King Street, Melbourne. Alphonse and Jason had given the tourists a fearful thrashing and after many years of ducking and diving, the moment of truth had arrived. Brickell happened to stash the tablets in Jason's garage just at the time Jason was convicted and went to jail. No result on Lewis, and now Jason was in jail. Brickell was sent back to Jason's to steal the tablets back.

Next, he was sent to visit the Bandidos' headquarters to do a deal. Unbeknown to Brickell, the Squirrels were watching as he took the ferry from Mornington to Geelong, then went on to Sloan's. When Brickell returned he was to meet Strawhorn. Surveillance had reported to the Drug Squad that when Brickell left the Bandidos' headquarters, he was carrying a black leather satchel which looked like it contained heavy, bulky items. Strawhorn was onto him. When they met he demanded to see the satchel and opened it in front of Brickell. In the bag were four long-barrelled Smith & Wesson revolvers. Where did these come from? Brickell caved in and confessed: he had purchased the guns on credit to sell on. They were obsolete—the Bandidos were now using fully automatic weapons. Good to see bikies upgrading their hardware to state of the art while the coppers were still armed with their old .38 revolvers.

Here was a bloke on bail for serious firearms offences in possession of a pile of shooters and now he was in debt to the

Bandidos as well. Matters had taken a definite turn for the worse for Brickell. Strawhorn seized the pistols and told him it was his problem how he paid the Bandidos. He'd deceived him and he was on his own. Brickell was even more firmly in Strawhorn's clutches than before. Strawhorn decided not to lay charges; he preferred to have the drop on him. So a detective senior sergeant in the police force, who has just taken possession of four illegal revolvers, hasn't receipted them, has made no paper record of them and hasn't charged the bloke in possession of them.

Strawhorn returned to the office with the briefcase and threw it on the ground, saying, 'Look what I just got from Brickell.' The bag was opened, displaying the four revolvers. The serial numbers had been removed. There was no doubt they were stolen. Malcolm entered the revolvers in the miscellaneous property register. They had to be lodged in the safe and a record of their seizure made, for the simple reason that if anyone saw the revolvers, there had better be a very good reason for their presence in the office. This presented a problem. Strawhorn clearly hadn't thought this through. How was he to explain taking possession of four revolvers without charging anybody? The pistols were in the system and nothing could be done about it, the cops needed an explanation and quickly.

The guns were secured in the office and a story was cooked up to explain how the firearms came to be in the Drug Squad's possession. No firearms were found at Brickell's house; instead the cops alleged these particular firearms were found in a nearby park and supposed that maybe they were Brickell's. The story became more complicated however when the police said that they had seen an unidentified male bury the guns near Brickell's house and the Drug Squad sat off waiting for the mystery man to return. A search warrant was issued on Brickell's house and when there was no show Brickell was arrested. He was taken to the Mornington Police Station and interviewed about the guns, making a 'nil' statement in his taped interview. He was never charged in relation to the guns. The whole sordid episode was a lie from start to finish to cover the unexplained presence of guns in the Drug Squad office.

Also at this time there was a hell of a stink in the force; police had started making two records of interview for the same offence with a crook who was an informer. The first was the *real* interview, where the crook inevitably spilt his guts and dobbed in his mates. Someone then came up with the bright idea that once the crook had tipped in he would be allowed to make a second record of interview in which he would offer 'no comment'. The second interview theoretically enabled the crook to demonstrate he hadn't lagged, covering his tracks when inevitably his mates ended up pinched. It was insurance for an informer; he could show he was staunch. This idiocy led to tears. On more than one occasion the second record of interview accidentally came to light during court proceedings and there were acquittals as a result. An order was issued that there were to be no more bogus second records of interview. In direct contravention of that order, two records of interview were made with Brickell and he was released with no charges. The four pistols were destroyed. The trouble was that Brickell still owed the Bandidos, and you don't lash bikies unless you're deranged. He had to pay and that was all there was to it.

The Drug Squad had Brickell well and truly by the balls and he had no hope of an earn anywhere else. He came to them a few days later offering to get a machine gun for $4,000. At the time the going rate for machine guns on the black market was about $1,000. Coppers are always keen to get machine guns off the street for obvious reasons, even if there is no pinch involved. Without further ado, a cheque was drawn for Brickell to purchase the machine gun, which he did, handing it over for destruction. They knew the money for the machine gun was for the debt to the Bandidos with the added bonus of Brickell making an earn of $1600 on the side. This was how it worked. Many double dealings, with crooks making an earn, were subsidised by the taxpayer. Brickell had evened up with the Bandidos but the Drug Squad was all over him like a cheap suit.

Never being one to miss an opportunity Strawhorn announced to Brickell he was to load Kim Sloan of the Bandidos so that in their upcoming raid the Drug Squad could be certain of a good result. Strawhorn gave Brickell 1,000 ecstasy tablets. These were the tablets from the Carl Williams bust that had been earmarked to load Jason Moran. Here they were, those very same tablets, being used now to load Sloan. Brickell visited Sloan at his house and placed a plastic bag containing the 1,000 tablets behind a potplant near the front door. A very ordinary load if ever there was one.

In parallel the Drug Squad was running a major operation into the Bandidos. The gang had a factory/clubhouse in Geelong with a secure shed attached. A camera monitored remotely from Melbourne operated around the clock, watching the bikies' every move. As with virtually everything in the Drug Squad matters soon became complicated. Those running the operation, codenamed Schild, decided to sell the gang a kilo of pseudo, notwithstanding the order from on high that pseudo must not be used because it disappeared so often. The operation had an undercover in the Bandidos. The cops watched from Melbourne as the package was delivered and one of the bikies placed it in the shed and locked it. Only a couple of the bikies and the Drug Squad knew about the delivery so what came next was extraordinary. That very night there was a burglary at the shed and the only item stolen was the pseudoephedrine.

Heaven knows who stole it but one must ask: Who knew? And who had a motive? The answer to both of these questions is the Drug Squad. Otherwise, if the shed was monitored, why wasn't anyone seen doing the burg?

When the Bandidos found out they had been burgled, all hell broke loose. They even employed an ex-copper private detective qualified to dust for fingerprints. Without access to the fingerprint archives this was a fairly pointless exercise. The burglar never surfaced.

The day of the raids arrived, coordinated to go off simultaneously. The main targets were Sloan's house and the clubhouse. The warrant on Sloan's house was executed by Steve Paton. Malcolm was ordered to search the clubhouse shed and spent the day searching, for no result. But a large number of ecstasy tablets had been found at Sloan's house and he had been arrested and charged. From the very moment he was arrested and shown the tablets, Sloan cried: 'Load!' He was furious by the time he reached custody. He blamed Paton, because he was the copper who 'found' the tablets.

Sloan pleaded not guilty at his trial, but was convicted and copped a jail term. They all knew he was not guilty but he still copped a substantial whack. This bloke was not the type to go quietly. Malcolm had a feeling that this was not the last they would hear of Mr Sloan.

Later, when Paton was charged with theft and trafficking, Sloan went on the attack, and Paton as chief witness at his trial was discredited. The allegations of Paton's trafficking had started before Sloan was the subject of any investigation. Therefore it was at least arguable that Sloan had been loaded. The matter ultimately ended in the Court of Appeal, where Sloan was acquitted. He received an ex-gratia payment from the Government.

Chapter Twenty-six

THE FRASER EQUATION

'This is a court of law, young man, not
a court of justice.'

—Oliver Wendell Holmes Jr

As a lawyer, I had always been extremely busy, my days filled with running from courts to clients, jumping on and off planes and generally not having time to scratch myself. The more experienced I became the harder and more serious were the cases I defended. I had what outsiders might see as a jetsetting lifestyle, travelling to exciting destinations, but I worked seven days a week on tight schedules. It was through this lifestyle that I started using cocaine on an occasional basis as a social thing. On reflection, it was a trapping of my success. As they say, a cocaine habit is God's way of telling you that you have too much money.

Meanwhile, Strawhorn wasn't happy that he still couldn't get a result with the Morans and was really putting pressure on Brickell, who was also getting desperate. One day he blurted out that he could purchase an ounce of cocaine from me, his lawyer. I was unfortunately at that time known to be addicted to cocaine.

Brickell told Strawhorn that he had, on occasion, paid me with coke for legal services and could score from me for $6,500 per ounce. When Strawhorn heard this he nearly wet himself. What a pinch. The Morans were brushed aside and all of a sudden Operation Regent ceased investigating one of Melbourne's greatest underworld families and had moved to a drug-addicted solicitor.

The excitement resonated throughout the Drug Squad. $6,500 was taken from the drug fund and on 25 June 1999 Malcolm and Firth met Brickell at Spencer Street Station car park. Brickell was instructed to visit my office at 550 Lonsdale Street, purchase the cocaine, and return with the drugs. Brickell was told that he would not be wired for the meeting with me. There would be some surveillance on him, but no listening devices—yet! He was told it was a non-evidentiary purchase; he was merely required to make the purchase and bring it back to the police for analysis. At this stage there would be no corroboration of any aspect of anything Brickell said. It was Brickell's word only that he could buy from me. Nor was there forensic evidence by way of fingerprints or DNA from this purchase.

Looking back on the whole exercise, the Drug Squad dropped the ball here, because they had no way of corroborating Brickell had even visited my office. They watched Brickell enter the building but other than that had no idea what he did until he emerged again. They only had Brickell's say so and his word was questionable at best. When Brickell returned to the car park, he claimed that though he went to my office no transaction took place, but it would later at Brickell's address in Rosamond Street, Balaclava.

Surveillance was on me and I was seen around the corner from Rosamond Street talking on my mobile. I jumped back in the car, drove to Rosamond Street, which is a dead end, and was seen outside talking to Brickell for a short time. No transaction was observed.

In the drug world if you are selling ounces you do not do home deliveries—the purchaser always goes to the vendor. Secondly this address had no attachment to me. Why would I go there?

This is what actually took place. I went to Brickell's place to score from him. He told me to wait in the street. He came from the house and as I was sitting in my car he slipped me some coke, not the other way round. Even more important was the fact that after my arrest Malcolm raided Rosamond Street and located what could only be described as a drug house. It contained a large hydroponic set up, a lot of cocaine and assorted other drugs. No wonder Brickell didn't want me go into the house, I would have seen the cannabis set up.

Brickell met the police for a debrief a short time later and handed over a bag of cocaine that he asserted came from me. Even at the time Malcolm had doubts. But Malcolm and Firth took possession of the cocaine and were delighted with Brickell. The cocaine went back to the office where there was jubilation among the senior officers. They had purchased an ounce of cocaine from a leading barrister; the fact that it was me, who had so often been a thorn in their side, made it even sweeter. They had what they needed and Operation Regent swung into action. Malcolm prepared an affidavit in support of an application for a listening device warrant and submitted it to His Honour Mr Justice Barry Beach in the Supreme Court. When an application for a listening device goes before the Supreme Court, evidence is by way of affidavit. It's clear now that the major factor in their application was the evidence of Brickell visiting me, which was supported only by his say so. There was no other evidence from any crooks or informers of me trafficking. It was out of left field and should have been treated with due caution.

Beach granted the application with very strict conditions. No professionally privileged conversations were to be listened to or recorded. The Drug Squad did both, practising deliberate deception, by maintaining two logs of my conversations: one to demonstrate compliance with the Judge's order if they were challenged, the other containing everything said in my office.

The other element of the order they ignored was that there was to be no dissemination of any listening device product. This part of the order was emphasised, yet other officers in the Drug Squad were allowed to listen to my conversations with clients. They regularly recorded conversations that had absolutely nothing to do with the investigation.

If I had been paying close attention to my life at that stage I would have realised that listening devices had been installed in my office. I can remember arriving in my office early one morning to find dust on my table from the ceiling tiles, which had been moved. The same in my boardroom; I should have seen the small hole in the wall over the powerpoint. But no, although I noted the sloppiness of their work, I didn't draw the obvious conclusion. I was not so out of it though that I didn't notice that my copy of the book *Walsh Street* had gone missing.

Here is clear evidence of the flouting of the good judge's instructions. One day a police inspector visited me. Unbeknown to him or me the conversation we had was recorded. It was about his son, who was in a bit of bother—nothing serious. In blatant defiance of Beach's order this conversation was recorded and the inspector questioned by ESD about his dealings with me. This conversation was nothing more than a client talking to his lawyer.

This total disregard for the Judge's order threw up some interesting results, particularly in the case of the trial of a young man for attempted murder. Early one morning he wandered into the Underground nightclub in Melbourne's notorious King Street. He was filmed at the door greeting his bouncer mates.

The allegation was that he then walked into the club and went downstairs to a booth where without uttering a word he shot a bloke twice. He then allegedly popped the shooter back in his pocket and turned and walked out and up King Street. The security footage revealed he was in the club but a few minutes.

The coppers recognised him from the tape and arrested him. I was instructed to act and he was granted bail. Ultimately we ended up in the Supreme Court facing a trial. My instructions remained the same from day one: 'Not guilty, not me.' No doubt about those instructions and he maintained that stance when he was acquitted.

We all headed back to my office for celebratory drinks. My articled clerk at the time came to my office and asked if he could enquire whether he really did shoot the bloke. I hit the roof and told him in no uncertain terms that our instructions had always been not guilty, and the jury had agreed. End of story. Under no circumstances was he to pop the question. In direct contravention of that directive the clerk headed back to the conference room and a couple of drinks later asked whether he really had shot the bloke, to which the young man replied, 'Of course I did!'

Malcolm has told me that when the coppers heard the recently acquitted man admitting his guilt the whole joint went up in the air. They were furious. There is no such thing in this state as double jeopardy, which means in spite of the post-acquittal admission of guilt nothing could be done. The acquittal stood and he could not be charged with any other offence. Goes to show, you shouldn't eavesdrop on other people's conversations lest you hear something you'd rather not.

When this conversation surfaced as part of the brief in my prosecution the young clerk got the proverbial kick in the arse for disobeying my instructions. I know it may sound odd to those outside the legal profession but what lawyers think of the case or the client is immaterial. You don't have to like or believe clients, just follow instructions. I had my instructions—not guilty—and that is the result we obtained. Never second-guess the jury.

Now let's return to my case. I was overheard discussing with my local cocaine supplier the fact that he intended to import drugs from Benin in Africa. I was charged and convicted of being knowingly concerned with the importation of a commercial quantity of cocaine. I have yet to be convinced that there was a serious case against me and that the subsequent prison sentence was appropriate.

Immediately before my arrest Strawhorn decided that just in case there was a hiccough with material taped in my office, they needed another purchase from me. If the importation fell over they had two traffics of a couple of ounces which was still a good pinch. Belt and braces.

Malcolm harboured real reservations. The Drug Squad caught Brickell lying on numerous occasions but they still wanted to believe him. He'd been fucking the cops around but after a bit of pressure he agreed to score another ounce.

It was the night before my arrest: Friday, 10 September 1999. They had been on my case for months and only one thing was obvious, I had a raging habit. They still had only the one sale to Brickell and that was without any real evidence. Malcolm wouldn't have wanted to be betting a sheep station on that being kosher.

I was having dinner at a restaurant called 2BC in Greville Street, Prahran with some friends that night. Brickell told the coppers he needed another $6,500 to buy the ounce. The price alone was odd because the going rate for top quality cocaine at that time was more like $4,000. There are none so blind as those that will not see.

Malcolm claimed they were sitting in the front window of the Jokers Hotel in Chapel Street watching Brickell walk down Greville Street toward 2BC. A couple of minutes later, Brickell and I emerged and spoke briefly. Nothing changed hands and Brickell turned and walked back to the Jokers Hotel where he gave an ounce of cocaine to them. Once again, this was a non-evidentiary purchase: no surveillance, no electronics, no forensics, no fingerprints. That the meeting had happened was purely on Brickell's say so.

He also says that it never crossed his mind to search either 230 or Brickell before sending them off to purchase drugs, or to search them on their return after they did deals. If they did this they would have found an ounce of cocaine already on Brickell before he got to me. With 230 they would have discovered money and drugs in his car after his transactions. How often they were deceived we will never know.

The day before I was arrested Malcolm wrestled with what he considers dirty work at the crossroads. Brickell faced Frankston Court charged with the original pistol offence back from when he turned informer. Brickell had many priors by then and was a double agent, something I had not the faintest idea of in spite of the fact I was appearing for him. He went before court, pleading guilty to one count of possessing a loaded pistol, and was fined the princely sum of $5,000 with no jail time. Malcolm never understood what happened.

After court, Brickell was at the Checkers Inn in Port Melbourne (known to the locals as the House of Twisted Faces because all the old crooks drink there) celebrating with the Painters and Dockers. Boy, didn't he have a lend of the P&Ds with his double dealing. He was hanging with them and lagging at the same time. Then the Drug Squad followed me to Checkers, where they watched me have a beer with Brickell. He'd been given two ecstasy tablets to make it look a bit better on my arrest. As they watched from the car, Brickell poked something into my jacket pocket while we were drinking. It turned out to be the ecstasy tablets Strawhorn had given Brickell.

I was ultimately convicted of being knowingly concerned with an importation of a commercial quantity of cocaine and went to jail for a maximum of seven years and served four years, ten months. As for Brickell, I have since ascertained he was never charged with any drug trafficking, suffering no penalty for all his wheeling and dealing, including the business with the machine gun. I have since looked at my own brief of evidence and was not at all comforted to discover the parade of police working on my case that ended up in the nick for corruption.

Chapter Twenty-seven

A COUPLE OF NASTY SURPRISES

'Nothing makes it easier to resist
temptation than a proper bringing up, a
sound set of values and witnesses.'

—Franklin P. Jones

Towards the end of 1999, out of the blue, Paton resigned. Malcolm was amazed when Strawhorn merely brushed the issue aside, confidently stating he'd be back in no time. Malcolm chased up Paton to find out why. He said he was leaving Victoria Police and was going to Queensland to join the force there, refusing to elaborate further. Three weeks later, Paton returned to work and not another word was said. What happened we'll never know. Following Paton's return life rolled on as if nothing had happened, until December, when it was apparent something was seriously amiss. Paton was continually at loggerheads with Strawhorn and took extended leave prior to Christmas.

At about this time Malcolm was called into Strawhorn's office and the door closed. This was unusual because Malcolm and Strawhorn never met behind closed doors; conversations were always in the open with nothing to hide. Strawhorn had his serious face on and Malcolm sat waiting for what was coming. Strawhorn produced a page from the back of his note book and asked him to look at a series of dates which tallied with purchases of pseudo and Sudafed from Sigma in the next column. Malcolm had no prior knowledge of the document or its contents. It specified details of purchases of large quantities: between half and two and a half kilos of pseudo, on various dates, together with large quantities of Sudafed. Strawhorn explained that he had been instructed to carry out an audit of all chemicals purchased by the Drug Squad over the past twelve months and asked whether Malcolm could furnish any details outside of the official records. Malcolm confirmed that he had no knowledge of the document, which was separate to police records.

It was suggested to him that these purchases had all been made by Paton, and that Malcolm, as Paton's supervisor and superior, must know about them. Strawhorn asked what his involvement was in these unauthorised transactions. Malcolm protested his ignorance. Strawhorn pointed out that the date that Brickell first came on the scene coincided with the beginning of these transactions and occurred thereafter, every two to three weeks, before stopping abruptly. The dates that Brickell was on bail accorded exactly with the dodgy purchases and when he hit the nick they stopped. When Brickell was out the purchases fired up again. The inescapable inference was that Paton and Brickell were up to no good and they were keeping the rest of the Drug Squad in the dark. Strawhorn stated as fact to Malcolm that Paton had made these unauthorised purchases and on-sold them to Brickell, potentially netting them a squillion dollars between them.

After more intense questioning, Strawhorn appeared satisfied that Malcolm knew nothing about them. Malcolm was to visit Paton at home and let him know that the joke was up; he had been caught out, and the best thing he could do was resign immediately. Strawhorn added: 'Better an ex-Drug Squad detective charged than a current serving member.' As Paton's sergeant Malcolm agreed to the home visit.

Then Strawhorn once more turned on Malcolm, questioning his innocence. As Paton's sergeant, ESD and Inspector Newton weren't going to believe that he was not in it up to his eyeballs. Malcolm could see what was coming. He was going to end up wearing this. He stared mortified at the details of the sheer quantity of drugs sold without his knowledge right from under his nose for almost a year. He then turned his mind to the other goings on in the Drug Squad that would become immediately apparent to anyone investigating this matter.

Visiting Paton at his home, Malcolm asked him to come for a drive and they headed to the local park for a heart to heart. He explained what had transpired in Strawhorn's office. Paton immediately went on the defensive, asserting that it was all Strawhorn's idea. Strawhorn had ordered him to make the purchases and directed him that every time he purchased anything from Sigma that he was to double up. Paton agreed to throw in the towel immediately and said that fact could be conveyed to Strawhorn.

Malcolm was in quite a quandary, with Paton saying it was all Strawhorn's idea and Strawhorn accusing Malcolm of being in cahoots with Paton. It was clear what was going to happen. He would be the meat in the sandwich if this ever unravelled. He couldn't see any way out if this pair of vipers ganged up on him. Later that evening he drove to Strawhorn's to deliver the news. To Malcolm's surprise, all Strawhorn said was, 'Thanks for doing that.'

Little did Malcolm know he had been used unwittingly to leak information (while an investigation was underway) that amounted to a warning to Paton to resign. It was a deliberate tactic to stymie the ESD investigation. It was becoming clear Ethical Standards were already involved in a major way and there was going to be a lot of explaining to do. The way Paton and Strawhorn were both positioning themselves, there was going to be one bloke left out on a limb: Malcolm. The next day Paton turned up at the office, bringing his children with him so no one could question him.

Let's go back a little now. Approximately six months prior to Paton's permanent exit from the force, Mark Moran was murdered. Ron Iddles from the Homicide Squad, probably one of the best investigators in the Victorian Police Force, rang Strawhorn. He knew Strawhorn had been working on Moran and asked for all the surveillance and intelligence he had on him. Strawhorn made his first mistake by lying to Iddles. He said the Drug Squad had not been working on Moran at the time of his death. Iddles hung up and thought to himself: That's got to be a lie. And more importantly: Why would Strawhorn lie to me? What's his motivation?

That lie marked the beginning of the end of the Drug Squad. Iddles then made it his business to ascertain precisely what the Drug Squad had been up to with Mark Moran. The obvious answer was the last thing Strawhorn wanted to surface—all their transactions had been off the books and off the record.

WHERE DID THE LIST OF DISCREPANCIES COME FROM? FATE played a hand as it so often does in these situations. Graeme Sayce was an ex-copper from the Drug Squad and didn't like Strawhorn at all. Sayce resigned from the Police Force and took a position at Sigma Pharmaceuticals. One thing that must be said about Sayce is that he is a straight up and down copper—fanatically honest. That's his approach, to do everything correctly. When Sayce commenced work at Sigma he carried out, for his own benefit, a review of the drugs purchased by the police. Being an ex-copper, Sayce rang Strawhorn and told him that the purchases didn't add up. The volume of chemicals sold to police far and away exceeded what could be used in legitimate operations. In other words, there was something rotten in the state of Denmark. Strawhorn made his second mistake when he told Sayce to mind his own fucking business. He wasn't in the Drug Squad anymore and he should piss off.

Around that time, Strawhorn invited Malcolm and another officer, Allison, for a cup of coffee across the road from Police Headquarters. Strawhorn mused that 'an ill wind was going to be blowing through the place', and he saw himself leaving the Force. It was time to move on. Malcolm didn't read too much into this comment but Allison questioned him further. Strawhorn was tight-lipped and clearly anxious but didn't elaborate.

Sayce went on to conduct a detailed audit. There was a huge discrepancy between what had been purchased legitimately and what had actually changed hands. Sigma maintained their own records of all purchases, legitimate or otherwise, and they did not accord with any of the official records at the Drug Squad.

Not long before Malcolm was called into Strawhorn's office over the pseudoephedrine transactions, Sayce rang the Drug Squad trying to contact Strawhorn, who was unavailable, so he ended up speaking with an Inspector recently transferred from ESD to the Drug Squad on promotion. Sayce detailed his revelations and the Inspector began investigating, later appraising Superintendent Dave Newton of his findings.

By now the damage was done, a full ESD investigation was in train. But Strawhorn hoped to smooth everything over and correct all the paper work so that the investigation would come to nought. He would attribute any inconsistencies to Paton, who had left the force, distancing himself from him entirely.

Chapter Twenty-eight

THE END IS NIGH

'Life is mostly froth and bubble,
Two things stand like stone,
Kindness in another's trouble,
Courage in your own'

—Adam Lindsay Gordon

You'll remember 230 had gone to ground. It was obvious he had gone cold and was in fear for his life. His utility had been torched outside one of his houses. He was paranoid about his living arrangements and would tell nobody where he put his head down. He refused to deal with the Drug Squad, particularly Strawhorn, so Malcolm went to see him off his own bat.

Malcolm wanted to reassure him that he was not being sold down the river nor being given up to Lewis to be knocked.

Eventually, ever so reluctantly, 230 came back on board and agreed to a couple of small jobs for Malcolm. Lewis Moran had hashish for sale and Kayak started purchasing it in ten-kilo lots. The location of the hashish was identified and warrants were executed. The Drug Squad deluded themselves that everything was back on track but again 230 went cold and wouldn't cooperate. He vanished and wouldn't answer his phone. Malcolm eventually tracked him down and met with him off the record.

At this point, Malcolm made a fatal blunder, irrevocably setting his compass firmly towards oblivion. He floated the suggestion that if another informer, Jacob Schentzer, was willing to buy hashish from Lewis, then 230 had a reason to meet Schentzer and do some drug deals. This was a common Drug Squad tactic. If you have two informers, try and get them together in the hope they'll strike up a relationship and commence doing business. This widens the informers' circles and the police net, thereby increasing the odds of the coppers landing more pinches down the track.

From the first meeting 230 did not like or trust Schentzer and did not want to do business. Malcolm believed he needed the two working together to get results. Finally Malcolm agreed, stupidly, to be the conduit between the two for their respective drug businesses. Amazingly, Malcolm had no problem with this, believing he was furthering investigations and only doing what was ordinarily done by others every day of the week. No one knew what he was up to, trafficking flat out, albeit for little financial gain.

Malcolm allowed 230 to purchase ten kilos of hash which was on-sold to Schentzer by Malcolm. This, according to 230, enabled him to repay some of the money he had owed Lewis since the first raid on 230's house. The price for the hash was $35,000. There is always a hiccough though—the hashish was found to be of poor quality. It was all dried out and appeared to have been sitting around for a very long while. It was most likely the same hash Lewis and the Munster had secreted in a container on the wharves years ago. The newspaper wrapped around the hash bore dates in the 1980s.

Malcolm explained to Schentzer the hash was from Lewis and he could not take it back. You couldn't just swap it over.

Lewis was not a supermarket. He was stuck with it and had to pay: no ifs, no buts. Schentzer eventually came up with $2,500 a kilo and the deal was settled.

230 WAS THE CLASSIC DOUBLE AGENT; NOT ONLY WAS HE informing for the Drug Squad, he had done a double back-flip. Unbeknown to the Drug Squad he was in bed with ESD, who had Malcolm and his mates under the microscope, watching their every move. It's likely that what tipped 230 over to ESD was Strawhorn pushing him for more and more intelligence, more dealing and more money. The more Strawhorn pushed, the more 230 resisted. The bloke was a walking time-bomb in Malcolm's view and Strawhorn wasn't playing him the right way.

At the same time Malcolm's life was going off the rails. The pressure was enormous. He not only became physically sick but psychologically ill as a result of the subterfuge and double dealing. He was receiving counselling and became so ill that a year before his arrest his wife urged him to see Ethical Standards and spill the beans. He refused, because he feared he would lose his job and be unemployable in any police force. He'd be a rat in the ranks. And he was terrified of Strawhorn. He knew those with a lot to lose would do anything to protect themselves. Malcolm lived with an overwhelming sense of foreboding. The world as they all knew it was about to end, but he couldn't find the exit door.

MALCOLM HAD FIRST MET JACOB SCHENTZER AT A PARTY SOME years earlier. They got talking and Malcolm told him he was a cop. During the conversation Schentzer said he owned a computer shop. As it turned out police needed new computers, and a deal was done. It was all above board, with computers purchased at the right price and everybody happy. When Malcolm moved to the Drug Squad Schentzer approached him with the news that two major crooks, Ezmund Mouseek and Izzy Kraznov, wanted to talk to him. They had substantial information to pass on. They were both serving lengthy sentences and wanted a get out of jail card. Malcolm used this opportunity to cultivate Schentzer as an informer. Every good copper has a web of informers and most good pinches originate from hot tip offs. The big busts are usually more arse than class.

Informers were supposed to be paid by the force, but often, with limited funds and the lack of a big bust, no money was forthcoming. So, on many occasions, drugs seized in raids were passed to informers to keep them sweet. Malcolm was no exception to the rule, giving drugs to Schentzer to sell for profit. In the cold hard light of day this behaviour is reprehensible. It just puts more drugs on the street and everyone knows it.

Strawhorn's top drawer was regularly used to give Malcolm drugs. When he had the occasional spring clean he would ask, 'Does anyone want this for any of their informers?' Malcolm was given hashish, amphetamine and cocaine, which he gave to Schentzer in lieu of payment.

In the meantime, while Malcolm was on sick leave, 230 continued to contact him. Unbeknown to Malcolm he had been ordered to engage Malcolm in any criminal activity possible. In Australia the defence of entrapment does not exist, therefore when police get a bee in their bonnet about a punter and can't catch him doing anything naughty, an agent provocateur will pester the bloke until he caves in and does the undercover's bidding. Hey presto, the coppers have their pinch. It troubles me that police all over this country engage in this behaviour and neither their ethics nor the legality of their actions are ever challenged. Entrapment creates serious issues. Many times clients have instructed me that an undercover has driven them mad to commit a crime and in the end, just to shut them up, they've done what was asked of them and copped a whack for their troubles.

Malcolm reached the point of no return. At a meeting with 230 Malcolm told him Schentzer had a friend, Claude Vanonou, who was expecting a shipment of half a million ecstasy tablets. 230 could purchase direct from Schentzer and continue trafficking under his green light. Malcolm added that there would be a good mark up on the tablets and he'd make plenty. 230 was even given a sample of the expected shipment.

Over the next couple of weeks numerous transactions were organised through Schentzer to 230, Malcolm being the intermediary. The first transaction was 1,000 tablets at eighteen dollars per tablet. The money was paid by 230 to Schentzer via Malcolm. Malcolm physically took possession of the tablets and delivered them. Malcolm thought the deal went down without a hitch but 230 covertly recorded every conversation and relayed the tapes to ESD. He pestered Malcolm to do more with Schentzer. Next time a couple of thousand tablets were ordered for $36,000. Again Malcolm did the pick up and delivery.

The second deal between 230 and Malcolm was classic entrapment by ESD. Malcolm had trafficked a sufficient size to attract a jail term. After the 2,000-tab deal 230 backed up almost immediately with an order for 10,000. Malcolm had implemented similar traps dozens of times during his career but he didn't tumble to his own. Schentzer was unhappy supplying such a large quantity; he smelt a rat even if Malcolm didn't. He thought it was a setup by Strawhorn but Malcolm reassured him it wasn't. The tablets were going to 230 for sale under the green light. Both would make a big whack. Schentzer was right of course; it was a setup.

These dealings are proof positive that after years of being around and taking part in corrupt activities almost on a daily basis Malcolm had completely lost any sense of moral perspective. This whole twisted saga was normal behaviour within the Drug Squad. After all, major traffickers were regularly given the green light and the coppers all scored an earn. This was the way of the world at the Drug Squad.

The 10,000-tab transaction went ahead. Malcolm was to meet 230 at Caulfield Park and deliver the money. At about 9 pm, 230 contacted Malcolm, saying he was on his way and to meet him at the park. Malcolm started walking to the meet in the dark when he heard a rush of police cars tearing into the car park and shortly afterwards was surrounded by a large number of heavily armed coppers and thrown face down to the ground. His hands were cuffed behind his back, just like in the movies. Detective Inspector Peter De Santo from Ethical Standards stood over him with his foot on his head pointing a cocked gun at his forehead saying that he was fucked and the time had come for him to start talking. If Malcolm had been oblivious to his position, this was one hell of a wake up call.

The game was up but Malcolm was still cocky enough to reply, 'What's in it for me?' De Santo told him: 'No deals.' This was a big bust, make no bones about it, and Malcolm had managed to land himself front and centre. It didn't take long for him to realise he had no option but to render whatever assistance possible, if he was to have any kind of a future at all. The cops hung around the park. Malcolm was told to phone Schentzer and tell him he'd met 230 and had the money. ESD reckoned that once Schentzer knew the money was available he would pick up the pills from Claude Vanonou, an Israeli national who dealt ecstasy all over the world. Vanonou was in Australia solely to set up an ecstasy-importing business and what ESD wanted more than anything was to have Schentzer collect the pills so they could identify Vanonou and arrest the pair on the hop.

The script ran like clockwork. Malcolm, Schentzer and Vanonou were all arrested. After the arrests Malcolm was bundled into a car with De Santo in the back seat. He was handcuffed and was heading to Police Headquarters in Flinders Street when without warning De Santo detoured to Malcolm's house, where the coppers tipped the place upside down. They found nothing. Needless to say Malcolm's wife Gillie was shattered. She couldn't believe her eyes. Here was Malcolm looking the worse for wear, handcuffed and browbeaten.

Although Malcolm was totally corrupt I have to sympathise with him at this point in his story. All of a sudden you're on the precipice, staring into oblivion, but funnily enough your first thought is not for yourself, rather for your family. In my case I had two young kids and I knew then that I could never forgive myself for what they would go through. Malcolm voiced exactly the same sentiment. We each have an albatross around our necks for the rest of our lives.

At Flinders Street the penny dropped that he was gone. Malcolm was well and truly in the shit and had no option but to cooperate fully. On the other hand he had to try and salvage whatever benefit he possibly could, so commenced lengthy and acrimonious negotiations.

Bail refused, remanded in custody and taken to court the next morning—you can imagine the excitement, a Drug Squad sergeant pinched with corruption amid a big drug bust. Nothing better than coppers and a drug deal to send the rumour mill into overdrive, to say nothing of the media. They were in a frenzy; it was headline news everywhere.

Bail was refused on the grounds of the seriousness of the offences and Malcolm trotted off to jail. How the mighty had fallen. He believed the Drug Squad was bullet-proof. Now he'd come unstuck in the most spectacular fashion. As a copper, jail is a very difficult place because there's no shortage of blokes you helped put there who would love to square the ledger. Coppers are in constant danger and are usually immediately placed in protection away from mainstream prisoners. In protection Malcolm was in with the rapists, paedophiles and the criminally insane: terrific company.

Again I'm able to sympathise to some degree because he was banged up in the same unit I'd been in, with the same crooks—not a pleasant existence by any stretch of the imagination. Don't get me wrong, I have no sympathy for the actions that landed Malcolm in the poo but believe me, in the nick, he needed eyes in the back of his head to survive.

A few days later Malcolm's head stopped spinning and he got down to tin tacks, retaining lawyers and commencing negotiations. But nothing was negotiable unless Malcolm gave Ethical Standards every detail of the sordid story of the Drug Squad chapter and verse. He agreed to debriefing by De Santo for over a month. When Malcolm decided to tell me his story he made a Freedom of Information application for the transcript of his debrief and surprisingly I received a copy of most of it—very interesting reading indeed.

While reading the debrief we both noticed chunks excised which were obviously too hot for general consumption. One thing that sticks out like the proverbial sore thumb in the transcript is the extent of the corruption within the Drug Squad, and the amount of money, drug dealing and other illegal behaviour that went on. At the time of this criminality, there were over 65 police in the Drug Squad. The corruption was massive. Many police had been making a fortune, crooks were being loaded and wrongly jailed and thefts during raids were standard practice. Why cover it up?

Chapter Twenty-nine

ON HOLIDAYS

'Vile deeds like poison weeds,
Bloom well in prison air,
It is only what is good in man,
That wastes and withers there.'

—'The Ballad of Reading Gaol', Oscar Wilde

A copper's life in jail isn't easy, I know. I watched former police arrive and witnessed with my own eyes what happened to them. Gone is the swagger, the overbearing self-confidence. These men are terrified. They don't have the brotherhood to back them up. They are alone and scared, usually with just cause, and it shows. It was bad enough being a lawyer in jail; I can only imagine what it's like for an ex-copper, because after all, everybody in jail is there as a result of a police investigation.

Shortly after his arrest and some heavy soul-searching, the realisation dawned that the best thing to do was cooperate with Ethical Standards. Malcolm indicated that he would plead guilty from the outset. He was spirited off to meet with Ethical Standards and that first interview ran all night. By morning

Malcolm found himself banged up in the Melbourne Custody Centre. Welcome to the real world. No more lodging miscreants in the cells. He was on the receiving end of their 'hospitality', another matter altogether.

The Custody Centre, known in the trade as the 'Yellow Submarine' because of its colour, is a shit-hole—every bit as bad as crooks over the years have complained it is. Having been lodged there myself I can attest to the undesirability of the place. This is where I was literally caged for some time. That is placed in a cage about three feet by three. Yes, this was in the last year of the twentieth century. A short time later Malcolm fronted the magistrate with his co-conspirators: Schentzer, Vanonou and the financier of the drugs, Ohien. He was formally charged and remanded in custody, bail refused. No plea was entered to the charges.

Later that morning Malcolm was unceremoniously chucked into a blacked-out prison van and taken off to Port Phillip Prison. Upon arrival he was banged up in solitary confinement, the 23-hour lock down in Charlotte Division, the solitary punishment unit: the safest place to put a cop. No visitors or phone calls were allowed. Other prisoners knew of his arrival and Malcolm tells me he is still haunted by the taunts from crooks at all hours of the day and night. Some of the threats sent shivers down his spine: 'Why don't you neck yourself, you cunt? Because if you don't we will. When we get hold of your missus she will be raped to a standstill. If we find your boys, they're off too.' Old time crooks always said the family was sacrosanct but not these scum bags. The screws provided Paton's wife's phone number from supposedly secure files to a crook who spent the night screaming out the number for all to hear and pass on to their mates outside.

This has an all too familiar ring. Day one in Port Phillip I was approached by Leslie Camilleri (the Bega schoolgirl killer) who chested me and said, 'You are a cunt and I'm going to kill you.' As the new boy on the block you don't know the ropes and the screws are certainly no help so you do what everyone in jail does: kick along with it.

Sitting in solitary is a sobering experience indeed but Malcolm was somehow able to marshal his thoughts sufficiently to call for Ethical Standards. Superintendent Steve Fontana turned up. Fontana was able to settle him down enough to spend the next hour giving him a rough outline of the evidence he could give. Once again, he confirmed his guilty plea.

Five or six days later, and before he saw Ethical Standards, Paton turned up at Charlotte in a cell near Malcolm. Every now and again, in the hour of exercise time when they shared the small exercise yard, each tried to figure out what the other knew about his case. Paton played dumb, other than to allege Strawhorn had set him up. Paton wasn't talking much, so Malcolm didn't either, particularly about 230.

Now though Malcolm at least had somebody to talk to during that hour, breaking the monotony of twenty-three hours in lock down. It was during his time alone that the enormity of his predicament really impacted on him. He had totally fucked his entire life. What the hell was to become of him? At this stage, the answer was simply: 'Buggered if I know!'

Malcolm had about a month before getting another hearing for bail. During this time he was moved for a week from Charlotte to Sirius East, the maximum-security protection unit, one down from the punishment unit. Sirius East at that time had notorious prisoners such as murderers Raymond Edmunds, 'Mr Stinky' and Peter Dupas. He was on tenterhooks the entire time. These men are dangerous psychopaths and being a copper made him a prime target. Malcolm was still a serving police officer. He hadn't been sacked, which made him the classic sitting duck. Protection is a misnomer. These blokes are dangerous and because some of them will never be released they have literally nothing to lose and behave accordingly.

Worse, Kim Sloan of the Bandidos Motorcycle Gang, who had been loaded by the Drug Squad, was at Port Phillip at the same time as Malcolm. When protection prisoners receive visits it is supposed to be in a segregated area, or at a separate time to mainstream prisoner visits, for obvious reasons. Malcolm's family were visiting when Sloan appeared and threatened to kill him in front of his family and everybody else in the visiting area. Needless to say this alarmed his family. The visit was moved to a secure room. What the hell were mainstream prisoners doing having visitors at the same time as protection? Just another Port Phillip fuck up, no big deal to the screws.

Sloan was removed before the visit ended so that Malcolm could be escorted to Sirius East without further commotion. But he'd had an indication of what was to come if he ended up in jail. He was shaken, his wife was in tears and his boys were terrified.

Another incident arose in Sirius East before the bail hearing that carried a warning of what a jail term might bring. Malcolm was in the exercise yard when a bloke called him to the wire fence. He had been warned by other prisoners not to cross the yellow line on the concrete as prisoners from the next unit regularly hurled boiling water and/or shit at you. Malcolm moved closer to talk to the prisoner, who was calling him by name, when he saw a shiny knife slide down the man's tracksuit sleeve and into his hand. He paused and turned back towards the unit. A large fat prisoner standing near the fence started quickly toward him. Malcolm got away back to the unit. Later he was told the plan had been for the fat prisoner to push Malcolm against the fence so he could be stabbed from the other side. The two conspirators were rounded up and shipped off to another prison.

Malcolm and I witnessed the same technique for management of violence in jail. Tip the offender off to another institution, usually without any penalty, only for him to reoffend there. Unless of course you were killed, then they were charged.

AT MALCOLM'S HEARING HE WAS GRANTED BAIL. NOW IT WAS time to deal with Ethical Standards—no easy task. They start with the premise that you lie every time you open your mouth and that they are the sole occupants of the moral high ground, above reproach. There was much toing and froing between Ethical Standards and Malcolm's lawyers for nearly a year before they sat down and thrashed out the final draft of Malcolm's statement.

Malcolm made it abundantly clear on the night of his arrest he would do a deal and plead guilty. He did so because as an experienced officer he knew a sentence discount applied for an early guilty plea. At all times, from the moment of his arrest, there was no doubt about the plea. The major part of the deal was that Malcolm would give evidence against Strawhorn. He knew this was a massive move against the brotherhood but was prepared to do it all the same. He couldn't undo what had gone before but was prepared to do whatever he could to try and put right some of the wrongs done by the Drug Squad.

The other big ticket item Ethical Standards was after was for Malcolm to make a statement to Dr Perry, the Ombudsman, about Graeme Jensen's murder by the Armed Robbery Squad. He conducted a taped interview revealing what happened at the Jensen murder and all that went with it. It was obviously too hot to handle because nothing ever happened with it. I have been told the Ombudsman is now in possession of another statement corroborating Malcolm's evidence.

Malcolm was charged with trafficking a commercial quantity of a drug of dependence on 29 July 2001, as was Paton in early August 2001. They were both on bail by the time Strawhorn was charged on 18 March 2003. Strawhorn had not been suspended, and was still a serving member of the police force, notwithstanding all the shit swirling around the Drug Squad. Strawhorn denied everything and in the end, Paton and Malcolm both gave evidence against him.

The real kicker was John Brickell, coming out of the woodwork and giving evidence. Also, 230 ended up not only informing on many significant criminals, he went on to upend the Drug Squad coppers who had dealt with him, turning Crown witness against the lot. Add to that Graham Sayce, who you'll remember had been digging into discrepancies at Sigma. Now I have dealt with Sayce many times over the years and he and I have never got on, but one thing is certain, he's as straight as a die. If he reckons he's right, he won't back off—he's like a terrier after a rat. Strawhorn could not have found himself a worse foe because once Sayce started investigating Strawhorn he had right on his side and after all, right is might.

The other significant aspect of Malcolm's deal was, while on bail and well after he indicated a willingness to plead guilty, he had said he was prepared to give evidence against me. A conference was held prior to my trial with the Crown Prosecutor, Richard Maidment SC, that looked at Malcolm's predicament of being on bail. Malcolm didn't much relish having his whole life raked over by defence counsel and a heap of shit chucked at him about his corrupt practices. As matters transpired he only gave evidence at Werner Robert's (my co-accused's) trial, but not for long, because nobody was allowed to cross-examine him about his predicament and guilty plea. To say he was amazed is an understatement. If the jury had been appraised of all the Drug Squad corruption which had become a matter of public record chances are the verdict in my case may well have been different.

Malcolm's case went before the County Court on a plea of guilty in November 2003. He received a sentence of six and a quarter years with three and a half years minimum.

After sentencing Malcolm was taken to the Melbourne Assessment Prison, where he stayed for about one month in the protection unit, which is an even bigger shit-hole than Sirius East. 'Sentence Management' was the next chapter in Malcolm's story. This body supposedly discusses placement and management options with you. What a lot of bullshit. Any decisions about placement are already set in stone—no discussion, no arguments; off Malcolm went to the sex offender and paedophile's jail at Ararat.

Ararat is a shocking jail. The blokes there are by and large gutless low-lives who prey on women and children and don't have the ticker to take on a bloke. Most of the ex-coppers are housed in the same unit. It's a vile existence. Every day you get threatened by somebody, even if it's just an abusive aside. You develop a sixth sense, eyes in the back of your head. The real wild cards in the Ararat prison are the former hard men who have become police informers and have jumped the witness box, committing the ultimate sin and turning Crown evidence. In the criminal code, these blokes are 'dogs', the ultimate betrayers and can't be put anywhere near the prison mainstream. The problem this presents is these are genuinely violent men. Some are in for double murder, like Peter Reid the cop killer, and they're in the same unit as the coppers. These blokes have absolutely nothing to lose because they're serving gigantic sentences and if they don't like the fact that they got a big sentence because of a copper's misbehaviour, then an ex-copper can become the logical target.

By the time Malcolm arrived at Ararat, Paton was already there and had been for several months. Paton had always resented Malcolm because he was a senior detective and Malcolm was a detective sergeant, so Paton had to take orders from him. The normal chain of command was not what Paton was used to. As Strawhorn's lackey, he was the one who gave orders and even detective sergeants obeyed. They did not get on well throughout their time inside.

Luckily Malcolm did not suffer any physical harm in jail but witnessed on a daily basis blokes taking drugs, bashings, stabbings, threats and sexual assaults in the showers. In our society you are supposed to be incarcerated, as punishment not to suffer even more punishment. Jail by its very definition is *additional* punishment. Malcolm experienced firsthand what the crooks he locked up over the years had experienced. There was no attempt at rehabilitation. There was no incentive to make you want to reform your ways—there was no encouragement. When Malcolm told me his views on jail I found that his experiences accorded exactly with my own. Jail is nothing but an advanced criminal college, to society's detriment.

You marked time in a vacuum until your release. Any education offered was so limited as to be almost non-existent. The screws didn't care if you took drugs, as long as you pulled your head in, and that seems to be the case across the entire spectrum of the jail system. We both witnessed this, at different jails. Ararat is a state-run jail. While it is a protection prison, it is still awash with drugs, and that doesn't mean blokes having a joint occasionally. Blokes are shooting up on a daily basis. They have no shame, no fear. Screws deliberately turn a blind eye and the sooner the general public realises this is what happens in jail, the better.

Every week Malcolm was subjected to 'random' piss tests. While Malcolm was tested weekly other blokes known to be users were never tested. Why test him? The answer is simple: jails are only allowed a certain number of positive tests per month before they are sanctioned, so they target those they know don't use.

Malcolm felt he was treated more harshly than other crooks. The screws did not like the fact that he was an ex-copper. Anti-semitism was also alive and well and living in Ararat.

Finally, after three and a half long, lonely years the day of release arrived. He was excited but at the same time, apprehensive. Gillie had been a pillar of strength to him from day one, all the way through Malcolm's trials and tribulations, and frankly, he doesn't think he would have made it without her love and support. In fact, she was the catalyst behind Malcolm contributing to this book.

Malcolm was released early in the morning and there was Gillie in the car park waiting for him. The relief was immense but so was the anxiety. He was a disgraced former copper, just look at any media report. There was no career to go back to and the future would be a real unknown.

By the time this book is published Malcolm will have been home for nearly four years, and life, while a struggle financially, is good. All the monkeys are off his back, he suffers none of the fear and apprehension that went with the double dealing and the dishonesty. He is leading, for the first time as an adult, a normal life. It doesn't matter how hard it gets financially, there will be no going back.

Chapter Thirty

A NEW BROOM SWEEPS CLEAN...OR DOES IT?

'There is no allurement or enticement,
actual or imaginary, which a
well-disciplined mind may not surmount.
The *wish* to resist more than half
accomplishes the object.'

—*The Passions*, Charlotte Dacre

Rosenes' journey through the Victorian police force is only one member out of approximately ten thousand serving coppers. But if he could go this way, it really begs the question, how many others are in a similar position. The answer is far too many.

Matters finally became so bad at Drug Squad Force Command that the politicians could no longer ignore the obvious. Members of the force were dropping like flies to Ethical Standards prosecutions. Something had to be done and pronto. Finally, on 14 December 2001, the Drug Squad was disbanded and into the breach stepped the newly constituted Major Drug Investigation Division (MDID), supposedly manned by officers who would not be tempted like their predecessors. How wrong can you be!

Senior Detective David Miechel found himself seconded to the new unit fresh from the disgraced Drug Squad, which begs the question: who was responsible for screening members of the new unit?

Detective Sergeant Paul Dale joined the MDID after its inception and was Miechel's immediate superior. Terence Hodson was one of Miechel's registered informers at the MDID and recipient of the green light to traffic as long as he remained an informer. Miechel was Hodson's registered handler and as such had a valid reason to visit him regularly. Informers are an integral aspect of all policing. They help make all units work more efficiently. After all, who's going to know what crooks are up to better than other crooks? As Hodson and Miechel became closer they started to chat and conversations turned to them maybe doing a bit of business together. Hodson would supply information on the whereabouts of drugs and/or money and burglaries would be organised. Hodson provided the whereabouts of a safe house containing over a million dollars worth of drugs. I have since found out in excess of $800,000 in cold hard cash was also on offer in the house. The plan was to pinch the drugs and money, split the money and thereafter use Hodson's drug business to sell the stolen drugs and whack up the takings. Talk about free money!

As it so happens, both Miechel and Dale were involved in a surveillance operation run by the MDID on the very same house. They knew all about the surveillance and when the time was right to strike. Who better to know what the coppers are up to than the coppers themselves?

Grand Final night, 27 September 2007, was the big night. They were all set to go. The MDID were ready to strike the next morning as the culmination of its operation so it was now or never. No coppers watched that night, there was no need: search warrants had been issued and the raid was set for the morning. The 'friendlies' whose house was used as the observation post were out for a Grand Final celebration. As investigating officers, Dale and Miechel had access to the covert telephone tapes, giving them perfect intelligence on the movements of all concerned. They even had copies of the floor plan of the house to make sure the bust would be quick and efficient.

Earlier in the day Miechel had volunteered to change the covert tapes of the target house, giving him an excuse to monitor the movements of the people in the house and the friendlies. Everything appeared in place. Hodson and Miechel headed off to Dublin Street, East Oakleigh, dressed in dark clothes and equipped with burglary tools, guns and dog repellent spray. As always in these situations Murphy's Law intervened and as Miechel and Hodson were committing the burglary a neighbour who hadn't been taken into account heard strange noises coming from the house and called the local uniform coppers. Needless to say the local cops weren't in on the giggle so they hot-footed it to Dublin Street in double-quick time, where they arrested Hodson and recovered a heap of drugs. Guess what, no money was found.

Miechel bolted as the local cavalry appeared in tandem with the Dog Squad to track the fleeing burglar, which Rover did and bit him hard. Miechel received rather nasty injuries and apparently has gone right off German Shepherds ever since.

Immediately upon his arrest Miechel demanded to talk to his sergeant, Paul Dale, and tried to claim he had been on duty. Hodson, seeing what was happening, decided to get in first and lag on Dale and Miechel. He confessed that there was a criminal agreement between the three of them and agreed to give evidence against both coppers. This was one hell of a pinch.

Dale had the perfect alibi. He was attending a dinner party with numerous witnesses. Good bloke—he tried unsuccessfully to distance himself from Miechel and was prepared to hang him out to dry in order to protect his own skin. Something to do with rats and sinking ships I suppose.

All three: Dale, Miechel and Hodson were charged. Miechel was refused bail and ended up not seeing the light of day again; he is still in prison, in spite of protesting his innocence all the way to the verdict. He gave a 'no comment' statement and made no admissions. Dale furiously protested his innocence but was also refused bail. Apparently he cried on one of his bail applications, when recounting how difficult jail was for him.

Miechel's silence left Terence Hodson as effectively the only evidence against Dale. He had done a deal to plead guilty and give evidence against both police in return for favourable treatment at court, and was immediately granted bail. Dale's bail application had been vigorously opposed by the DPP on the grounds that he was a threat to witnesses. Bail was refused in the first instance in the Supreme Court but when Dale appealed the decision, it was granted by the Court of Appeal with a special condition that he have no direct or indirect contact with any witness. Such bail conditions are as useful as a hip pocket in a nightdress. The Crown Prosecutor, Gavin Silbert SC, put it to the court rather forcefully when he warned the court Dale posed a very real risk to witnesses: 'to put it crudely, organising an execution from prison has to be more difficult from prison than outside'. The court ignored this warning and Dale was released.

Not long after the burg a brief nominating Hodson as a registered informer was stolen from the Drug Squad offices. Haven't we heard this story before? Not surprisingly these documents ended up with crooks all over Melbourne. There were even copies of this document floating about while I was in jail. So it seemed he was a 'dog' who was unearthed and should cop his right whack. Perfect subterfuge for what happened next.

Terry Hodson had been married for years to his wife Christine and on the night of 15 May 2004 one of them answered the front door of their home in Kew and allowed an unknown person in. The person admitted must have been known to the Hodsons or why would they let them in? The house was like Fort Knox, for good reason. The next day Christine and Terence Hodson were found in their loungeroom, kneeling, hands tied behind their backs, shot in the back of the head. A professional hit if ever there was one.

With the murder of the Hodsons the case against Dale collapsed and he was discharged. If that doesn't stink to high heaven then nothing does.

Jump forwards and Carl Williams is cooling his heels in jail for ordering multiple murders. He watched as the trigger man, my old client Victor Brincat, did a deal with the coppers and got a hefty discount with a minimum sentence fixed. In normal circumstances he would never be released. Williams was serving over thirty years with no end in sight so he decided to test the waters for a discount on his sentence.

The police took Carl out of Barwon Supermax jail and with George was taken to a beachside location where Carl and George told all about their involvement in the Hodson murders. Dale and the hit man (who has no name thanks to ridiculous suppression orders—yet he was recently convicted of a double murder bearing remarkable similarities to the Hodsons' murders) were charged with the murder of the Hodsons. A key claim in the case was that Dale paid Carl Williams $150,000 to organise the hit. It was extraordinary that Williams was allowed to leave the most secure jail in the state for a debrief. Anything could have happened. But it is clear the coppers were as keen as mustard for Williams to tip Dale in.

Another wild card surfaced with 'little Tommy' Ivanovic, a mate of Carl's, in for a road rage murder. Both made it abundantly clear to me while I was at Port Phillip Prison that they had a bent copper on the payroll, and they didn't hesitate to nominate the copper. You don't get favours from a detective sergeant for nothing. Tommy turned and was scheduled to give evidence against Dale. Who knows what was in it for him?

But before anything else happened Carl Williams was murdered in Barwon's Supermax prison, just when the closed circuit TV was not being monitored. Williams was bashed to death. Don't forget this is Supermax. Something rotten there.

With Carl's death the prosecution against Dale has folded again. Yet another stroke of luck for Dale. Because the charges are to be withdrawn it doesn't mean it's all over, far from it. There will certainly be a coroner's inquest and it remains to be seen whether Mister No Name heads down the same track as Carl and offers to turn Crown evidence in return for a discount on his current sentence and indemnity for the Hodsons' murder. Watch this space.

Miechel was sentenced on 18 August 2006 by Justice Betty King in the Supreme Court at Melbourne. Because he pleaded not guilty he could not expect a discount as is the case if you accept your culpability and enter a plea of guilty at an early date. He was convicted of one count of burglary, one theft, two counts of trafficking a large commercial quantity of drugs, one of trafficking a commercial quantity of drugs and two of simple trafficking. The trafficking of a large commercial quantity is the most serious drug offence and carries a maximum of life imprisonment. In the end Miechel copped a sentence of fifteen years with a minimum of twelve to serve.

Finally, I wonder if Miechel will chance his arm and go for a discount by putting his hand up to give evidence.

Chapter Thirty-one

WHERE TO FROM HERE?

'It is the absolute right of the State
to supervise the formation of public
opinion.'

—Joseph Goebbels, Nazi propaganda minister

What does the future hold? There has been a continued and steadfast opposition to the establishment of any type of Anti-Corruption Commission. As recently as April 2010 the Premier of Victoria John Brumby flatly refused to entertain the prospect of an anti-corruption body, because all they do is create a 'lawyer's picnic'. His constant mantra has been the Office of Police Integrity (OPI) is more than sufficient. The facts state otherwise.

While writing this book, on an almost weekly basis a new corruption allegation has reared its ugly head, and I have been left with no option but to draw a line under the issues constantly bobbing up otherwise I will never finish. Before I do though two matters have arisen which cannot be overlooked.

In February 2010 the Director of Public Prosecutions dropped its prosecution for perjury against former Assistant

Commissioner Noel Ashby. Prior to that a prosecution against former Police Association secretary Detective Senior Sergeant Paul Mullett, was discontinued. The only scalp salvaged was media advisor and unsworn member Steven Linnell, who received a wholly suspended jail sentence in return for his undertaking to give evidence against Ashby.

After the spectacular unravelling of the case against Ashby, Linnell is now appealing his penalty on the basis that there was never any offence he could be found guilty of, leaving the government with a bill that would choke a horse and nothing to show for it except embarrassment.

This case received blanket exposure in all media and was one of the greatest balls ups one could imagine. The case against Ashby ended up being an example of professional ineptitude the likes of which I hope we never witness again and while Paul Mullett and I never got on I am prepared to say from my research and interviews there most likely never was a case against him. Clearly the whole investigation against him was politically motivated to get rid of a pain in the Government's neck.

Amazingly, in a piece of spin that could only be described as breathtaking, the OPI claimed the operation a success. How extraordinary; little wonder they make so many fuck ups!

Three persons became of interest to the OPI: Ashby, Mullett and Linnell. The plot was of Shakespearian proportions; this was last man standing stuff, there would be blood in the streets.

Ashby and Mullett were both stationed at Flinders Street and knew each other well. Ashby had resigned from the Police Association and was ambitious for the forthcoming post of Chief Commissioner. The incumbent Chief Commissioner, Christine Nixon, was making it clear her preferred replacement would be former Australian Federal Policeman Simon Overland.

Overland had been recruited together with Luke Cornelius from the AFP and from day one at Victoria Police his ambition was obvious. From the outset the Police Association thought Overland was a desk-driving copper without operational experience. He had never faced an angry man therefore he could not possibly know how to represent the cop on the beat. The same thinking applied to Cornelius.

Ashby's ambition knew no bounds—but that's not a criminal offence. Nor for that matter is the extraordinary amount of bad-mouthing recorded in phone taps put in place by the OPI. It was clear Ashby was planning to rise to the top and if he had to walk over hot coals to get there then so be it.

Mullett and Ashby had known each other for years and talked regularly. It helped that Ashby was in charge of negotiating the new Enterprise Bargaining Agreement on behalf of the rank and file coppers so it was common for the two to meet. Never being one to let an opportunity pass him by, Ashby saw an opportunity to garner the support of the Police Association to apply political leverage in his quest for power.

Ashby, in an effort to curry favour, provided Mullett with snippets of information which in the wash up were of no significance whatsoever. The line of communication flowed from Linnell to Ashby and finally to Mullett. Notwithstanding what the media has said this case was never about Mullett, even though his belligerence always makes a good headline.

The info passed on was little more than scuttlebutt. If the three had exhibited enough smarts they could have stopped this fiasco dead in its tracks. But the Paul Mulletts of the world crash through or crash—he doesn't have a conciliatory bone in his body.

Both Mullett and Ashby's phones were 'off' (being listened to) by now and a conversation was recorded in which Mullett spoke to Peter Lalor, formerly of the Major Crime Squad and later St Kilda CIB. Lalor was a person of interest to OPI because of a possible link to the murder of male prostitute

Shane Chartres-Abbott, gunned down outside his house in a professional hit. It was suspected Mullett tipped Lalor off that he was being investigated for allegedly providing Chartres-Abbott's address to a professional hit man. Mullett vigorously denied these allegations and to this day no improper relationship with Lalor has been established.

The OPI was hot to trot; it had a real live one and couldn't help itself. Summonses were issued for public examinations of Ashby, Linnell and Mullett. Don't forget, to date the OPI has precious few runs on the board and those that have been successfully prosecuted are small fish indeed. But the fish don't come much bigger than an Assistant Commissioner and the feared Paul Mullett. The stage was set for a battle of titanic proportions.

Once the summonses were served the three still didn't realise their phones were 'off'. Ashby and Linnell were clearly panicked when they received the summonses. Ashby was recorded telling Linnell what to say, a potentially fatal mistake, and when these conversations were put to Ashby in the witness box he denied them, as did Linnell. The tapes were played in court contradicting their sworn statements and both were gone. Linnell immediately did a deal to shelve Ashby in return for a non-custodial sentence. The OPI were cock-a-hoop. Ashby was as good as in the bag.

Mullett kept his cool and fought doggedly on.

Justice Murray Wilcox QC was appointed to conduct the public hearings and at their conclusion recommended criminal charges against Ashby, Linnell and Mullett. The first crack appeared when the Director of Public Prosecutions got hold of the brief; it was clear there was no case whatsoever against Mullett. There was a huge back down and the DPP withdrew all charges against him. The case against Mullett was certainly smelly but never sufficient for a criminal prosecution. In his usual fashion Mullett didn't go quietly.

Who cared about Mullett, Ashby was done for, gone a million. He had demonstrably lied under oath and the prize witness had tumbled and agreed to give evidence against him. What could possibly go wrong?

Enter Phillip Priest QC, a black letter lawyer with a sound background of many years conducting criminal trials and one dogged customer. Rest assured Priest would leave no stone unturned, and he didn't.

The trial was listed in the Supreme Court and the hearing day arrived. The press gallery was packed. There had been a whisper around the traps that there would be some fun and games on day one. Priest rose to his feet about to drop the mother of all bomb shells. No one had seen it coming, least of all the OPI.

The two men responsible for the public hearings were then OPI head, George Brower, a very experienced public servant and lawyer, and former Federal Court judge Murray Wilcox QC, a judge of over twenty years' experience. When you have a bloke like Priest on the job everything had better be water-tight or he will locate the leak.

The OPI charter essentially provides for investigation of transgressions by police and where appropriate have them dismissed from the force, without necessarily launching criminal prosecutions. On this occasion criminal sanctions were front and centre—the motivation behind the public hearings. The OPI strayed into unfamiliar territory and paid the price.

No matter what the reason, Brower and Wilcox made a fundamental and fatal blunder that effectively finished the OPI as a credible body. Put very simply, for Wilcox to have the capacity to administer the oath to witnesses, he must in turn have been properly authorised pursuant to the OPI Act. Without this authorisation Wilcox had no power to conduct hearings or administer the oath, leaving the OPI with a big fat nothing from its public hearings. Had Brower properly authorised Wilcox we would have finished up with a different scenario altogether. Instead he failed to do so, rendering all 'evidence' taken of no evidentiary force or effect. In other words the DPP was powerless to pursue Ashby. He had technically not perjured himself, because of the fatally flawed 'oath'.

The case against Ashby was withdrawn once the enormity of Priest's submission finally sunk in. Ashby won, compliments of an own goal kicked by the OPI. He won on a technicality. He was not acquitted by a jury after hearing all the evidence. He had not been found 'not guilty'. When Ashby jumped the witness box at the public hearing he thought at that time he was subject to the oath to tell the truth and as the second highest ranking police officer in this state one would expect him to abide by the oath. Instead Ashby lied on oath and was caught out. If Brower and Wilcox had attended to all necessary details prior to the hearings Ashby would have been gone a million. He should thank his lucky stars for Phil Priest.

The rest is history: Simon Overland succeeded Christine Nixon and became Chief Commissioner. The animosity from the Police Association toward Overland remains.

When Overland appeared in front of the news cameras the night Ashby walked free all he could muster, when asked his view of the day's catastrophe, was to say it was 'bad luck'. Bad luck indeed! After the OPI's debacle the political fallout was substantial. One of the morning newspapers had started running a campaign for the establishment of an anti-corruption body, but the Government continued to stonewall.

History has shown how ineffective the OPI has been and the interesting twists and turns the 'brotherhood' have employed to avoid their investigations. The OPI clearly lacks the power and legal ability required. Then there's the Ombudsman, again under-resourced, and while reports to government have come thick and fast, the capacity to radically change the cultures and systems of the police remains lacking.

The dissatisfaction was palpable; something needed to be done, pronto. This issue was getting away from the Government. The Opposition was screaming for a Crimes Commission when out of the blue, in the first week of June 2010, the Premier did a back flip that would have done an Olympic gymnast proud, announcing the establishment of the Victorian Integrity and Anti-Corruption Commission (VIACC).

Now, don't go getting all excited by this announcement because the Commission is a long way from even being established. Add to this the concerns of many lawyers and academics that the proposed model is overly complex—if you want something to be ineffective make its rules arcane, thereby stymieing efficient and effective implementation. The government then says it is doing something while really it is not. The old smoke and mirrors trick that has already been employed with the ESD, OPI and the Ombudsman. There remains a steadfast refusal to establish a Royal Commission with wide-ranging powers to publicly examine the issues and make recommendations for prosecutions as was so successfully done in Queensland all those years ago with the Fitzgerald Royal Commission. The question of political obfuscation looms large on the horizon.

After the kicking the Victorian Government copped at the Black Saturday Royal Commission no doubt they won't exactly be falling over themselves in their haste to establish another Royal Commission.

The final and most comprehensive report made by Ceja stated that 87 per cent of the drugs and chemicals dealt with under the Controlled Delivery Scheme remain unaccounted for. There remains a yawning gulf of missing drugs and chemicals worth many tens, even hundreds, of millions of dollars. As I've said, there is a very large hole somewhere full of ill-gotten gains.

Don't hold your breath for anything to happen quickly, or even at all, unless the public continues to stridently demand a Royal Commission, followed by the establishment of a Corruption Commission. It is the minimum the people deserve.

Chapter Thirty-two

A BRIEF FOR THE PROSECUTION

'The community is ill-served by this
escalating transfer of power from
the public to the dominant political
parties, and the parties disinterest in
ethical constraints and resistance to
oversight and accountability even by
independent anti-corruption bodies.'

—Tony Fitzgerald QC

'The State opposition concurs with your sentiments regarding the need for a Royal Commission into police. Labor has repeatedly called for a royal commission into police corruption and will continue to do so in the coming budget session of parliament and beyond.' Opposition leader John Brumby in 1997.

Researching this book, I read a number of reports to Parliament by the Ombudsman and the Office of Police Integrity. Police corruption in Victoria is as old as the Colony itself and it is clear that insufficient has been done over the years to address it or stamp it out. We have zero tolerance for a number of offences—that should include police corruption.

I read Malcolm's debrief to Ethical Standards and listened to his story. The litany of corrupt offences was sickening, particularly in view of the clinical and unemotional manner in which it was told. Malcolm's account exposed criminal behaviour on a scale never before realised.

Add to that the spectacular demise of the Armed Robbery Squad and the Drug Squad, in its various guises, and it is blatantly obvious that the issue of corruption will not go away until we have a fair dinkum go at rooting out the corrupt elements continually sullying the reputation of the majority of excellent coppers.

Senior police regularly jumped in the witness box, giving evidence of colossal values attributed to drugs found on crooks, yet when it came to Wayne Strawhorn's turn to be sentenced the value attributed to the drugs he trafficked was a pittance. Why was this? Easy answer: one rule for coppers and another rule for the rest. If you think this is hysterical then ask yourself how someone sworn to 'Uphold the Right' traffics a commercial quantity of a drug purely for financial gain (not addiction) and serves only four years. Wouldn't you have thought the fact that he was a senior copper would have been a severe factor to warrant a sentence well into double figures?

To explain how sentencing works I need to be technical for a moment. Three levels of drug trafficking offences exist in Victoria. For our purposes I'll restrict myself to amphetamines. After all that's what Malcolm and the rest of the Clandestine Laboratory Unit put into the community compliments of the Chemical Diversion Desk.

1. Trafficking a drug of dependence. Trafficable quantity three grams, including admixture. Penalty up to fifteen years' imprisonment.
2. Trafficking a commercial quantity of a drug of dependence. Trafficable quantity 100 grams pure or 500 grams including admixture. Penalty up to twenty-five years' imprisonment.
3. Trafficking a large commercial quantity of a drug of dependence. Trafficable quantity 750 grams pure or 1 kilogram including admixture. Penalty up to a maximum of life imprisonment.

The term 'admixture' means the drug plus cutting agent, so you end up sentenced on the total weight of powder, not the amount of the pure drug present.

Drug Squad coppers always hit the witness box regaling the court with their extensive and unassailable expertise in properly ascertaining the real value of drugs involved in a particular case. As a general rule it did not matter whether you cross-examined these coppers up hill and down dale, their word was gospel and the numbers accepted.

Let's use the Drug Squad's own figures to work out the real value of some of the drugs already mentioned. Earlier Malcolm stated that 1.2 kilos of pseudo produced a kilo of pure amphetamine. This assertion is based on years in the Clandestine Laboratory Unit, dealing with dozens of cases of amphetamine manufacture.

Using figures from Detective Sergeant Stephen McIntyre's calculations mentioned earlier, the 1.3 kilos of pure pseudo that was stolen from a locked safe in a locked office at the Drug Squad would equate to one kilo of pure speed on the street, valued at over two and half million dollars. Who had access to the office and the safe? Were those in the frame questioned? And did they answer or did they refuse to cooperate? Where did the drugs come from? Was it a legitimate purchase or otherwise? What the hell was it doing in the safe? The most important question stands: What was the outcome of the investigation of an incident that led to over two million bucks' worth of drugs reaching the streets?

At Strawhorn's trial he was convicted of trafficking two kilos of pseudo to Mark Moran, which equals 1.66 kilos of pure speed. The value was put at $12,000. Perhaps this was the cost from the chemical company. But if we use the Drug Squad's own figures for its street value it would be valued at over four million.

As it turns out though, with PAS ('Paton and Strawhorn') Chemicals in full flight, a cornucopia of chemicals was purchased and on-sold to who knows who. To give you some idea of the extent of the black market dealings, the following unauthorised purchases were put to Malcolm by ESD after his arrest: 28 October 1999—one kilo pseudoephedrine; 13 December 1999— one kilo pseudoephedrine; 14 December 1999—half a kilo pseudoephedrine; 7 January 2000—one kilo pseudoephedrine; 8 May 2000—720 packets of Sudafed; 9 May 2000—360 packets of Sudafed; 19 May 2000—two kilos of pseudoephedrine; 20 June 2000—50 packets of Sudafed; 26 June 2000—500 packets of Sudafed; 7 July 2000—504 packets of Sudafed; 13 July 2000—720 packets of Sudafed; 3 August 2000—600 packets of Sudafed; 21 August 2000—600 packets of Sudafed; 28 September 2000—eight litres of acetic anhydride; December 2000—two lots of 720 packets of Sudafed.

Remember the day Malcolm was greeted by a storeroom full of unauthorised packets of Sudafed that disappeared as soon as he queried their presence? Malcolm calculated fifty to sixty packers were present, each holding 72 boxes of 100 tabs, equalling 7,200 tabs per packer. If every three boxes of Sudafed produces two grams of pseudo the total amount present in the storeroom was 2.4 kilos of pure pseudo. Applying the McIntyre calculation the two kilos of pure speed you can produce from this has a street value in excess of six million. Has this ever been investigated? And if so what was the outcome? If no investigation, why not? We are not talking peanuts here. Somewhere, there is a very large hole filled with an obscene amount of money.

How the penny didn't drop with the so called Controlling Committee of the Controlled Delivery Scheme beggars belief. Someone must have noticed the vast amounts of chemicals unaccounted for. I find it amazing that no one in a position of control ever appeared to contact the chemical companies and make enquiries as to amounts sold and to whom. If anyone had bothered, the whole house of cards would have come down very early on. But even more importantly where should the buck have stopped? Who was in charge?

Don't forget the Ceja Report calculated that 87 per cent of all drugs purchased and sold through the Controlled Delivery Scheme were unaccounted for. On this basis the true value of the illegal dealings by Drug Squad members, using their own figures, has a street value of some hundreds of millions of dollars—a mind-boggling figure indeed.

There is damning evidence that organised crime operated within the police force, the proceeds of which have disappeared without trace. A starting point should be the Australian Taxation Office. Have any of these coppers or transactions been reported? And have any of these blokes been audited or investigated by the Tax Office? As a lawyer, every time you break wind you cop a tax audit. I haven't heard of any coppers being audited.

ESD checked Malcolm's bank accounts and didn't find anything untoward. You have got to be joking. Only honest people with nothing to hide put their money in legitimate accounts. What about assets and lifestyle? If the rest of the police investigated criminals like that they'd never catch anyone, but that was the extent of the ESD investigation. No wonder the pundits continually scream coppers should not investigate coppers.

There remain so many unanswered questions that the only way the stench can be cleared is with a Royal Commission. If the Government sticks to its usual stonewalling, the question must be asked: What has it got to hide? The answer is that it doesn't want corruption on a grand scale *ever* hitting the headlines.

Drug trafficking is not the only serious crime disclosed here. By far the most serious is murder, and there's more than one. The question of what really happened at Narre Warren on 11 October 1988 has never been adequately explained or any closure provided for Graeme Jensen's family and friends. Who has ever really pursued the relationship between the murder of Jensen and the awful deaths of Constables Tynan and Eyre a few hours later, early in the morning of 12 October 1988. History has shown, clearly in my view, that the police murders were a direct response to the actions of the Armed Robbery Squad the day before. I am going to be unpopular for saying this. It is an unpalatable truth no one will admit: the Armed Robbery Squad has the blood of Tynan and Eyre on their hands. The senior ranks of the police at the time must also accept responsibility; if they had reined in the Robbers the Squad would not have become a law unto themselves, believing themselves judge, jury and executioner, which they were.

And what of the deaths of Jed Horton and Gary Abdullah? How Abdullah was shot 'accidentally' seven times beggars belief. The longer these sleeping dogs are allowed to lie the more corruption is seen to be tolerated.

What about the Paul Dale case and the deceased witnesses and the stuff up with the OPI case against Ashby? Then there are the blokes who were loaded, and don't forget, finally, nothing ever happened to anybody regarding evidence that went missing and exhibits that were tampered with or contaminated. All these events demand to be revisited. While there is no double jeopardy in Victoria and no one can be re-tried for murder, if Malcolm's version of events is correct, there has been the most serious perversion of justice one could imagine. More than one person has many awkward questions to answer.

Perverting the course of justice, loading suspects, missing drugs and money, coppers getting away with murder. The next Victorian Government must establish a Royal Commission into this utter disgrace.

This is one man's story, his journey through the Victorian Police Force. If only one member out of approximately ten thousand serving coppers can go this way, it really begs the question, how many others are in a similar position? The answer is far too many.